ISLINGTON

CW00540090

Please return this item on or before the
be liable to overdue charges. To renew
access the online catalogue at www.is
your library membership number and F

I.D.13

22/12/14

3/17

TRANS SC 2118
24/9/18.
13/10/18
16 OCT 2019

Islington Libraries

020 7527 6900   **www.islington.gov.uk/libraries**

THE
Princess
Alice
DISASTER

JOAN LOCK

ROBERT HALE · LONDON

© Joan Lock 2013
First published in Great Britain 2013

ISBN 978-0-7090-9541-5

Robert Hale Limited
Clerkenwell House
Clerkenwell Green
London EC1R 0HT

www.halebooks.com

A catalogue record for this book is available from
the British Library

2 4 6 8 10 9 7 5 3 1

Printed and bound in the UK by
Ashford Colour Press Ltd, Gosport

Contents

'Where are you coming to!'

The light is beginning to fade as the *Princess Alice* pleasure steamer sails up Erith Reach on her return to London. To warn approaching vessels of their presence, a lad puts a taper to the wicks of the red and green port and starboard warning lights, then hoists a white light on the masthead.

The band is thumping out a rousing, patriotic song, 'We don't want to fight, but by jingo if we do!', which is intended to issue due warning to the Russians who may be thinking of invading Afghanistan. Despite being tired after a long day pursuing pleasure, the passengers sing lustily, in competition with several middle-aged and elderly ladies giving their all to 'Onward Christian Soldiers!'

The children, boisterous earlier on, have begun to tire, worn out by a day on the river and amongst the attractions of the Rosherville Pleasure Gardens and the resorts of Gravesend and Sheerness. Some are asleep in their mothers' arms, despite the couple having a noisy row over by the paddle box. Some mothers' heads have also started to nod.

The *Princess Alice* follows the long, north-westward curve of the Thames as it approaches Tripcock Point. Ahead, to the right, are the surging flares of the monumental Beckton Gasworks, the largest in Europe. To the left, over the misty marshes, passengers can glimpse the distant lights of their next stop, Woolwich. A large, Cardiff-bound collier passes them going downstream, followed by a tug travelling so fast that the barge it is pulling lifts out of the water.

The band is now playing a jolly polka, 'Good Rhine Wine', and some of the young ladies try to dance to the lively tune. But the deck is too crowded for them to make much of a showing. When the tune finishes the musicians stand up, collect their instruments, and go below for a break.

The *Princess Alice* rounds Tripcock Point and enters Gallions Reach where, to the left, is moored *The Talbot*, a large, red-painted, gun-powder barge. Beyond her, a row of colliers wait to unload at Beckton Gasworks. After the jolly music ceases, all that can be heard is the swish of the paddles and the pounding of the engines. The evening is growing a little chillier.

Robert Haines, the double bass player, has been obliged to wait at the top of the stairs until there is room for him and his bulky instrument to descend. He doesn't mind. He is interested in boats and the river life. But he does begin to wonder why that huge collier seems to be heading straight towards them? He shrugs. It will veer away in a minute, they must know what they are doing. He turns to go below.

Suddenly, there is a commotion up front. Warning whistles screech.

'Ease her!' a man's voice shouts urgently. 'Stop her!' Then, frantically, 'Where are you coming to! GOOD GOD! Where are you coming to!'

CHAPTER ONE

Today's the Day!

Miss Susannah Law was a wealthy, middle-aged lady, and a generous one who had promised the poor women in her Clerkenwell Mission Bible Class a day out down the River Thames on the *Princess Alice* pleasure steamer.

Although August 1878 had been unusually wet, September dawned brightly, encouraging Miss Law to set the outing date for Thursday the 5th. But when she saw what a beautiful day Tuesday the 3rd was promising to be she changed her mind and sent messengers around to announce, 'Today's the day!' Thirty women and several children turned up.

The cheerful early morning sun also inspired Mr Edward Leaver of Lambeth. He decided that this was just the day 'for a blow on the river down to Sheerness' for him and his four children.

Inspector King, of the Thames Police, was persuaded to complete his week's holiday in a similar manner and took along his wife and two children, his mother, his father (a naval pensioner with a wooden leg), and his brother.

It was no sudden decision for Miss Maria Scholz, German governess at the Queen's College Institution for Young Ladies in north London. As a reward for their good work she had long ago set the date for taking eight of her pupils, ages eight to thirteen years, down the river on the *Princess Alice*. The parents of three of the girls were half a world away. Thirteen-year-old Rosa Hennessy's father was a surgeon in India, while the parents of 14-year-old Fanny White and her 13-year-old sister Eva, were in Shanghai.

Many passengers boarded the popular paddle steamer at 10.30

a.m. at Swan Pier by London Bridge, others a little later at North Woolwich, which sat opposite the historic town of Woolwich[1]. At that time North Woolwich, on the marshy north bank of the Thames, had only a sprinkling of houses and a pub, the last of London's pleasure gardens and the terminus of the north London railway line.

Many who boarded the *Princess Alice* here had already braved the train journey from Islington, Clerkenwell, Dalston and the East End, despite the recent terrible rail collision at Sittingbourne in Kent. Railway accidents were frequent occurrences and passengers were becoming increasingly nervous about them. What a relief to be gliding down the river on a pleasure steamer, a much less dangerous and more pleasant way to approach the attractions of Kent, 'the garden of England'.

True, there had been an accident on the Thames on this very spot a year ago when, in a fog, a boat had overturned while carrying workmen from Woolwich to North Woolwich. Nine men had drowned. But the *Princess Alice* was a large and sturdy, professionally manned, paddle steamer – quite a different matter.

Most of the *Princess Alice* passengers were upper working class or lower middle class; many were women and children: facts that would influence their fate later that day. One or two were higher up the social ladder. Among these was Mr Samuel Lowry, 'a gentleman' from Highbury, who was in the habit of amusing himself by taking trips on the river.

All were welcomed onboard by the captain, 47-year-old William Grinstead, who was considered to be one of the most experienced and careful of the captains employed by the London Steamboat Company. This was now a leading firm in the Thames pleasure-boat business, having been formed two years earlier from an amalgamation of several smaller firms. The royal names (the *Duke of Teck*, the *Duke of Cambridge*, the *Princess Maud* and the *Princess Alice*) of the boats created an aura of glamour and respectability.

Princess Alice was the second daughter of Queen Victoria, and had been a tower of strength to her mother as Prince Albert lay dying. But none of this weighed on the minds of the happy crowd boarding the vessel named after her. It was a lovely day and they were going to have fun.

The bright day had persuaded Captain Grinstead to bring

along his wife, Jane, elder brother, Charles, and 14-year-old son, John. Even the company's superintendent, Mr William Towse, was coming with his wife, eight children, mother-in-law, children's nurse, a cousin and a friend.

The scene down at the Millwall Dock that morning was a less happy one. Captain Harrison, the master of the 890-ton Tyne collier, *Bywell Castle,* was trying to get his ship released from the dry dock where it had been repainted. Congestion was delaying his departure. His way out was blocked by other vessels and he was all too conscious that he had to get back home to Newcastle-upon-Tyne to pick up a cargo of coal bound for Alexandria in Egypt. As part-owner of the vessel, he was particularly aware that wasted time was wasted money.

Captain Harrison had already paid off his regular crew, intending to sign on a new one when he got back to Newcastle. For the journey home, he had taken on some temporary men or 'runners'. He did not view these men as inferior to the regular seamen. On the contrary, he thought them 'a superior article' being steady, sober and dependable men who would rather not be away from their wives and families for long periods. They were also cheaper to employ than keeping on a full crew.

The captain was not familiar with the Thames, his usual route being from Newcastle to the eastern Mediterranean and back, so Dix, a Thames pilot, was onboard, although, strictly speaking, there was no obligation to hire one. They just had to wait for their way to be cleared, hoping that by the time it was, they would not have missed the evening ebb tide.

After leaving North Woolwich, the *Princess Alice* steadily steamed its way down towards the Thames Estuary, first passing the Essex marshes and the monumental Beckton Gasworks. Despite this distraction, much of the talk onboard was of the Sittingbourne railway disaster. An express train bringing trippers and holiday makers back from Ramsgate, Broadstairs, Margate and Sheerness, had collided with a freight train that had been shunted into its path. Five passengers had been killed and many seriously injured. The newspapers graphically described mangled bodies strewn across the track and luggage, picnic food and toys spilling from torn carriages.

The *Princess Alice*'s ultimate destination was Sheerness, where

11

the Thames opened out to the sea. Here, Londoners could paddle on the beaches, breathe air many times fresher than that of their city, saunter along the pier and promenade and watch the white sails and black smoke of the ships entering the Thames as well as the ferries shuttling back and forth from the Continent.

However, many passengers intended to disembark earlier at the port and resort of Gravesend, which offered many of the attractions of Sheerness apart from the sea breezes. Or, earlier still, at Northfleet, for the famous Rosherville Pleasure Gardens.[2] Here, they were welcomed by a billboard quoting a line from a popular music-hall song:

ROSHERVILLE GARDENS
The Place to Spend a Happy Day!

Listed beneath were some of the many attractions on offer; these included an Italian garden, an archery lawn, bowls, a maze, a lake with ducks, cliff walks, an aviary, a bear pit, a theatre, a baronial hall with food and dancing, a floral bazaar, a shooting gallery, a fortune-telling booth, a photo saloon and an exhibition of the skeleton of a whale which had strayed into the Thames.

The setting of these pleasure gardens was extraordinary: twenty acres of disused chalk quarry bounded to the rear by cliffs and to the front by a Thames-side promenade from which the busy river traffic and the distant Tilbury Fort could be viewed.

The gardens, a favourite cockney haunt, had inspired music-hall songs, were mentioned in novels and in a Gilbert and Sullivan comic opera.[3] There was a Rosherville perfume and even a poem about the gardens, by Reverend G. Crolly, which began:

If in London streets you grill
All is cool in Rosherville
If in London time stands still
He wears wings in Rosherville

And so on for twenty more similar couplets.

Unsurprisingly, quite a number of the *Princess Alice* passengers decided that, indeed, Rosherville *was* where they would like to spend a happy day. After all, the vessel did not arrive at

Sheerness until 3 p.m. and would be leaving again at 4.15 p.m. Meanwhile, *they* would be enjoying the many delights on offer in the pleasure gardens: dancing, dining, attending the music hall, taking a turn at archery or just appreciating the lovely flowers and scenery.

Quite a number of the passengers boarding at Sheerness for the return journey had been holidaying at the resort. Among these, were young P.C. Cornelius Briscoe, his wife, Jane, their 5-year-old daughter, Sarah, and 18-month-old son, Benjamin. Back in Dalston, Briscoe was something of a local hero, having recently won both the Humane Society and Bow Street Awards for rescuing a drowning child from the Regent's Canal.

When the smart little pleasure steamer reached Gravesend Town Pier at 5.55 p.m. Hopgood, the regular helmsman, went ashore. He had already asked the captain if his friend, John Eyres, could substitute for him, so that he could have a night off. The captain agreed. A decision that was to have far-reaching consequences.

By the time she left Rosherville, at about 6.30 p.m., the *Princess Alice* was packed. Not only had some of those holidaying at Sheerness and Gravesend decided to return to London this safer and more pleasant way than by rail, but many who had come down for the day on the sister ships, the *Duke of Teck* and the *Duke of Cambridge*, had opted to return on the *Princess Alice*. She was, after all a smarter, faster, more popular boat and was leaving a little earlier.

The twenty-three mile journey back to London was scheduled to take just over two hours along a river which wound its undulating way north-westwards. Firstly, it passed the new Tilbury Docks, then large tracts of marshland punctuated here and there by factories and warehouses; a riverside situation was a great advantage when it came to transporting goods.

Back at Millwall Dock, the *Bywell Castle*'s path had at last been cleared and she had begun to make her way out of the outer dock. Alas, as she did so, a barge drifted across her path and there was a collision. Fortunately, the damage to the barge proved minor and the collier was allowed to continue on her way. With the aid of a line attached by a waterman, she was pointed downstream. Her lights were lit and she was on her way towards the sea at last. She was under the control of Dix, the pilot, while Hardy, one of the runners, was acting as lookout – a necessary precaution when the ship's raised forecastle meant that the helmsman had no clear view ahead or astern.

Erith was one of the busier riverside towns on the *Princess Alice*'s route home. Once a popular resort, it was fast becoming industrialized. As if to compensate for the parade of factories and warehouses on their journey, as they rounded the left-hand curve into Halfway Reach, passengers saw one of the river's most impressive sights: Crossness Pumping Station. This handsome, Romanesque building in cream, red and black brick, boasted an adjacent, free-standing chimney resembling a particularly tall and slender Florentine campanile.

Londoners were both proud and grateful for what the Crossness Pumping Station represented. Proud because it looked so splendid and because its four rotative beam engines (named Victoria, Albert, Alexandra and Albert Edward) were the largest in the world. Grateful because the new system carried sewage away from central London and emptied it in this backwater. This 'Sewage Palace', as Londoners dubbed it, was as magnificent inside as out. Its twin, Abbey Mills Pumping Station, on the north side of the Thames, was equally exotic to look at but, unlike Crossness, was not visible from the river. However, its outfall was just around the next bend, Tripcock Point, in the stirringly named Gallions Reach. Right next door, in fact, to that other British engineering feat, the Beckton Gasworks.

At about 7.35 p.m. there was still sufficient light for Mr Henry Reed (an Oxford Street stationer who had left an assistant in charge of his shop) to make out the features of his niece in a photograph shown to him by his wife, but not enough for him to read the inscription on the back.

The Reeds noticed a kindly gentleman sitting a few rows behind them on the upper saloon deck who was showing great interest in the toys which a group of still-lively children brought him to admire: dolls, tops, trumpets and picture books.

Young and pretty Miss Emma Eatwell had been persuaded by Mr Huddart, the proprietor of the Half Moon Street Hotel in Mayfair, to come for the day trip. She had found him rather heavy going and retreated below decks but was now trying to get back to their place in the bows.

Children of the workers at Lawes chemical manure factory at nearby Creekmouth on the River Roding were enjoying themselves mightily. It was their Treat Day. Swings had been hired. There had been running and jumping competitions followed by a delicious tea in their schoolroom, then final rides on the swings and more energetic indoor games complete with party masks and paper hats. The party was still in full swing at 8 p.m.

Meanwhile, onboard the *Princess Alice*, there was the competition between passengers singing the patriotic song, 'We don't want to fight but by jingo if we do!', and the hymn-singing middle-aged and elderly ladies (possibly the Bible-class party led by Miss Susannah Law and her younger sister, Jane).

Some passengers turned to watch the passing, Cardiff-bound collier and a tug going so fast that the barge it was pulling was lifting out of the water.

Robert Haines, the double bass player, who didn't mind being held up at the top of the stairs when the band went below for their break, was shrugging and turning to go below.

All was quiet except for the pounding of the engines and swish of the paddles. Suddenly, Mr Henry Reed heard a commotion up front and climbed onto a seat to get a better view of what was happening. He was promptly told to sit down. Edward, the elder son of the Leaver family from Lambeth, also heard the disturbance and dashed out of the saloon where they had been sitting. A frightened Emma Eatwell rushed up to the saloon deck.

'Ease her!' a man's voice shouted urgently. 'Stop her!' Then, frantically, 'Where are you coming to! GOOD GOD! Where are you coming to!'

Warning whistles began to screech and passengers to scream as the huge hull of the Tyne collier loomed above them.

And the 890-ton *Bywell Castle* kept coming, ploughing into the *Princess Alice*'s side just forward of her paddle box then, with a terrible scrunching and grinding into her engine room and saloon, while the whistles of both vessels continued to screech and the passenger's screams reached a crescendo.

The front of the *Princess Alice* tipped forward, pitching passengers into the water, where they became a seething, thrashing mass of frantic people pulling each other down. Most of them wore boots and restrictive clothing – particularly the women with their long skirts – and very few of them could swim. Four men, aided by the upward slant of the deck, managed to seize the *Bywell Castle*'s anchor chains and climb up onto the collier. Another grasped them, but fell off.

The boat hung like that for a few moments. The collier's second mate, William Brankston, dashed forward and slid down a rope onto the deck of the *Princess Alice* where all was confusion. He tried to get people to the ropes, but they retreated up to the higher part of the vessel and he was pulled at and jostled by the terrified passengers. He got hold of some women and attempted to put ropes around their waists because he knew they would be unable to climb up them. Then the vessel canted over and there was an ominous roar as the fires were drowned out. The vessel broke in two, nose and stern going in the air, as she sank in the centre.

Brankston found himself in the water, but managed to climb a rope. He was hauled onboard by the scruff of his neck. The first mate, who seemed surprised to see him, exclaimed, 'Wherever have you been?'[4]

Passenger Robert Spencer had realized that a collision was inevitable and managed to swing out one lifeboat. He placed Miss Mary Ann Relfe and her sister, Jane, onboard, but had no knife to cut the rope which fastened it to the sides.

As the *Princess Alice* broke in two and sank it took the lifeboat and its occupants with it along with all the passengers trapped below, while those remaining on deck were tipped into the water. The crew of the *Bywell Castle* threw down anything the drowning people might cling to – planks, boxes, chicken coops, lifebuoys, ladders and a carpenter's bench – and dropped ropes down the ship's sides for them to climb up.

The *Talbot* powder barge sent out a lifeboat, and several small craft, including those belonging to the Beckton Gasworks, rushed to their aid. But there were few of them, it took time and they had to push some desperate people away lest they themselves were swamped.

A steward who could swim put his girlfriend on his shoulders and jumped in. But she slipped off and though he dived after her again and again he never found her. Two young brothers managed to swim to the ropes and pull themselves up to the deck of the *Bywell Castle*. Their sister actually swam to the riverbank, a fact that was later reported in terms of great wonder.

One man who reached the north shore with a lifebuoy around him stated that he had jumped overboard after telling his wife to throw their children and jump after him, but he had lost them all.

Miss Emma Eatwell was half an hour in the water before being picked up. Her host, Mr Huddard, had managed to grab hold of one of the ropes, but slipped off, as did others. However, he managed to get hold of a piece of wood the size of a table and hang on until rescued.

Young Edward Leaver, who had run out of the saloon on hearing the commotion, also managed to climb the rope, as did a Mr Childs, with his son in his arms, but someone above him fell and dashed the child from his arms.

Unsurprisingly, Inspector King of the Thames Police could also swim. He managed to save his wife and reach the bank, only to find that the woman he had saved was not his wife.

All that was known at Woolwich was that the *Princess Alice* was late. They had heard warning whistles, but that was not so unusual. The river was busy and near misses were common. Woolwich was a place of many tragedies, but most of them, being due to explosions at the Woolwich Arsenal, were seen as well as heard. The first they knew of the *Princess Alice* tragedy was when a lifeboat was rowed up to the jetty. It contained five shivering adults, one child, and five bodies.

By then it was too late for anyone at Woolwich to rescue anybody. Estimates from eyewitnesses of the time it took the *Princess Alice* to sink after impact varied from two to four minutes, the time taken for hundreds to drown, not much more. Twenty minutes after the accident there were no survivors left in the water. All to be found at the site then was a flotsam of hats, umbrellas, shawls and toys, and all that could be heard was a band playing in the distance at the North Woolwich Pleasure Gardens. Once the tragic news spread, that music ceased abruptly.

Living at Woolwich at the time was W. T. Vincent, a reporter for the *Kent Messenger* newspaper. The town had kept him well supplied with copy from its many tragedies. There were the spectacular explosions and more minor, but sometimes more lethal, Arsenal laboratory mishaps, as well as – being a garrison town

THE PRINCESS ALICE DISASTER

with lots of young men cooped up with weapons to hand – many assaults and murders. But W. T. Vincent realized that *this* was something else.

The next day, hundreds of reporters arrived by train and some managed to get on the special 2 a.m. train put on for relatives. But earlier that night, W. T. Vincent had had the story all to himself. Later, he was to claim that by the following morning – with the help of the electric telegraph – he had informed the people of every civilized land on earth about the sinking of the *Princess Alice*.

As yet, of course, he had no idea how many had lost their lives, but he quickly realized that this was *huge* and began his first report, time-lined: Woolwich, Tuesday, Midnight: 'One of the most fearful disasters of modern times occurred this evening on the River Thames at Woolwich'.[5]

CHAPTER TWO

Collision

Abraham Deness was sitting on the main hatchway of his spritsail barge,[1] the *Bonetta*, having just unloaded a cargo of bricks at Beckton, when he saw the *Princess Alice* rounding Tripcock Point and hugging the south shore of Gallions Reach as she did so.

Soon after came the screeches of her warning whistle and the anxious shouts of 'Where are you coming to? Where are you coming to?' Then the answering call, 'Port! Port!' from a large collier, which he saw bearing down on the pleasure steamer.

Deness yelled out to his mate, James Hodgman, who was down below washing up the tea things. 'For God's sake come up and save lives!'

The pair jumped into their small boat and rowed to the crippled steamer as fast as they could. Deness was to say later:

> The *Princess Alice* disappeared almost immediately. I was close under her stern when she went down, and those I picked up jumped out of her. I saved eight lives. Would to God I could have saved the lot! I hardly know how to describe the scene to you. It was too dreadful. I can compare the *Princess Alice* to nothing else than a cloud. One moment she was there, and the next moment clean gone. I can compare the people to nothing else than a flock of sheep in the water.
>
> The river seemed full of drowning people. I went right in the midst of them, but from their frantic exertions to save themselves I hardly thought I should get out again alive. The shrieks and shouts of the people were piteous to hear, and would have quite unnerved me but for my desire to rescue some of the poor

creatures. The people were calling out all around me. "Save me, save me! For God's sake, save me!"

I rendered all the assistance I could. My boat is a small one, only 12 ft long, and I hung more on her than she was able to carry. She was very nearly level with the water, and I dared not attempt to row ashore. Another boat took two persons from me.[2]

Deness saved nine men and one girl, but had to transfer them onto another boat while he got rid of the water, then take them back and row them to Beckton Gasworks.

Joseph Smith, the master of the 75-ton schooner, *Ann Elizabeth*, from Goole, had also been anchored on the north shore near Beckton Gasworks, seen the collision and launched his lifeboat. He saved eleven (nine men and two women) and took them to the Gasworks.

At around 8.45 p.m., the inhabitants of Creekmouth, which overlooked Tripcock Point and Gallions Reach, had been startled to hear a noise 'like the boom of a big gun'.[3] Some of them ran to the river wall, where they saw the light in the back of the pleasure steamer rise in the air then disappear and heard the terrible screams and shrieks of those struggling to stay afloat.

A Lawes' factory manager promptly ordered five boats to the scene. The children's party, which had moved into the school-room for more goodies and games, was brought to a halt. The children were given sweets and sent home and the schoolroom was prepared to receive survivors.

Soon, there were eighteen soaked, injured and exhausted passengers in the Creekmouth schoolroom, one of them fran-tically lamenting that his wife and children were gone forever. They were dried, tended to and fed with the Treat Day helpers' celebration supper before being settled into hastily improvised beds and cared for throughout the night.

Twenty more were taken to the two rows of workers' cottages in this isolated spot. The Creekmouth residents donated their own shirts, trousers and waistcoats to them. Beds were vacated and the victims watched over all night by people who had to leave for work at 6 a.m.

The local curate told the *Essex Times* how touched he had been by the care given by 'these rough-looking people':

I myself saw horny-handed men with hearts soft as a woman's gently bearing poor shipwrecked men and women in their arms, bending over them, bathing their wounds and soothing their mental agonies as they best knew how.[4]

Soon it was only bodies that were being brought in and by morning thirty corpses, mostly female, lay on sacks on the factory floor, where the bodies of three children joined them.

Mr Trewby, the manager of the Beckton Gasworks, picked up several survivors and took them to his home where fires were lit, blankets and brandy provided and the women offered dry clothing. Some of them were sent home by van or cab.

Those taken to Beckton Gasworks included William Driscoll, a passenger who had jumped into the water with his little girl. He related how he had seen a man struggling to get into a lifebuoy and put out his hand and grasped it. Seeing a rescue boat he had called out, 'For God's sake, save my child!'[5] The boat had moved towards them, put out a scull for him to grasp, then taken them onboard. A sailing barge took them in while their boat was bailed out, then they were taken to Beckton.

Mr Childs, whose 3-year-old son had been dashed from his arms while he was holding onto a rope, had swum towards the shore, been picked up and taken to Beckton, as had a Mr Gill from Edgware Road. In the water, after taking off his overcoat and jacket, he found that the swimming power he had exercised as a boy (but not used for many years) had not failed him.

Mr Gill later wrote to *The Times* that among the number next to him in the boat which picked him up he found a charming little boy, about four years old, who had been separated from his mother and three sisters, who were lost.

When we reached the shore, we were hauled up to the pier of the Beckton Gas Works, where a band of good Samaritans in the shape of workmen of the place, stripped off our dripping clothes and gave us a most salutary roasting before the burning kiln fire. I was then carried on the back of one of them, naked except for a coat thrown over my shoulders, to the house of the foreman of the Gas Works, Mr Sidney Smith, who treated me and my little companion with a delicate yet hearty kindness which I shall never forget, and which I am glad to be able to here record.[6]

Mr Henry Reed, the stationer from Oxford Street, could not swim, but had managed to get hold of a plank to which he and his wife clung until they were picked up by a waterman who rowed them upstream to Greenwich. There, they were able to get a train to London Bridge and then a cab to Oxford Street where they arrived before 11 p.m. – earlier than they had expected to get home in the first place.

Other survivors and bodies were taken to Woolwich, some on the *Duke of Teck* pleasure steamer that had been ten minutes behind the *Princess Alice* but arrived on the scene too late to actually save anyone. Several survivors were also taken way downstream to Erith in the *Bywell Castle*'s larger lifeboat, which they eventually managed to launch.

After the first rowing boat had brought its startling load of survivors and bodies into Woolwich, rumours had quickly spread. An ironclad had collided with a liner, or was it a schooner? A ship had run ashore, or was it a pleasure boat? But the recurring mention of the *Princess Alice* having sunk began to gain acceptance. Those at the pier had realized she was late. Crowds began to gather, someone went to fetch the police.

More survivors and bodies began to arrive. Police Inspector Phillips arrived on the scene and called out the rest of his small force. But they still had no idea of the scope of the tragedy.

Despite his dramatic electric telegraphs to the world, even the *Kent Messenger* reporter, W. T. Vincent, still had no idea how many had perished and how many had been saved. Survivors had been taken to so many different places and some of them had found their own way home by various routes, which made arriving at any sensible figure extremely difficult both for Vincent and the authorities.

The fact that there was no passenger list, indeed no proper record of exactly how many had been onboard the doomed craft, was to make the question of how many died a long, ongoing puzzle. From the very beginning, all sorts of guestimates were bandied back and forth, all of them too awful to contemplate.

The first four bodies to arrive at Woolwich were placed in an outhouse of the Ship and Half Moon Hotel, while six female survivors, wrapped in blankets, sat shivering and dazed before the fire in the kitchen of Steam Packet Public House. More bodies were laid in the office of the London Steamboat Company at

Roffs Wharf. Soon there were nineteen in there. The mayor ordered the town hall to be opened up and the townsfolk (many very poor after the closing of the dockyard) threw open their homes to offer what warmth, dry clothes, food and comfort they could. Mr Brown, of Robson's Warehouse in the High Street, fully re-clothed three of the male survivors.

Back at Swan Pier by London Bridge, anxious relatives were trying to discover why their loved ones had not returned from their day out, but still expected to see the *Princess Alice* approaching any minute. Eventually, they were informed that there had been an accident and, when no further information was forthcoming, the crowd turned en masse and began to run towards the company's offices near Cheapside. There, a scanty list of survivors began arriving by electric telegraph.

One man and his brother-in-law, having no luck at Swan Pier, Bennets Hill or Fenchurch Street, where they had heard that some survivors were turning up, went to London Bridge Station, but found that no incoming train was expected until morning. There was, however, a hop-pickers train[7] leaving at 2.30 a.m.

'The railway inspectors put on a first class carriage, which conveyed about a dozen men and four ladies, "all on the same melancholy errand", to the Arsenal Station', he wrote to *The Times*. 'We were then taken by the station inspector to the pier, where commenced the work which is not yet finished, that of finding three persons who are most dear to us. Then to the town hall and then to the police office where the inspector telegraphed home for us.'[8]

The following day *The Times*, which had obviously received W. T. Vincent's late-night telegraph, led their report with the words: 'One of the most fearful disasters of modern times occurred last evening on the River Thames at Woolwich'. It went on to describe the accident as far as was clear, pointing out that it occurred 'at the very spot where the fatal collision between the *Metis* and the *Wentworth* had occurred some ten years earlier'.[9]

In their midnight dispatch they related some of the survivors' harrowing stories, such as that of William Alexander Law, who lost his girl off his shoulders, and that of the man who had asked his wife to throw in his children but lost them all.

The newspaper also made a guess as to the numbers lost: 500. But they also quoted the number given at Woolwich wharf: 'as many as six hundred and fifty'. And it was becoming obvious that no matter how many were lost, the great majority of these were women and children.

A further dispatch, time-lined 1.15 a.m., announced that four of the saved had just been brought over to Woolwich from Barking Creek. These included Mr Edward Leaver of Lambeth, 'who is in great anguish at the loss of four sons and daughters'.

Even those saved had no idea what had happened to their loved ones. Edward Leaver Junior feared that his family, whom he had last seen in the upper deck saloon, were lost; Thames Police Inspector King frantically sought his wife, parents and brother, and governess Elizabeth Randall had no idea of the fate of her fellow governess, Maria Scholz, and the six young students they had taken on a day out down the river.

Mr Childs had not lingered at Beckton but managed to get home to Edgware Road that night. Early the following morning, reported the *Daily News* of 5 September, Paddington Police brought round the telegram they had received from Woolwich Police, which informed Mr Childs that his 6-year-old daughter, Alice, and her 7-week old brother had survived. His wife, Emma, however, and their 3-year-old son, who had been dashed from his arms, were dead, as was his brother and his brother's girlfriend. But the *Standard* and *The Times* of the same day carried different news. Mrs Child and their 7-week-old daughter had survived and were in the Plumstead and Woolwich Infirmary. Indeed, *The Times* even carried Child's own statement to that effect. In fact, Mrs Childs and the baby *had* survived. The rest had perished.

CHAPTER THREE

Indescribably Hushed

The little town of Woolwich, 'somewhat dull and grimy at all seasons' was now, 'indescribably hushed', reported the *Standard* of 5 September 1878. 'The people stand in groups upon the pavement, discussing the calamity which befell last night.'

Every train brought more frantically anxious relatives and friends in search of their loved ones and more sightseers and reporters. Apparently, one could tell which was which by the faces among them that were 'drawn with anxiety, swollen with prescient grief'. Frantic crowds gathered at the town hall and the office of the London Steamboat Company where the bodies lay and at the pier where more were being brought in. Inspector Phillips tried to control the emotional crowds around the little round house at the foot of the pier that contained thirty bodies. The police were kind, but they might have managed better, commented the *Standard*.

> Round the door there was an ugly squeeze, and when parties came out they had a struggle to make way. One elderly woman asked again and again with pitiful simplicity and earnestness, "Is there a stout female in there about 40-years-old?" Half a dozen times I heard a patient inspector reply that no such person lay inside but the old woman asked again, always in the same words, of those who came out.

According to that newspaper, the arrangements were much worse at the town hall, even though police from Woolwich Arsenal had been brought in to assist. Indeed, the situation was simply scandalous.

> Childish common sense might have prepared a better system
> for meeting the emergency ... the street was thronged but no
> policeman tried to keep a passage. Two powerful constables
> stood before the door, resisting by main force the rush of people
> who tried to enter but no way aiding those who came out.

Only five or six were let in at a time and it took them twenty
minutes to examine the bodies. 'We have been here three hours,
and there are fifty people before us yet!' complained one tearful
woman and, it was alleged, policemen even began losing their
tempers and assaulting those trying to get in.[1]

The *Daily News* and *Morning Post* were more understanding
of the police problems saying that it was no easy task repressing
'the ardour inspired by grief and despair among those engaged
in the dismal duty of traversing rooms full of corpses in the hope
of recognising the one they might claim'.

The melancholy search for loved ones was made more
harrowing by the fact that the bodies were so scattered. After
trying Woolwich Town Hall, the couple who had come down
by the hop-pickers train at 2.30 a.m. crossed to North Woolwich,
continued along to Beckton Gasworks, went from there to
Creekmouth, then on to Rainham and Erith by boat. 'At all those
places the same result, many corpses but not those we sought ...
Our search is not over yet'. they told *The Times*. 'No better father
and mother sat on that boat than those we mourn.'[2]

The two-mile trek from North Woolwich to Beckton and
Creekmouth was particularly unpleasant. The area was ugly and
the terrain difficult. The first pathway through the marshes was
a narrow causeway. On one side there were poor and weedy
fields strewn with watercourses and bits of broken railway.
On the other, a muddy stream. Beyond, on the other side of
the Thames, were the outskirts of the town of Woolwich, half-
hidden under a smoky haze.

On the river itself, steamers stood waiting to collect the next
load of bodies dragged up from the depths by the watermen or
gathered from the riverbanks. Many London watermen had
come down to drag for bodies, each of which would earn them
at least five shillings, and they could make even more by taking
sightseers to the supposed site of the accident.

The steamers also brought in some of the flotsam of hats,

bonnets and shawls which still floated on the surface of the river.

Beckton Gasworks was surrounded by a coal-blackened laby-
rinth of sidings, tramways, rails and sheds through which, after
viewing the bodies held there, the anxious relatives were guided
by watchful overseers, to another causeway. Twenty minutes later
they reached Barking Creek, through which the River Roding, a
slough of mud and water, emptied into the Thames. There, specu-
lative boatmen awaited them, loaded their crafts to the gunwales
and ferried them across to the little village of Creekmouth and
the Lawes Patent Manure Factory. Here, at the far end of a dark
and murky shed, a large room had been set aside for bodies, half
of them still unclaimed.

Four survivors still remained at Creekmouth, including Mrs
Gollifer, who was too weak to be moved, and a Mr Hagger, who
had saved her. He had a terrible gash behind his ear, but no idea
how he had received it, and wounds and bruises all over his
body. There were also two unclaimed small boys, one of whom
seemed to the *Standard* reporter to be 'dull with terror and grief',
and could only say that if he was taken to Kensington he would
find his aunt. This, a 'good natured workman' was about to do.[3]

After Creekmouth, the many searchers, driven on by anxiety
and dread, were obliged to carry on downriver to Rainham, a
quiet little village isolated among the marshes on the north side
of the Thames and only reachable by a long, circuitous walk or by
boat. Then it was on to Erith on the south side. To make matters
worse, more bodies were beginning to wash up elsewhere along
the Thames as far upriver as Limehouse.

Searchers became more and more confused and overwrought,
not knowing where to go next. More than one person began
to recognize the same body that had in any case become more
similar as a result of increasing decomposition and the state of
their clothes. Still they came. 'At an early hour of the morning',
reported the *Standard*, 'the Factory of Messrs Lawes was again
besieged'.[4]

A few survivors remained in the Plumstead Infirmary where
Dr Rice, Mr Makie and the matron, Miss Wilkinson, had been up
all night after the accident, preparing beds to receive as many as
a hundred.

'Unfortunately', reported the *Morning Post*, 'only a very few
of them found occupants'. Sixteen had arrived however. Among

them were: Benjamin Smith, who had a bandaged face due to an injury to his nose, received when he surfaced through the wreckage; the very poorly Mrs Emma Standish and a Mrs Child, whom the *Daily* News had reported dead along with her 2-year-old son and who were now miraculously alive.

Despite the fact that her husband and two other children had been missing, Emma Childs had acted 'with exemplary patience' throughout the night, said the *Morning Post*, and had not given way until the morning, 'when her husband was found to be alive'.

They found another (unnamed) patient had not been so stoical, despite her son having identified her and brought along with him a letter from his father (content not specified). Her other children were missing and 'the kindest assurances of their safety would not satisfy her, as she instinctively felt that they were subterfuges to hide the horrid truth from her for a little time longer'.[5]

Lone children had also ended up at the infirmary. These included a little girl, who could only say she had been in the boat with her Aunt Lizzie, but later revealed her name was Mabel Hepburn and that her mother kept a sweet shop in London. Then there was 'a splendid little lad, apparently a foreigner, about four years of age, who has not spoken since his admission. I, however,' wrote one of the *Standard*'s special correspondents, 'tried him this morning with a few words in French, and the poor little fellow burst into tears, without, however, answering me'.[6]

The west Kent coroner, 69-year-old Charles Joseph Carttar, had been informed of the accident on the evening it occurred by a police sergeant from Greenwich Police Station who knocked on his door to announce: 'We have word up from Woolwich, sir, of a big sinking in the river'. He added that the Woolwich inspector thought hundreds had been drowned.[7]

Carttar told the sergeant he would be at Woolwich early next morning.

The coroner was not a well man; he suffered from vascular heart disease, which affected his circulation and caused his legs to swell up at night. Now he was to preside over a protracted inquest on the country's worst-ever civilian disaster with the eyes of the world upon him.

Fortunately, he was very experienced, having presided, during the previous forty-six years, over many inquests in this volatile area. Indeed, only the year before he had conducted the famous inquest into the death of a wealthy heiress, Harriett Staunton, as a result of which her husband and three others were charged and convicted of causing her death by starvation. (Although sentenced to death, they were reprieved due to disagreement among medical men, some of whom claimed that the cause of death could have been tuberculosis.)

Mr Carttar opened his inquest on Wednesday 4 September, the day after the disaster, at Alexander Hall in Woolwich. After swearing in the nineteen-man jury of shopkeepers and tradesmen, he began by pointing out that no words of his could adequately describe the intense feeling of sorrow and distress occasioned to the relatives by the dreadful calamity on which they met to inquire. They could only alleviate it by having the bodies identified as soon as possible and handed over to the relatives. The inquiry as to the cause of the accident could wait. After going into his reasoning on this at length and, his voice breaking, he finished by reiterating that their main duty was first to have the bodies identified, then to ascertain how the deplorable occurrences had come to pass by which so many human beings had been hurried into eternity.

The ever-knowing *Standard* had news for him there, having begun its coverage on 5 September 1878, with the words, 'It is now clearly understood how the *Princess Alice* was sunk, though the cause of the disaster has yet to be investigated'.

Carttar took his jury to view the fifty-eight bodies still scattered around the various venues, then began to take formal identification evidence on seven of the eight who had been recognized.

The first to be identified was 45-year-old William Beechey, who had, perhaps, the oddest of reasons to have been on the boat: a sudden whim. He had left his workplace at a city stockbrokers at 4.30 p.m. and 'was supposed to have taken a train to join the *Princess Alice* at some point on her voyage upriver as he had proposed to a fellow clerk to do so the previous day', reported *The Times*.[8] When he failed to return home that evening his wife, alarmed by his absence, had contacted his employees, who sent down a fellow worker to look for his body and who now identified him.

The next witness, Henry Drew, a warehouseman from Tottenham, was 'one of the saved'. He identified the body of his 2-year-old daughter, Martha Helen, but was still looking for his other two daughters, who had been given the outing as a treat when their brothers were taken to see a cricket match at Lord's. His wife was also 'one of the saved'.

An 18-year-old boy, William James Elliott, from Clapham, identified his father, but was still looking for his mother and her friend. He told the coroner that he and his young sister had no money, so Carttar ordered that he be given £5 from the £19 found in his father's pocket.

Freddie Pollard, the 18-year-old *Princess Alice* knife-boy, was identified by his elder brother, while boot-maker, John Marsh of Clerkenwell, swore to the identity of his 60-year-old mother-in-law, Zillah Waddilove, who had been one of the St John's Mission's Bible party. Two men identified their sons: mariner Matthew Mountain, from Poplar New Town, swore to his 23-year-old son, William Frederick, who had been a second steward on the doomed vessel; while Hampstead grocer Mr Hill, that of the body of his son, 22-year-old Thomas Wheeler Hill, a mathematical instrument maker who lived in South Norwood. Mr Hill had been alerted to his son's possible plight when he received a telegram from the young man's landlady saying he had gone for a holiday and failed to return.

The jury were taken to view the site of the collision although, as yet, nothing could be seen of the wreck. They were then instructed to reconvene on the following day at 2 p.m., this time at the smaller, but rather more comfortable and convivial, board-room at the town hall. With its large, horseshoe-shaped windows, tasteful carpet and brass chandeliers, it was a decidedly more pleasing chamber in which to work and they were going to be there for a very long time.

As the *Princess Alice* body count continued to rise, the question of where to put them became ever more urgent. The person chiefly tasked with sorting this out was the London Steamboat Company's Superintendent Towse who had, himself, lost his wife, his mother-in-law and four of his eight children.

One of Carttar's first moves was to ask for assistance from the military that now used the dockyard buildings. They made available a large iron shed in which to place the bodies and, during the night, all those that had been found on the south shore were taken there.

CHAPTER FOUR

Yes, But How Many?

The awful trek to find bodies of loved ones was made much easier when all those found on the south side of the river were taken to the shed in the Woolwich dockyard.

There, Woolwich Police Inspector Phillips organized a system which made identification a less painful procedure. As each corpse was brought in a police clerk took details of sex and apparent age and attached a number to them. Watches, jewellery and small articles were removed and placed in glass-lidded cigar boxes which bore the identical number. These were placed in a separate room – dubbed the 'Black Museum' by the Press – which also held hats, umbrellas, scarves and shawls. Here, relatives could view the artefacts. If they recognized them they would be taken to the body bearing same number, thus saving them from the dreadful experience of viewing numerous corpses just to pick out those they sought.

Once formally identified before the inquest jury, the body was removed to another shed where it was released to the relatives. From there, it could be taken to London Bridge, free of charge, by the South Eastern Railway.

Thus, by the second day after the disaster, the crowds, who previously had been so desperate for information that they grabbed hold of anyone who looked the least official, had calmed down.

There was a marked increase in the incoming flow of bodies due to the number being brought up by steamboat from Erith and to those surfacing from the river bed. Many of the shops had begun displaying placards offering rewards for help in finding the missing.

Naturally, the scenes at the dockyard remained, as the *Standard* put it, 'harrowing in the extreme'. A Mrs Wood, of Denham, recognized her son, Charles. 'It was most piteous to hear the poor lady beseeched to be allowed to touch her son's hand, which she was allowed to do.'[1]

Although those bodies found on the south side of the river were now all taken to Woolwich dockyard shed, the same was not true for the bodies found on the north side, simply because the south side was in Kent while the north side was in Essex (with the exception of North Woolwich which was included with Woolwich town and thus in Kent), and it was against the law to move unidentified bodies from one county to another. Therefore some bodies still lay at Beckton Gasworks and the factory at Creekmouth.

The south Essex coroner, Mr Charles C. Lewis, tried to clarify the matter, even going up to London to consult the officials at the Board of Trade and the Home Office, but no one there was prepared to sanction the move of all the bodies to Woolwich or tell them how to handle these exceptional mass inquests. So he decided to open his inquest for the purposes of identification, issue burial certificates, then send the bodies over to Woolwich. 'I will then adjourn until your inquest is over,' he wrote to Carttar, 'and then I shall hope to conclude the case without having all the evidence repeated'. (He was referring to the fact that once most of the identification was completed the inquests were obliged to go on to decide the cause of death as well as that of the accident.)[2]

Efforts were made to ease the plight of the relatives arriving at North Woolwich by the north London railway by sending over a list of the saved, compiled from various sources, to be read over to them. If those not lucky enough to receive welcome news proved to be very poor, some of the watermen took them across the river to Woolwich, free of charge, to begin their search. There, just inside the dockyard, were now eight or nine service wagons behind which were clerks who took the descriptions of those sought and compared them with those of the bodies found so far.

Besides the inquests at Woolwich and in the schoolroom at Creekmouth, there were to be other inquests on bodies which turned up further away. One had already taken place at Poplar on two bodies that had been washed upstream and into East

and West India Docks. One body was that of a, so far, unidentified woman. The other had been recognized as that of Edward
King, father of Police Inspector King, the man who thought he
had saved his wife but found, on reaching the riverbank, that it
wasn't her. He was now in search of his wife's body and those of
the rest of his family.

Unsurprisingly, the news of the sinking of the *Princess Alice*
rapidly came to dominate the newspapers. There were initial
dramatic headlines such as 'Terrible Collision on the Thames',
'The Catastrophe on the River', and 'Fearful Collision on the
River'. The text below the headlines soon followed a familiar
pattern: a general run-through of the current situation then,
under separate headings 'Narratives of Survivors' or 'Personal
Narratives', then 'Latest Particulars and Inquest'.

The same survivors, such as Oxford Street stationer, Mr
Reed, and Mr Childs, whose son had been dashed out of his
arms, told their stories or 'narratives' to several newspapers, or,
one imagines, they were just picked up by them. The *Standard*
managed to strike a particularly tasteless note by describing such
tales as 'thrilling personal descriptions'.

There were also the endless lists. At first, these were merely
hastily put together roll calls of the missing, giving their names,
ages and addresses plus occasional brief details. For example,
from *The Times* of 5 September:

> Enquiries were yesterday made for the following persons, who
> are missing and supposed to be drowned in the *Princess Alice*.
> The list reveals more clearly than any comment could the kind of
> loss which the collision brings upon very many families:
>
> **Edward King,** aged 64, a wooden-legged Greenwich Pensioner.
> His brother-in-law and friends make inquiries. He was on a day's
> excursion to Sheerness. His address was Woodbine Cottage,
> Woodland Street, Trafalgar Road, Greenwich.
>
> **Alfred,** son of the last, aged 19.
>
> **Mrs Fanny King**, sister-in-law of the last, aged 29, 20 Wootton
> Street, Cornwell Road, Lambeth.
>
> **Edward King**, six months old, child of the last.

Mr Robert Everist, aged 38, 2 Croydon Road, Barking Road, Essex.

Mrs Everist, aged 32, his wife.

Robert Everist aged 10, son of preceding.

John Everist, aged 8.

Willie Everist, aged 4 and

A baby, 15 months, child of Robert Everist the elder.

The enquiries were made by Mr Hawkins, son-in-law of Mr and Mrs Everist. They had gone on a day's excursion to Sheerness from North Woolwich.

Mrs T. Lee, 28, 2 Kilburn-baths, Kilburn. She was staying at Sheerness with her husband and cousin. They came up by train on Sunday, but she, in consequence of the railway accident on Saturday, was afraid to come and preferred to travel by boat. Her husband and cousin arrived safely and are now looking for her.

But soon the lists of the missing included personal descriptions and the clothing worn. On Friday 6 September *The Times* told its readers:

The following list of missing persons who have been inquired for is to be added to the list we published yesterday:

William Potter, age 33; height 5 ft 10 in; very stout; dress, brown tweed suit, side-spring boots. Address, 12 Suffolk-street, North-street Poplar.

Caroline Dyble, age 43; dress, black silk jacket, gold watch and chain, gold brooch and earrings. Address, Rose and Crown, Dorset-street, Fleet-street.

Alice Hammond, age 20; fair; dress black, braided jacket, brown Holland dress,[3] silver earrings, locket and chain, new side-spring boots. Frederick Villa, Barking-road, Canning-town. E.

Disney Perou, age 51; hair dark, large scar on left check, black suit; on person, gold watch and chain, diamond ring on finger. The Rising Sun public house, 87, Sidney-street, Mile-end.

Walter Brodrib, age 11, complexion and hair dark, eyes blue; dress light plaid suit, straw hat, low shoes with buckles, gray ribbed stockings, white shirt, flannel bandage around chest. Address, 12 Goulborne-terrace, Appleford-road, Kentish New Town.

Annie Summers, aged 30; height, 5 ft 3 in; complexion fair; eyes light blue; dress brown stuff, black silk jacket, side-spring boots; three gold rings (one wedding, one keeper, one fancy). No 7, Mornington-road, New Cross.

And so on, for about another hundred names. The authorities might not know how many were missing but the extent of the loss was becoming more and more evident due to the growing numbers being sought.

There were also lists of bodies found and identified before the coroner. With these, readers were given more of their stories, as in this from *The Times* of Friday 6 September 1878:

Edmund T. Moore, 45, keeper of the Alfred Tavern, Roman-road, Barnsbury, identified by his son Thomas H. Moore of the same address. Witness's mother was saved, but two brothers of his are missing.

Susannah Law, aged 52, spinster, Charterhouse-street, identified by her brother, John Law, manager of the Charterhouse-street branch of the London Joint-Stock Bank. Jane, sister of the deceased, aged 49, is missing. Deceased is one of the Bible-class party, which, according to witnesses numbered 48 or 50 persons of ages varying from 28 to 70. All but two of these have been lost.

S. M. Page, commercial traveller, East Dulwich, identified by his son W. S. Page, commercial clerk 1, Brixton-villas, Hindman-road, Peckham. This witnesses case, like Mr Towses, is of an especially sorrowful character. He is the only person saved out of a party of six, among whom were his father, his wife, aged 21 years, his son aged 12 months and his sister Florence aged 16 years ... when the collision occurred he and his wife, who had the child in her arms, were standing near the part of the steamer which was struck. Holding his wife and child with one hand, he seized the chains of the *Bywell Castle* with the other but finding the load too much for his strength, he told his wife to sacrifice the child. She refused to do this, and he was obliged to let both go.

As well as the lists of those sought and those found and identified were the lists of bodies found and not yet recognized. These appeared regularly in newspapers and were posted at the dockyard gates and grew longer and more prominent as time went by.

The clothing descriptions for the bodies found were much more detailed than in the lists of the missing; understandably so, relatives were unlikely to be absolutely sure of every detail of what they had been wearing that day. Typical of the lists on bodies found and not identified were:

Man, aged 40, height, 5 ft 9 ins; hard whiskers and mustachios; light summer overcoat, blue coat and vest, cloth plaid trousers, brown striped socks, low shoes; a silver, open-faced watch, gold guard, two lockets, one red stone, one wreath of hair, £2.10s gold, 8s silver, 10d bronze, one telescopic knife, brass, tooth pick, 12 postage stamps, key; ticket, Waterloo to Addlestone; pocket book.

Woman, 35, hair dark brown, height, 5 ft; dress, black cross-over, bugle and lace trimmings, pink flowers, necktie, white stockings, side-spring boots; four rings (left) one wedding, one keeper, two dress, ruby and green stones, a small brooch, shell setting, half-circular comb, pair of earrings, pair of studs, initials C.[4]

Incidentally, these lists are useful sources for anyone interested in what the upper working and lower middle classes wore for a day out in the mid-nineteenth century. Amongst the interesting facts to be gleaned is that so many of the passengers, male and female, were wearing the fashionable side-spring boots. That is, elasticated at the ankles rather than buttoned or laced.

Looming increasingly large among the questions posed by the press and many others was just how many had been onboard the ill-fated pleasure steamer and therefore how many had been lost. Numbers fluctuated wildly, even going as high as a thousand in one instance. The *Morning Post* of Friday 5 September made a concerted effort to work this out by comparing estimates gathered from various 'authorities'.

One authority states that there were 800 passengers, while the ticket collector at Gravesend, who happened to give unusual attention to the number of passengers onboard, expresses his belief that the *Princess Alice* left Gravesend with about 600 people. Captain Fitzgerald, the Thames harbour-master, estimates the loss at 400; the superintendent of the Woolwich police at about 300; but the steamboat officials estimate the loss at from 400 to 500. It is probable, however, that the loss will be nearly 600 lives.

Oddly enough, they did not reveal *how* they came to that final estimate, but did say that, so far, 'not more than 70 survivors are known of with certainty but the number of dead bodies recovered is upwards of 100'.

Opinions on who was to blame for the accident were also prompt to surface. As might be expected, *The Times* letter writers were soon in full flow on this subject, and on the other big question – why the huge loss of life?

As for blame, Mr W.H. Crispin wrote that the week before the accident he had gone to Gravesend in one of the saloon steamers, which had been crowded with passengers. The tide was against them both up and down. However, instead of the steamers keeping to their own side, 'they ran first one side the river, then the other, to "cheat" as the captain called it, the tide'. Until a law was passed to prevent such erratic proceedings, he concluded, accidents such as that to the *Princess Alice* must happen.[5]

'Nemo' claimed the accident was due to ignorance of the 'rule of the road', and 'Marine Insurance' claimed that such accidents were incessant due to careless navigation but were only noticed when there was loss of life.[6]

The Times chewed over these points, but concluded that perhaps it would be better to wait until the matter had been thoroughly investigated before coming down on any particular side. The *Standard*, of course, felt no such compunction. One of their reporters declared:

> Waterside people know no better than others how the calamity happened, but they have a strong conviction founded on experience. They say that the officers of the London Steamboat Company are careful beyond all others. That watch is always kept with vigilance, and the crew are picked men. Upon the

other hand, it is declared that the crew of colliers leaving London are always worked out, dead with sleep, and that the lookout, always careless, is in no state to do his duty as he goes down the river. I give the statement for what it may seem worth to those who are concerned in such matters.[7]

Of course, the opinions of 'waterside people' may have been somewhat biased, influenced by their familiarity with the *Princess Alice* crew and the London Steamboat Company, which operated among them and which had brought much needed work and trade to the area.

CHAPTER FIVE

The Vultures are Gathering

'Gentlemen, before proceeding with the business before us; it is my paramount duty to read to you a gracious message from Her Majesty, which has been communicated to me through the Lord Lieutenant of the county', announced the coroner on opening the Woolwich inquest on its second day, Thursday 5 September. [1]

Right from the start, Queen Victoria had been repeatedly telegraphing the Board of Trade for news of the tragedy, wanting to know how many had been onboard and asking that messages of condolences be sent to the relatives of those who had lost their lives. These were passed to the Lord Mayor, Earl Sidney, the Lord Lieutenant of Kent and the London Steamboat Company from whence they were disseminated via newspapers and other means.

She, too, wanted to know just how many had been lost, as did the Grand Duke and Duchess of Hesse, who had just arrived back in London from Eastbourne, where they had been holidaying. The day after the collision their secretary sent a letter from Buckingham Palace to the London Steamboat Company saying how they had read 'the accounts in the papers with very great sorrow' and hoped that their sympathy be conveyed to the survivors and that the loss of life would not be as great is it was feared to be. The Duchess was, of course, the Princess Alice after whom the fated pleasure craft had been named.

After reading out the Queen's message, Mr Carttar went on to explain the reason that they were holding a jury viewing and inquest on every victim, even though the task was almost insurmountable. He said that he and his fellow Essex coroner had asked for but not received any official advice on the necessity of doing it this way, so they had just gone ahead. Also, they had realized that had they not done so, there might be 'an unseemly scramble for property on the part of people who might have no right to it whatever'.[2] He and the Parish authorities had therefore come to the conclusion that they ought to pursue their painful and arduous task to the end if the jury agreed. They did.

Carttar also complained that he was overwhelmed with letters containing all sorts of silly and impracticable suggestions. All these did was waste valuable time and he asked it to be known through the press that he should receive no more.

One of these letters was from a Kent plumber who suggested that some bodies might be brought to the surface if a heavy piece of cannon was fired over the river where, it was supposed, some were thought to lie. He had witnessed it done and had seen a body rise 'almost perpendicularly'. Another letter writer offered his patented Fresh Meat Preservative, which could preserve the bodies for some time.

Mr Harrington, the jury foreman, spoke up to announce that after the previous day's adjournment, in compliance with instructions, he and Inspector Dawkins had taken a steamboat down to Erith to collect the fourteen bodies left there. He reported, 'I am sorry to say they [the bodies] have been treated in a different manner from what has been the case at Woolwich'.

In fact, some of the bodies at Erith were rather more damaged than those landing elsewhere – possibly due to buffeting when carried a long distance downstream. More disturbingly, some had been undressed, which, said *The Times*, 'somewhat retarded their identification'.[3]

By the reopening of the inquest on Friday, 6 September, it all seemed to be getting a little too much for Mr Carttar. Three days of viewing bodies of men, women and children and listening to a relentless succession of bereft relatives giving their tearful evidence of identification, were obviously taking their toll. As he spoke of the magnitude of the disaster and the dreadful loss of life, and praised the military, the people of Woolwich and others for their assistance, he was suddenly overcome and covered his face with his hands. When he recovered, the sad procedure continued. But, upset or no, Carttar was not going to let any dubious witnesses go unchallenged.

Thomas Gray, who claimed a body to be that of his wife's

niece, Harriett Gurr, aged forty, admitted that he had no real reason to assume that she had been onboard the *Princess Alice*. He knew nothing of her movements apart from the fact that she had gone to Gravesend on the Monday. It was only when he heard of the accident that he had become concerned. His wife, however, had had 'a presentment' and had ordered him down to Woolwich where, he claimed, he had seen her niece among the dead. He had no doubt about her identity.

The coroner was not satisfied and urged Mr Gray to consider that a mistake was possible.

Mr Gray was not happy: 'I have no doubt about the identity of my niece'.

But Mr Carttar persisted. 'You are, I doubt not, speaking as you believe, but I should like some better evidence.' He went on to describe a case 'not long ago' in which sixteen persons had sworn most positively to the identity of a body of a man. There had been a public subscription for the widow and her dead baby had been buried in the same coffin with the corpse. Three months later, the husband suddenly appeared alive and in good health. Therefore, Carttar insisted, it was necessary to be particular.

'Mr Gray could not see the argument,' reported the *Standard*, 'and lost his temper. He had been sent to recognize his wife's niece and he had done so'.

However, in answer to a question from the jury foreman he admitted that had there been no accident they would not have inquired for some days longer.

It was revealed that the niece usually wore a hunting watch so Mr Gray was sent off to examine her property.

Next came a surgeon, Mr Arthur William Kempe, who presented an erroneous death certificate which, he said, had been issued for the body of his surgeon-dentist father. A fellow surgeon had identified him as Arthur William Kempe, but in fact his name was William Hussey Bloomfield Kempe. 'This mistake was most serious, pointed out the *Daily News*, 'as the deceased had insured his life; the name was corrected, of course'.

When William John Anchorn identified his father and mother to the court's satisfaction 'a spectator' stood up to declare that the mother's name had been wrongly given as Ellen Elizabeth when it should be Ellen Flin. *He* knew that because she was his sister. The son said he had never heard the name Flin connected with his family or his mother. The objector was called forward to explain 'that property might be at stake'. Since he had no proof of his claim he was told that the name could be changed if some was brought.

'A lady, who indeed had no close interest in the remains she claimed', reported the *Standard*, 'was painfully anxious about "the property" – a wedding ring, a keeper ring with two emeralds and a small diamond, silver earrings and suchlike. The police eased her mind by the assurance that these things were safe, and she departed happy.'

It seemed that Carttar and Williams Lewis had been right to ensure proper identification. The vultures appeared to be gathering.

Mr Gray reappeared complaining that he had been unable to find the official charged with keeping his niece's things, but someone spoke up to say he had just left Inspector Ford in his proper place, whereupon Mr Gray found he had been looking in the wrong direction. 'This gentleman', commented the *Standard*, 'evidently thought himself a public benefactor in identifying his wife's niece, and declared aloud, on setting out once more to find Inspector Ford, that if this search was not successful he would go home'.

The *Standard* continued its graphic descriptions but mostly in a somewhat kinder tone:

> The testimony of Henry Beadle had touches of extreme pathos. A gaunt and dirty old man deposed to the finding of his wife, and the coroner's close questioning could do no more than raise a quiver of his unshorn lip, and a dogged repetition, 'Oh I know her – oh I know her, sir!'
>
> Mary Jones gave her evidence firmly until it came to the point when her husband went 'for a ramble with a friend' after doing his work. Here she broke down suddenly and piteously, but in a few seconds her firmness returned. The companion of this sad ramble had escaped and he stepped up to the table. In that dry and husky voice that belongs to the street poor of London, with odd starts and bursts, and sudden stoppages he told how the pair went to Deptford, then to Gravesend, and thence the one to death and the other to do a battle with the stream.
>
> Louisa Boddington, an interesting young girl, claimed a

burial certificate for her mother, who had gone upon the pleasure trip of the Cowcross Mission. As a lady explained, this child is left without a sixpence to support four little brothers and sisters. Mr Catlin, who was seeking his own dead at the riverside, is willing to bury Louisa's mother if the corpse can be brought to him, and the exertions of the military and steam-boat authorities have provided for such a case.[4]

Poor old Fanny Robert, a spinster from Luton in Bedfordshire, who identified the body of her cousin, had been kindly looking after this cousin's seven children while she and her husband went on the *Princess Alice* to Sheerness. The husband was still missing and Fanny had been left holding the babies, all seven of them.

There came further evidence of whole families being wiped out. George Hunt, an office fitter from Kingsland in Hackney, identified the body of his 22-year-old son. His wife and four other children, two boys and two girls, were also lost.

And so it went on: sons and daughters identifying parents, parents identifying children, husbands identifying wives and wives identifying husbands, with occasional variations.

George Quinton, a cooper, identified Emily, the 10-year-old daughter of his employer, William Davies. William Davies himself, his wife, and five other children were all lost.

'The mother reached the shore alive,' reported *The Times*, 'but died thirty-six hours afterwards from exposure and exhaustion. She was perfectly conscious to the last and knew that all her family were lost. Her husband at the moment of collision said to her, "It's all over this time." The newspaper did not explain what Mr Davies had meant by 'this time'.[5]

Mrs Davies was not the only survivor to die quite soon after rescue. Sixty-one-year-old Mrs Emma Standish, who had been recovering in the infirmary, died on the Friday morning from 'chronic bronchitis accelerated by shock and immersion'.[6] Mrs Davis of Limehouse 'succumbed to her injuries in the presence of her friends' in one of the Creekmouth cottages[7] while Mr Vachel, 'a gentleman from Surbiton' died on Friday night at the house of a friend, Dr Lacey of Plumstead 'whither he was taken from the wreck at his own request'.[8]

Other departures from the norm of family identifications

occurred when Royal Artillery Sergeant Major Richard Sleet identified Farrier Sergeant James Burton and when Police Inspector William Jenkins identified the body of PC Cornelius Briscoe, 'N' Division's local hero who had rescued a drowning person from the Regent's Canal. His wife and children were still missing.

At nearly one o'clock the coroner decided to adjourn 'for dinner' but Mr Hughes, on the behalf of the London Steamboat Company, asked if he might summarize a statement of his which demonstrated how they had arrived at the number who were onboard at the time of the collision. This explained that, at various boarding points, a tally of passengers was taken by the pier-master, for the purpose of charging dues, giving a pretty accurate return and thus answering the burning question of how many might have drowned and how many more bodies they might expect to surface.

It was known that the *Princess Alice* was licensed to carry 936 passengers on the 'smooth water voyage', that is as far as Gravesend, but beyond that, in the estuary where the Thames began to open out to the sea, only 486 in the summer and 336 in the winter.

Mr Hughes's statement revealed that on Tuesday 3 September 1878, there had been 491 passengers onboard the *Princess Alice* when she arrived at Sheerness. Four had left there, leaving 487. Eighty-one of these had landed at Gravesend, reducing the total to 406, but seventy-nine people had then boarded at Gravesend, bringing the total back up to 485. At Rosherville, 138 had boarded, raising it to 623. To be added to that were twenty-nine crew and stewards, bringing the total up 652. And, to this, 'a few' needed to be added for the band. However, very young children were not counted nor were children in arms.

A juryman commented that, in fact, children up to the age of six or seven were not counted. The coroner disagreed saying that, in his experience, two children above the age of two were counted as one passenger, which meant that if 150 of the single tickets represented two people, this would raise the 652 total they had been given, to 802.

A juryman suggested that an aggregate might be obtained by taking the numbers of the parties, as stated by the witnesses. But the jury foreman said that very few tickets had been found on the bodies, so it seemed there must have been a number onboard *without* tickets. Another juryman pointed out that this might be accounted for by one member of a party having retained all the tickets and therefore *some* bodies might be found with several tickets on them.

In the end, it seemed that Mr Hughes's statement had not taken them much further forward except to convince them that, as feared, the number onboard had been very large, and therefore there were many more bodies yet to come.

Meanwhile, as Mr Carttar and his jury adjourned for their dinner, the Grand Duke and Duchess of Hesse (the real Princess Alice) were lunching at Clarence House, in the company of the Prince and Princess of Wales and the King and Queen of Denmark, prior to their departure that afternoon for Antwerp and thence home to Darmstadt.

CHAPTER SIX

Serious Accusations

Meanwhile, the *Bywell Castle* remained anchored off Deptford where she had moved from Barking Creek on the instruction of the owners. Captain Harrison and his wife, who had been a passenger, went back to their home in Hackney to await developments.

The unenviable situation of Captain Harrison had not been helped by an accusation from his own stoker, Purcell, that at the time of the collision the crew of the *Bywell Castle* had all been drunk. Purcell had first made his accusation on the night of the disaster. He had climbed onboard the *Bywell Castle*'s cutter with other crew members plus three of the saved from the *Princess Alice*. They had been hoping to rescue as many as forty, even though the boat was meant to carry only thirty. In the event, only five living survivors remained to be saved, but they took them, along with four dead bodies, downriver to Erith to avoid the heavy pull needed to go upstream. Purcell certainly appeared drunk. He proved a garrulous nuisance whilst onboard. But when he reached Erith he began shouting his accusations.

PC30 'R' of Erith Division had joined the crowd gathering at Erith's moonlit landing place and took the names and addresses of the survivors. After he finished, Purcell asked him insolently, 'Well, are you going to get me some brandy?'

When the constable said 'No,' Purcell asked where there was a pub.

'Just at the top,' said the PC.

'I will bloody well go and get some myself then,' Purcell said.

While the others helped move the bodies Purcell stayed at the pub where a local confectioner, named Harris, befriended him, took him home and gave him a jacket, as he was still in shirt sleeves.

'This is a sad affair,' Harris had murmured.

'By God it is, Guvnor,' Purcell agreed.

'How do you account for it?'

'It's the bloody booze.'

'You do not mean that?'

'I do, by God,' exclaimed the stoker.

Purcell had gone on to claim that that the Captain and the pilot had been boozing, 'all the bloody afternoon,' but he blamed the collision squarely on the second mate whom he had heard say, 'I'll see if I can handle this bugger,' before striding off.

Just after that, the collision occurred.

The arrival of another crew member stopped Purcell's mouth, for a while, but on the way back to the pub he returned to blaming the second mate who 'ought to be bloody hung'.

'Do you mean to say you were all boozed?' asked Harris.

'Every bloody bung.'

'Were *you* drunk?'

'I was, Guvnor, but by God, it brought me sober.'

Shortly afterwards Purcell collapsed on the floor. When revived, he was taken to the bar shouting, 'The beasts were drunk. The beasts were drunk!'

Settled into a high-backed chair he began to cry muttering, 'S'help me God I mean to tell the truth'.[1]

The other men told him to keep quiet and said they ought to get back. As they went down the causeway Purcell was sick then fell into the boat where he was left insensible. By now, the rest of the crew were also tipsy from being 'treated'. On their return journey they were all over the river. Fortunately, Robinson, a local man, took charge of the cutter and got them back safely.

The following morning the *Bywell Castle* moved up to Deptford where Captain Harrison made up his log: the first official account of the disaster.

Log of the steamship *Bywell Castle* from London towards the Tyne

Remarks

On Tuesday the third of September, 1878, John Hardy on the lookout on the topgallant forecastle. William Henry Haynes, Henry Gribben and William Brankston, Second Mate, at the wheel. Light air and weather a little hazy. At 7.45 p.m. proceeding at half speed down Galleon's Reach, being about the centre of the Reach, observed an excursion steamer coming up Barking Reach shewing [sic] his red and masthead lights, when we ported our helm to keep over to Tripcock Point. As the vessels neared, observed that the other steamer had ported and immediately afterwards saw that he had starboarded and was trying to cross our bows, shewing his green light close under the port bow.

Seeing collision inevitable stopped our engines and reversed full speed, when the two vessels collided, the bow of the *Bywell Castle* cutting into the other steamer which was crowded with passengers with a dreadful crash. Took immediate measures for saving life by hauling up over the bows several men of the passengers throwing ropes ends over all round the ship, throwing over four life-buoys, a hold ladder and some planks, and getting out three boats, keeping the whistle blowing loudly all the time for assistance which was rendered by several boats from the shore and the boats from another steamer, the excursion steamer which turned out to be the *Princess Alice* turning over and sinking under the bows. Succeeded in rescuing a great many passengers and anchored for the night. About 8.30 p.m. steamer *Duke of Teck* came alongside and took off such passengers as had not been taken on shore in the boats.

(Signed)   Thomas Harrison, Commander
             Henry John Belding, Mate[2]

This log was published in the newspapers.

Letters kept coming in to the newspapers, some correspondents offering the benefit of their expert knowledge, others brimming with ideas, opinions, accusations, justifications and advice.

Some had an axe to grind. John Orrell Lever, the founder of

the London Steamboat Company, insisted that, while he was not desirous of imitating the owners or the captain of *Bywell Castle* who, by the publication of their ship's log had, 'in the most un-English manner' attempted to prejudice public opinion, as far as he had been able to discover no blame whatever could be laid on the deceased captain of the *Princess Alice* nor on any of his crew.[3]

A virtual eulogy for Captain Grinstead came from S.R. Townsend Mayer. After describing the captain's great care of passengers, devotion to duty, calmness, skill, presence of mind in all circumstances and his seamanship, he drew a picture of the problems he daily faced.

> The difficulties of a return voyage from Gravesend to London Bridge in the evening, when the river is covered by every kind of craft, can be recalled only by those who have witnessed them. Barges, ladened, gunnel-deep, drift down the river diagonally, and being generally undermanned, they are almost helpless logs in an ebb tide, alike dangerous to their own crews and everything they meet. Scarcely has one of these been cleared, amidst such badinage and shouting of 'Ease her', 'stop her', 'back her', and 'go ahead' – and perhaps with a 'close shave' – then, what are far worse, sailing vessels and screw steamers unusually buoyant, because unfreighted, and all but umanageable as a their heads yaw from side to side in the strong current, have to be passed.
>
> With infinite patience and never failing promptitude and decision, Captain Grinstead would thread his tortuous course through these thousand and one obstacles in the growing darkness – never hurrying or losing his temper, yet always making way.[4]

One thing the captain *wasn't*, Mr Townsend Mayer assured readers, was a man to take risks just so as to make good time. What's more, he loved his job and his ship and was unhappy when away from either.

Abraham Deness, the Master of the *Bonetta* who had gone to the rescue of survivors, had already (at the end of his statement to the press) given his opinion as to who was to blame for the accident:

It is my firm opinion that if the *Bywell Castle* had not ported her helm she would have cleared the *Princess Alice*, and if the latter had not been there she must have gone ashore ... It was just dark, but moonlight – the moon was just showing itself. The *Princess Alice* was keeping her course in a proper direction, and had no chance of avoiding a collision than by keeping the course she was going in. If the *Bywell Castle* had not ported her helm she must have gone clear. There was nothing else in her way to the northward for three-quarters of a mile.[5]

A letter from Mr Mead Corner offered all kinds of technical data but emphasized that the public should clearly understand that the *Princess Alice* was only a little steamer – and he gave her tonnage and measurements to prove his point. It was necessary to be very explicit on this he wrote, because, 'to the inexperienced, these "saloon" steamers appear large boats'. However, her length was twenty-eight times her depth, which made her grossly top heavy 'thus the leverage exercised by passengers rushing from one side to another is immensely increased.[6] Imagine Blondin[7] on his rope with a sack of coals on his head'.

'A Flag Officer' agreed with 'Marine Insurance' that collisions were incessant on the river and, given the traffic, it was almost impossible it should be otherwise. Like Mr Townsend Mayer, the Flag Officer penned a vignette of river life at that time:

Steamers of all sizes and descriptions, sailing vessels, lighters, barges, and pleasure boats throng the reaches from before daylight till long after dark. Add to this fog and mists and, not least, the smoke from factory chimneys, and bear in mind that scarcely any obstacle will stop the traffic on the river. The rule of the road as applied on the open sea is almost useless.[8]

In any case, he added, boats like the *Princess Alice* were not calcu-lated to stand even a slight collision with a heavier vessel.

F.C. told *The Times* that he had commanded a ship around the Cape of Good Hope thirty-four times but, having seen an overcrowded passenger steamer leaving London Bridge for Woolwich, declared that he would not cross the river on her. 'Observer' claimed that 'on crossing London Bridge yesterday I saw the *Albert Edward* [sister ship to the ill-fated *Princess Alice*]

51

just about leaving Swan Pier literally swarming with passengers. Suspended aft, hung one small boat, capable of holding some dozen persons at the most. Comment is superfluous'.[9]

Suggestions for improving safety included semaphore on ships so they could indicate their intentions, lighting the Thames with electricity at night and electric lights fixed to the mastheads.

Naturally, the subject of life-saving, once a collision had occurred, also exercised many of the correspondents.

Passengers should *not* be allowed to go onboard a river steamer without a life-belt, declared the Flag Officer. This did not have to be cumbrous or unsightly. Indeed, a neat and handy cork belt fitted round the waist and over the shoulders would be quite adequate to support a person in the water for hours 'and in the case of a female, it might, doubtless, be made ornamental or attractive if desired'. He, himself, had been frequently on the river for years and had always worn an ordinary coat but one fitted with an air-tight lining 'that I could inflate it in a few seconds with my own breath'.[10]

Other life-saving notions included: a number of life preservers fixed on simple posts fore and aft which would float freely when the vessel was submerged; airtight seating on board which could then be used to support people in the water; and folding rafts recently trialled in Ostend Harbour.

Some survivors chipped in by explaining to reporters why they had not drowned. Mrs Dee and her child were kept afloat by her very stiff, quilted dress which was padded with wool, while Mrs Mary Brent, one of the only two adult survivors of the Bible party, claimed she owed her life to the buoyancy of her alpaca dress and petticoat.

One of *The Times* letter writers was concerned that there might be children left indoors when their parents had gone down river who might now be left to die undetected

While many children were lost, quite a few had been saved whilst their parents were missing. Finding out *who* young children were was sometimes a problem. The coroner's officer, PC Gilham, interrupted inquest proceedings to read out a letter from Dr Rice of Plumstead Infirmary, stating that a little boy who had originally given his name as Freddy Brady was now saying he was Freddy Lambert. Constable Gilham hoped the press would notice this.

The *Daily News* reported:

> Perhaps one of the most painful scenes is that which has been experienced at No.17 Ferndale-Road, the residence of Mr Elliott. He and his wife were amongst the excursionists, leaving their children at home. Our Correspondent went to the address indicated as above by a police-officer, and a child said, 'Sir, there is nobody in; but we see that there have been 120 persons saved, and surely father and mother will be home soon. I hope they will; don't you, sir?' and the child burst into a fit of grief.[11]

Many kind souls offered to adopt orphaned children. Miss Cayley of St Leonard's said she would take an orphan girl, as would Mrs Horsfall of Liverpool and Mrs Hope of Birkenhead. Mrs Ladds of Tunbridge Wells offered to take six children for six months. The East End Juvenile Mission (Dr Barnado's Home) promised to admit the orphaned children into their homes at Ilford or Stepney Causeway, as did St Saviours Home for Boys at Woolwich. The National Orphan Home at Ham Common said they would take two girls.

The *Princess Alice* disaster continued to dominate the newspapers, not only with the lists, narratives of survivors and statements of witnesses, but the subject percolated the news generally. Anything that could be linked was picked up and placed alongside, particularly any excursion steamer accidents or near misses.

All this dicing with death came as no surprise to the *Ipswich Journal*. According to them it was all down to steam, as they exclaimed dramatically:

> The excursion season has set in with its usual accompaniments of human slaughter. The French observation of our national character, that we take our amusements solemnly, will soon have a terrible meaning. Each year sees its long ghastly roll of victims and, if we do not amend, a man who goes on a holiday excursion, or for an Autumnal holiday, will feel that he travels with his life in his hands.
>
> The awful accident on the Thames on Tuesday evening is a warning and a lesson to us. We are a little accustomed to boast of the power over time and space which the use of steam

has conferred on us, and here we are reminded with terrible emphasis that there is a limit to our powers.[12]

They went on to discuss who was to blame for the collision but questioned whether, in any case, a crowded passenger steamer should be allowed to navigate the busy waters of the Thames in the dark? The *Ipswich Journal*'s opinions about the dangers of steam and potentially lethal excursions did not prevent them advertising, in the same issue, the Great Eastern Railway Company's Excursions for the following week to Brighton, London and elsewhere.

Readers were also informed which areas of the capital city had so far been most affected by the tragedy: south London (Walworth, Camberwell and Brixton), Islington, Whitechapel and Marylebone. Those passengers from the last, it was pointed out, would be of 'the superior working classes'. Woolwich, too, of course suffered quite heavily since many of the crew came from that area.

Then there was the news that the *Princess Alice* had been insured for £8,000 and that shares in the London Steamboat Company had taken a tumble. One generous shareholder correspondent to *The Times* suggested that one per cent of the next dividend should be handed over for the benefit of 'those poor children who had lost their parents due to the sad calamity'.[13]

A rather curious side note to this obsession with the subject was an item in the *Daily News* of Saturday 7 September titled 'The Foreign Press and the Thames Disaster' which began with the rather petulant remark: 'From foreign journals it appears that the frightful catastrophe in The Thames has awakened an amount of interest abroad that is seldom shown in British affairs'. Apparently, the 'earliest, fullest and most accurate accounts' had appeared in the Paris *Figaro*. They went on to list the other French newspapers that had given the subject proper attention, as well as those of Belgium and Germany.

With so much frantic newsgathering, not to mention the copying of each other's survivors' narratives, it is not surprising some mistakes or even some journalistic embroidery took place. Thus, Mr Robert Haines, the double bass player in the *Princess Alice* band wished to make it known to readers of the *Daily News* and *Morning Post* that the statement that he had been 'kept afloat by his instrument' was incorrect. He had, however, suffered severely from the effects of 'the immersion' and had since been an in-patient at the Charing Cross Hospital.[14]

Similarly, although having appeared on the missing list, Mr and Mrs Wickens wanted it known that they had *not* been involved in 'that lamentable catastrophe'. Neither ('despite rumours') had Mr Boncy, the *Princess Alice* restaurant contractor, been on board. He had intended to go, but had been too late.[15] However, there was reason to believe that Mr Buncy, his uncle who was the chief steward, had been.

Mr Henry Drew was particularly angry about this press licence. He wrote to the *Daily News*:

> Sir: In your today's impression you publish a statement purporting to be mine, sent by an anonymous correspondent, which my friends will, I am sure, from its style and phrase-ology, detect as an invention. As to the facts themselves: In the first place, I could not possibly have stated that I sat abaft the paddle-boxes, knowing that I was on the fore-station deck the whole of the journey from Sheerness. I did certainly, and most providentially, cling to a piece of board; but not a single thought had I of any other poor creature taking it away from me, nor had I, indeed, any opportunity of hearing or seeing any of the hundreds struggling round me after the ill-fated vessel had sunk. Surely the bare facts of my case, without embellishment, are sufficiently appalling to satisfy the public crave for harrowing details; and I feel, as a private individual, I have a right to expect from the press some respect for my feelings in this my calamity. As you have published the statement from an anonymous corre-spondent, I trust you will give this the same publicity.
>
> Yours faithfully,
> HENRY DREW
> The Hale, Tottenham[16]

His 'calamity' was that he had lost his three little girls taken on an outing while their brothers had the treat of going to a cricket match at Lord's. His situation was to become even more appalling on the day after his letter was published when his wife, who had been rescued, died from 'exhaustion and a broken heart'.

At times like these the newspapers were the only way many

people had of acquiring urgent information so, despite the mischief wrought by some of the over-enthusiastic reporting, some of it may have turned out to be of assistance to survivors such as the Leaver family of Lambeth. The father, being a strong swimmer, had been able to tread water until he was picked up and taken to Woolwich where he arrived bewailing the loss of his whole family. Meanwhile, the son, 19-year-old Edward, had gotten out from the saloon on impact and had also been saved, but landed in another place and dashed home to tell his mother that all the others had perished. Sadly, however, the rest of the Leavers, 18-year-old Benjamin, 15-year-old Albert and 14-year-old Ruth, all drowned.

CHAPTER SEVEN

Shameful Sunday

The red-painted rail of the *Princess Alice's* starboard paddle box had become visible at low tide and when the approximate position of the wreck was established by probing with poles a diver was sent below to examine it.

In spite of being hampered by the muddiness of the water he was able to report that the pleasure steamer had broken into three parts; the shorter forepart pointing downstream, the larger after-part upstream and the boilers in between. The roof of the forward saloon was missing but was found two days later downstream at Rainham.

Chillingly, the diver reported that the cabins appeared to be full of bodies standing erect and packed together by the doors through which they had obviously been trying to escape.

Raising the wreck was not going to be easy. The Board of Trade had never found themselves in the face of a task so difficult claimed, the *Standard* on 9 September 1878: 'Vessels of twice the size and many times the weight are handled briskly, and lifted with ease ... but these hulls are complete, the motions of which can be calculated and the chains adjusted to an easy principle'. It was a new thing, they claimed, even for Mr Wood, the experienced Surveyor of Moorings, to whose office the lifting of the wreck was entrusted, to deal with a steamer from which the boilers and machinery had rolled out, and which lay in two huge pieces.

But it seemed that one of the fragments, the forepart (which was about 90 ft long) was not going to be such a problem after all. On Friday night it was announced that it would be beached at low tide at around 2 a.m. The operation commenced under the dim and flickering light of lanterns and war rockets provided by the military who had been practising for this purpose on Plumstead Common.

But practical matters often take longer and are more complicated than one expects and to forecast them ahead of time is tempting providence. It had been hoped that two chains, suspended from the lighter, would be sufficient to raise the forepart, but these proved inadequate and caused the lighter to swing around dangerously. Another chain was affixed before the water slacked down, then, a couple of hours later, a fourth chain was passed under while a diver went down to adjust it. The lifting was again attempted, very slowly and carefully until, finally, at around 8 a.m., there was a sudden extra straining on the chain, then a slackening at the bows of the big lighter and, to a cry of 'Here she comes!', she was lifted from the bed of the river.

Very slowly, still submerged, she was towed from her spot in the middle of the channel towards the south riverbank, where she was deposited in five fathoms of water. This left the river a little safer for the early morning traffic of large, outward-bound steam and sailing vessels. One of these was the *Bywell Castle*, but without her captain who remained in London. A few minutes later the *Metis* steamboat passed carrying a pleasure party and, on seeing the part-revealed wreck, their band played a funeral march.

As the tide gradually receded, the crumpled bridge and twisted rails came into view, then the battered funnel. At this stage, only one body could be extricated, so it was decided to wait until the next tide, when it was hoped the forepart could be lifted to shallower waters.

'It was a lovely morning', the *Standard*'s special correspondent reported incongruously. 'The great buildings on the north shore loomed shadowless and pale, like painted things washed in with a flowing brush. Even the bleak south coast had a softness of colour which broad daylight would disperse, and the river stream was warm with dappled tint. It was a morning too beautiful for our work, and the ill-omened wreck we had to view took on a shape more dismal – if that could be', he finished lamely, his poetic muse suddenly deserting him.

The activity had caused bodies to surface and numerous

watermen were probing the site in the hope of raising more. After the wreck was beached, they augmented their income by offering trips to see the wreck at a shilling a head. 'All the water thieves in London are out', commented a police inspector,[1] his men even having to guard the ship's boiler, the metal being a great temptation.

The Thames Police endeavoured to keep order, aided by the fact that they had use of a chartered steamboat rather than their usual rowing boats. The want of such a vessel had been long felt, commented the *Standard*, 'but this affair has compelled the police to adopt what should have been only an ordinary thing for the officer in charge of a river like the Thames'. But the rapidly increasing flow of bodies meant the extra police drafted in were needed for many other duties at the dockyard, such as the search for a sufficient number of large-size shells to take the increasingly bloated corpses.

The harbourmaster, Captain Fitzgerald, had assumed some police duties. He sent out boats to patrol the north (Essex) shore for bodies that were then brought back to Woolwich. He also patrolled back and forth in the conservators' yacht, keeping an eye out for theft from corpses and preventing watermen taking more than one body onboard at a time. Stacking them, which they preferred to do, caused them damage. He towed the loaded boats back to his vessel, the *Heron*, making sure the faces of the dead were covered with linen rags for decency's sake.

Meanwhile, a deputation of Creekmouth inhabitants, accompanied by two police officers, approached him to protest against unclaimed bodies still being kept in their little village. The stench was sickening. The previous evening their coroner, Mr Lewis, had agreed that they should go to Woolwich and he had issued burial certificates. Mr Hughes, the solicitor for the *Princess Alice* had promised to forward shells and arrange for their removal, but nothing had been done. Fitzgerald sent them to see Mr Hughes again and told them that if they couldn't find him, to go to Mr Thomas who would see they got their shells.

It transpired that the lower part of the saloon of the beached wreck was full of mud and water too deep to allow the searchers to wade about. There was no hose to drain the vessel, so Captain Fitzgerald dispatched men to Woolwich for hammers and chisels. 'In the meantime', said the *Morning Post* reporter, 'the watermen poked about the cabin with boat hooks in the hope of recovering bodies, but they only succeeded in finding clothing and cushions ... soon, the deck was littered with a miscellaneous collection of battered hats, dripping umbrellas, babies bonnets, cloaks, crates of ginger beer, bottles, and boxes and drawers full of broken china.'

When the tools arrived he reported that:

> ... the rivets began to fly off, leaving holes through which the muddy water in the cabin shot through in jets. In a very short time the men, stimulated by the energy of Captain Fitzgerald, had wrenched away a portion of the plate, and the water speedily began to diminish in the cabin. As soon as it had sunk down to three or four ft the Thames Police crowded in and fished about for bodies. But none were found amid the debris, nor were any discovered in the closed compartment abutting the cabin. Several bags were found, one containing money taken by the steward[2] ... The stench arising from inside the wreck was of a most horrible nature, but the Thames Police and others worked manfully and expeditiously.

In the mud was also discovered the likeness of a girl, which from the newness of the gilt frame, had evidently been taken by some cheap itinerant photographer at Sheerness or Gravesend on the day of the disaster.[3]

Elsewhere, twenty-five bodies had been found, five of them men, one of them a uniformed soldier of the 11th Hussars. There were also thirteen women, one 'lad', three little girls and two babies. By noon, five more had been taken from the saloon: two women, one little girl and two boys, one of these Captain Grinstead's son, John James, who had been a call boy on the *Princess Alice*. They were all loaded onto the *Heron* and taken to the dockyard shed where they were placed male bodies on one side and female on the other – another method of helping streamline the identification process.

That weekend, the news of the expected raising of the wreck caused thousands of sightseers and grieving friends and relatives to descend upon Woolwich. They came by train, steamboat, cab and special omnibuses from London Bridge. They crowded the town, tramped and stumbled their way over the marshes and lined the riverbanks on both sides to stare at the site and the wreck of the forepart.

Doggerel relating to the disaster were sung and hawked about in broadsheets by street musicians, as were souvenir beer and mineral bottles salvaged from the steward's cabin, which were purchased at high prices, and carefully handled so as not to disturb their muddy crust.

This is a typical broadsheet of the time, but offered two ballads for the price of one. The first was:

THE LOSS OF THE *PRINCESS ALICE*
Tune: *Sailor's Grave*

> How many thousands have found a grave
> 'eneath the ever rolling wave,
> And day by day the list we swell,
> Another loss we have to tell;
> Above five hundred precious lives,
> Women and children, men and wives,
> In the midst of joy and pleasures' games,
> 'eneath the Thames their bodies lie,
> Both old and young were doom'd to die,
> The steamer sank beneath the waves,
> And hundreds found a watery grave.[4]

And so on for another five verses.

Pickpockets also arrived on the scene and were soon plying their distressing trade. There were fights between watermen protecting their 'fishing' rights, often fuelled by alcohol. Some sightseers rowed up to the beached wreck and tried to pry pieces off as souvenirs. Others even managed to gain access to the dockland shed where the bodies were still stowed.

Among those still searching for loved ones, the *Morning Post* noted, 'the fearful scenes which were enacted on the previous two days after the wreck, were not yesterday to be witnessed, as the calmness of despair seemed to have taken the place of the frenzied grief naturally manifested at first by the bereaved relatives'.

The Thames Police, led by Superintendent Alston, tried to control the unruly bystanders, including moving on an old man named Douglas Chellow, who paraded along the riverbank and in and out of a temporary mortuary carrying a placard bearing the words:

CAN WE BE MASTERS OF THE SEA IF
WE CANNOT KEEP A PLEASURE BOAT
AFLOAT ON THE THAMES?
THE RIVER HAS HAD HER REVENGE.[5]

But worse was to come. At low tide several ruffians climbed onboard the chief conservancy barge and impeded the rescue operations. Two drunken labourers began swearing and shouting and, faced with a couple of policemen, one of them drew a knife and threatened to slit up any bluebottle who tried to touch him. Touch him they did, and arrested them. The next day a magistrate informed the pair that their conduct in such solemn circumstances was simply disgraceful and, despite their protests that they had been drunk, sentenced them to two weeks' hard labour. Another man was charged with stealing from a body.

Those who went home early on the Sunday missed the raising of the larger and heavier after-part, which began to surface at around 7 p.m. At low tide a lifting barge had been floated over the wreck and divers helped place chains under the vessel from two side barges. At the second attempt, the battered wreck was raised and grounded on the riverbank.

As soon as the top of the saloon became visible, watermen grew busy probing for bodies. The first to be drawn out was a woman wearing a figure-hugging black gown and black kid gloves. She was followed by another, also in black, but with her gold jewellery shining in the evening sunlight.

The Times of 9 September 1878 wrote:

It is noticeable that the women's bodies chiefly are discovered in the wreck. Those of the men are hooked from the riverbed. Most of the men had a struggle for life. Many of the women seem to have remained in the boat, some huddled in a corner clutching their children, others fighting with each other for egress through the narrow doorway.

It seemed not to have occurred to them that men were more liable to be able to swim, so would be more likely to 'struggle for life', or that the women were probably looking after the children inside.

Mr Carttar reopened the inquest on the Saturday morning but first had to deal with the problem of the unclaimed bodies that had been out of the water some time and were now causing real health concerns. The weather remained warm, there was no refrigeration, and it didn't help that the water in which they had drowned was foul; the two marvellous new sewage outlets emptied into the river around the point that the *Princess Alice* sank and the water was further fouled by waste from the nearby Silvertown factories and fertilizer works.

The jury foreman reported that a meeting of the Local Board of Health had just passed a resolution saying that, on health grounds, the unclaimed should be buried as soon as possible and Police Superintendent Baynes declared that he could no longer justify exposing his men to the risks of working among the putrefying bodies. Issuing them with smelling salts was not enough.

The coroner told them he had received some thirty letters suggesting they should be photographed. PC Gilham told him that had already been done and that, apart from those brought in on Friday night, there were thirty-one still unclaimed.

Mr Carttar thought this 'an extraordinarily large number' to remain unidentified. It was not conceivable that there could be thirty-one people living in London who absence since Tuesday had not been observed by anyone. He could only suppose that people thought giving a description to the police was sufficient and that they would be informed when they were picked up. But given the state of the water and the effects of it on the bodies, it was not possible for police to recognize them from a description.

A juryman suggested that many of the deceased might live alone in London and all their friends be in the country, so it would take some time for them to become aware of the loss. 'That is true', Carttar agreed, but added doggedly, 'thirty-one unidentified bodies is, nevertheless, a large number'.

He decided that they should all be buried on the Monday morning. But, before they left to view the latest batch of bodies, he told them about a private communication he had received from the churchwarden at Erith. It justified what had been done with the bodies found there 'of which the foreman of the jury had

THE PRINCESS ALICE DISASTER

remarked a day or two ago that they were in a painfully different state from those landed at Woolwich'. The jury foreman said that he was sure his brother jurors would admit that they were 'much more exposed as to their persons than the bodies recovered here'. What had happened, Carttar explained, was that two women had been employed to deal with the bodies – 'to examine their linen for marks etc. – but it was subsequently felt that this was inadvisable and a stop was put to it. With that explanation I think the matter may be allowed to pass'.

A juryman agreed and the foreman said he was sorry if any expression of his had given unnecessary pain to anyone, 'but the point was one on which I felt deeply, and I thought it right to express my candid opinion'. Something he seemed ever ready to do.

Then, once again, came the endless parade of grieving relatives trooping across the tasteful carpet to stand under the brass chandeliers of the town hall's handsome boardroom and explain why they thought a certain body was that of their loved one.

They included: Edward Leaver, who identified his 15-year-old son, Albert; John Bolam, who identified his aunt, 38-year-old Mary Ann Bolam, who was yet another deceased member of the Bible party; and William Usherwood, who 'had some difficulty in making it clear how many of his family were lost'. While being questioned by the coroner and jury members 'his emotion overcame him, and he had to be furnished with a chair and a glass of water'.

There was a pause when Mr Hughes for the London Steamboat Company stepped forward to say he wished to correct a mistake made by the Sheerness people as to the number onboard the *Princess Alice*. He said it was quite true that 491 people went onboard at Sheerness, but they distributed themselves between the *Princess Alice* and the two other steamers, the *Duke of Cambridge* and the *Duke of Connaught*, so perhaps 150 should be deducted on that account. Therefore, the total number onboard when the *Princess Alice* left Rosherville might be set down at about 500, instead of 651. The children would be in addition.

The foreman: Would the 500 include the seven musicians?

Mr Hughes: I think so.

The foreman: I think not. It has been stated that the musicians did not travel with tickets.

The coroner: The actual number onboard must, I am afraid, always remain a matter of doubt.[6]

Indeed, as he spoke, bodies were arriving thick and fast and continued to do so, silencing, as one newspaper commented, those 'who in the teeth of all the evidence continued to assert that the total number onboard the steamer did not exceed five hundred' and also disproving the watermen's claims that bodies took nine days to rise.

As for the little boy at Plumstead Infirmary, the coroner was informed that neither Mr and Mrs Lambert nor Mr and Mrs Brady, whose names he had given, had had a boy with them. The little boy now said he was with his father and mother and a brother named Bob and a sister named Alice.

One hundred and twenty bodies were brought in on the Saturday and, by 6 p.m. on Sunday, a further 111 had been added. They came not just from Woolwich but, Barking, Erith, Rainham, Greenhithe and upriver at Blackwall and brought the total thus far to 503. One of the last two bodies recovered just off Woolwich Arsenal, at around 9 p.m. on the Sunday night, was that of Captain Grinstead, the much-respected skipper of the ill-fated *Princess Alice*. He was immediately recognized by an old acquaintance, Police Inspector Phillips.

CHAPTER EIGHT

Burial Monday

'A stranger entering Woolwich yesterday might have imagined that a terrible pestilence was ravaging the town, so large was the number of hearses which came in from the London Road, so subdued the demeanour of the residents' reported the *Standard* on Tuesday 10 September 1878.

Indeed the conduct of the people of Woolwich on Burial Monday was held to be in stark contrast to the unseemly behaviour of the holidaymakers on the preceding day. The shops on the route were closed and shuttered, quiet crowds assembled on the pavements as the church bells tolled. Men's hats were lifted and the eyes of the women were wet as army ambulance wagons rumbled by, driven by smartly uniformed members of the Army Service Corps wearing the pickle-haube.[1] They were carrying thirteen of the still unidentified dead. On each person's coffin was a metal plate inscribed with the police registration number that had been attached to their clothes and jewellery, their photograph and any laundry or other mark found upon their clothing.

Most of the long-term unidentified dead were women, a fact which much exercised one of the imaginative *Standard* reporters. Why was this when women's garments and personal adornments were so much more distinctive than those of men? Was it that the men were too busy working to provide for their families to attend? Or was it that men lost heart sooner, were less patient of the weary agony of waiting or sickened sooner over the dreadful task of identification? Men gave up in horror and despair, whilst women became totally absorbed with the object of their search was his conclusion. The fact that there had been more women than men onboard may well have also had something to do with this identification disproportion.

Sixty-one more unidentified bodies were buried that afternoon. Once again the route of the cortege, led by two mounted police officers, rumbled past the dockyard wall and the Arsenal Gates, out onto the Plumstead Road and up the hill to the new Woolwich cemetery at Wickham. It was a pretty place shaded by many trees, bright with flowers planted among the graves, and fragrant with the odour from its cedars, limes and Italian pines.

Beyond, the eye stretched away over green fields to the steep wooded slopes of Shooters Hill, where 2,000 to 3,000 people had gathered. Some were merely spectators, some relatives and friends still searching for their loved ones and some just wanted to bear witness for those as yet unnamed. Then there were the policemen drafted in to keep them in check: an inspector, five sergeants and fifty constables. But, this time, their crowd control skills were not needed, people were quiet and respectful.

The officiating clergyman, Reverend Adelbert Anson, stood at the top of the hill, outlined against the sky as he intoned the words of the burial service to the hushed and expectant crowd. They displayed 'great emotion' as he advised them also to be ready, 'for no man knoweth the hour', but assured them that souls redeemed by the Saviour's love could cheerfully face even sudden death, for they were always ready for the Master's call.[2] One doubts, of course, that many of the *Princess Alice* victims had cheerfully faced their dreadful, sudden deaths, but Reverend Anson was doing his best.

The dissenting body, which was numerous and influential in Woolwich, was represented by a well-known minister, the Reverend Thomas Tuffield.

As the coffins were lowered into the ground a Miss Broughton of New Cross (a member of Reverend Anson's congregation) scattered sweet-smelling flowers – heartsease, fuchsias and geraniums – onto each one.

Clergymen continued to pray over the graves as the skies grew dark and the atmosphere emotional.

What *The Times* referred to as 'a remarkable incident' occurred just after the first cortege had left the dockyard. Two (separate) relatives who had long been searching for their loved ones, suddenly recognized the bundles of washed clothing belonging to those already en route for the cemetery. The pair were placed in a cab to follow the funeral procession. At the cemetery 'due to the admirable system of registration' the bodies were claimed and taken back to the dockyard where a family burial could be arranged.[3] Thus, the body of William Alfred Codling was identified by his brother and Mrs Wayman was claimed by her brother-in-law.

It was not only the unclaimed who were buried that day, hence the many hearses traversing the riverside town. More than 150 private funerals also took place, including that of the *Princess Alice*'s chief steward Mr Frederick Boncy.

It was the police who had been responsible for the 'admirable system of registration' as well as the handling of the flow of bodies, which was now threatening to become overwhelming. Dock labourers brought in to replace striking Arsenal dock labourers had themselves just struck for a rise from six shillings a day to seven shillings and sixpence, for what was clearly a dreadful job. However, they were quite quickly replaced by thirty 'volunteer' soldiers.

Given the numbers and the rapid state of decay there was scarcely any time left for identification which, in any case, was becoming increasingly impossible. At that day's inquest the coroner had quickly signed burial orders for the seventy-three unidentified interred that same afternoon. And, despite the increased numbers, the police still had to search them, remove any jewellery and clothing, note their descriptions and take their photographs.

The *Standard*, which had at first severely criticized the police, now, in their intemperate fashion, went to the other extreme, saying that no words of praise for them could be too high. It would never be forgotten, they said:

> ... that in a time unparalleled in English history they performed a public service, the record of which should be handed down as one of the brightest spots in the annals of the nineteenth century. Many men who have been rewarded with decorations and titles have never gone through a particle of the terrible work that has been undertaken so cheerfully and carried out so admirably, by Sergeant Alstin and Inspectors Lucas, Meering, Phillips and Dawkins of the River and Metropolitan Police ... never shrinking

from what has appalled some of the most callous and hardened of the riverside men who have officiated as labourers for a portion only of that time.[4]

The Times agreed that the behaviour and the industry 'of the greater number of police was beyond all praise'.[5]

Mr Carttar opened his inquest at 10 a.m. on the Monday with more condolences sent by the Queen from Frogmore House in Windsor Great Park, the site of her mausoleum to the late Prince Albert. This was another proof, among many, said the coroner, that the sorrows and distresses of the relatives of the deceased were mourned over by Her Most Gracious Majesty, and it showed how affectionately Her Majesty sought to share, to solace and to alleviate the grief of her people.

Not sufficiently, of course, for her to come out of her seclusion to actually visit them. But there had been an attempt to attract royalty to the scene. J. Orrell Lever, the founder of the London Steamboat Company, wrote to the Prince of Wales offering to place the saloon steamer *Victoria* at his disposal should he desire to visit the scene of the accident now that the wreck was raised. If the Prince had any such inclination it would doubtless have been quelled by Lever's comment that by doing so the Prince might then see that Captain Grinstead was entirely free from blame. The Prince's private secretary replied thanking him for the offer but saying that His Royal Highness regretted that 'it was not in his power to take advantage of your proposal'.[6]

Back at the Woolwich inquest Mr Carttar said that now the dimensions of the disaster was becoming fully known he had one or two observations to make on the subject:

At the outset it was my wish and intention to have taken evidence of the identity of only a limited number of bodies, feeling that the ends of justice might be duly and properly attained by such a course. But when I found no less than fifty-three bodies awaiting the inspection of the jury the first day, I staggered under the magnitude of the task before me. My brother coroner (Mr Lewis), of Essex, had the same impression as myself, that possibly the viewing of a few bodies might be sufficient and he was kind enough to ask from the proper authorities some advice as to the course we ought both to pursue.

That advice unfortunately could not be given us, and we were of necessity thrown back on what may be termed the state of the law, which requires that on the body of every person who has come by a violent death an inquest should be held. It was felt, moreover, by the relatives of the deceased and others that the dead should be identified as far as possible in order to prevent an unseemly scramble for property on the part of people who might have no right to it whatever – that is to say people who might claim bodies with property, knowing that they could have them buried free of expense by the parish authorities.

I have, therefore, come to the conclusion that we ought to pursue our painful and arduous task of identification to the end if such a course should meet with your approval. It will not only have the advantage I have mentioned but it will be some consolation to the relatives and will tend to prevent fraud here- after. Of course, those beyond recognition we can only put aside as unknown. Their clothes will be sacredly preserved as a last clue possible to their identity. Do you approve gentlemen to the course I propose?[7]

Again, the jury did, which was a great relief to the coroner's mind. He clearly would have been even more relieved if members of the public would stop sending him letters containing silly and impractical suggestions. They were overwhelming him and wasting his time.

And so began another very long day listening to unbearably sad tales from unbearably sad people who stood in the midst of the semi-circle formed by their boardroom table, in the centre of which, the back-lit figure of the kindly, white-haired coroner, was framed by the large windows behind him.

Some names must now have been familiar to them. The bodies of Mrs Briscoe and her 5-year-old daughter Sarah had finally been found, as well as more children of the Leaver, Childs and Towse families, plus various Bible party members. Mr Henry Drew from Tottenham identified the last two of his three little daughters, telling the court that his wife had died from shock to the system and a broken heart at losing her children. William Quinton recognized Thomas Davies, his master's son. Of the Davies family of six there was now only one missing, he told the coroner, a 15-year-old boy.

The captain of the *Princess Alice*, William Robert Hartridge Grinstead, was formally identified, as was his 65-year-old brother, Charles Thomas, who, it was said, had rendered very active assistance at the Sittingbourne railway accident the previous Saturday. He and his wife had been staying at Sittingbourne with his sister, but they had left to join his brother's boat at Sheerness.

New stories emerged. Mr John Baker came up from Somerset to identify his son, John, and John's wife, Emma Jane, 'only married Tuesday week'. William John Richards identified his fiancé, 28-year-old Minette Bishop, adding 'we should have been married in a few weeks'.[8] John Charles Weaver, a 64-year-old musician onboard the *Albert Edward* pleasure steamer, came to identify his wife, Jane. He had had free passes for the *Princess Alice* for Jane and her friend, he said, but they went without waiting for him and paid their fares. 'I missed going with them.'[9]

The increasing problems with physical recognition and clothing discolouration led to more reliance on other means of distinguishing people. With Ellen Ridout, a 27-year-old milliner, it was her penchant for trinkets, 'which we all knew', said her brother Henry when identifying her, while with publican George Hughes of the Control Arms, Porters' Green, it was the wart on his nose.[10] Hugh Burns, over whose body there had been something of a dispute, was finally successfully claimed by his brother-in-law Joseph Sykes, who recognized Hugh's clothes, boots and the season pass for the local railway found in his pocket.

By the time the jury finally retired at 10.15 p.m., after a twelve-hour sitting, the Woolwich coroner had issued 123 burial certificates and the coroners at Blackwall and Poplar had added several more. Keeping an accurate account of the current total number of dead was difficult, however, particularly now that, commented *The Times*, 'they drift into strange nooks above and beyond the site of the catastrophe. Yesterday two were reported at Westminster, five at Blackwall, four at the Victoria Docks'.[11] However, it was clearly around 600, so there was no longer any hiding the size of the tragedy.

The following day, the status of the *Princess Alice* disaster as the country's dominant drama was challenged by news from the Welsh coalmines. Mining accidents, like those of the railways, were quite frequent occurrences. Already that year there had been a mining explosion at the Wood Pit near Wigan in Lancashire that had cost the lives of around 200 men and boys. Now it was the turn of the Prince of Wales Colliery at Abercarn in Monmouthshire: 370 men and boys had been working underground when massive explosions ripped through the mine. Eighty were rescued quite quickly and another ten (badly burned) a little later, but such were the fires raging through the 3 miles of tunnels that the rescue teams were soon ordered to withdraw. A number of those rescued died soon after of shock, after-damp and burns. The total loss of life turned out to be 262, the fires took two months to quell and the *Princess Alice* Mansion House Fund was duly expanded to include mining disaster relief.

CHAPTER NINE

Laid to Rest

Unlike most women onboard the *Princess Alice*, 20-year-old Miss Ella Hanbury *could* swim. Indeed, she came from America where, according to the *Islington Gazette* of 18 September 1878, 'encouragement is given to the practice of swimming by women'. She was not only an excellent swimmer but had 'carried off prizes for her skill in the art'. She was also a young woman 'of great personal attractions', very accomplished, able to speak four languages fluently and a talented musician. Ella lived in Mildmay Road, Mildmay Park, north London, with her brother, who was a merchant. She had gone down the Thames on that lovely early autumn morning with two brothers, one of whom was her fiancé, 24-year-old William Harrison, 'to whom she was deeply attached'.

After the collision, when it became obvious that the rope attaching their lifeboat to the *Princess Alice* could not be undone and they would be sucked down by the sinking steamer, William clasped Ella in his arms, kissed her and said, 'Goodbye, darling, we shall meet again in heaven'. By which, one presumes he was unable to swim. The pair sank twice. Only she came up the second time, when she struck out and managed to swim and float for two hours eventually ending up 2 miles downriver near Barking, where she was picked up. She was kept at Barking for several days while she recovered, before being taken home to Mildmay Park, only to relapse on Friday 13 September, when she did indeed go to meet her fiancé in heaven.

The Islington inquest jury verdict as to cause of death was 'congestion of the lungs and shock from immersion in the River Thames'. The grief at the loss of her fiancé, Mr Harrison, doubtless added to the shock, commented the *Islington Gazette*. As with Mrs Drew of Tottenham, who lost her daughters, a broken heart was deemed to be a contributing factor, as it probably was.

Bodies continued to beach on the banks up and down the river. On the day of Ella Hanbury's inquest, thirteen days after the collision, a Poplar inquest jury gave its verdict on sixteen bodies that had been 'found drowned off Blackwall'. Blackwall is on the north side of an acute curve in the Thames upriver from Woolwich, in the dockland area from which the *Bywell Castle* had begun its fateful journey. Among the sixteen 'believed to have been passengers in the *Princess Alice*', were one unidentified child, six identified women, one unidentified woman and eight men, two of them having been crushed before drowning.[1]

Funerals of victims taken home for burial began to take place, some with marked ceremony. The body of a 13-year-old student at a college in Highbury New Park was escorted to Highgate Cemetery by the school's principal, two of the masters and his schoolfellows who placed white wreaths and sprays and tokens of affection on his coffin and sang the hymn, 'A Few More Years May Roll' over the grave, then threw in more flowers.

The bodies of the students and tutor from Queen's College School for Young Ladies were also escorted by a large number of fellow boarders and the guardian of the two young White sisters whose parents lived in Shanghai. He had identified them, he said, by means of the absence of an ear lobe on one girl and the markings on their linen that he himself had made.

Two young temperance brothers were given a fervent send off with a rousing rendition of 'Rock of Ages', sung by large numbers of the East London Temperance Association and the Good Templars who regretted that these pure young men had been called away in the midst of careers of usefulness.

But possibly the most impressive of the funerals was that of Constable Briscoe of 'N' Division and his family. The cortege, formed outside his police station at Dalston, was headed by the divisional superintendent, nine inspectors, twenty-four sergeants, and over 300 constables plus 'H' Division's Police Band who played the 'Dead March'. At Briscoe's home, these were joined by the hearse, a mourning carriage and a local fire engine mounted by eight firemen and their superintendent. The *Islington Gazette* of 11 September 1878, estimated that there could not have been less than 8,000–10,000 present to see the burial of this local hero who, ironically, had been awarded a medal for saving a child from death by drowning. The local newspaper also revealed that one of the Briscoe children was still missing and that there was a third Briscoe offspring, 'a boy of tender years' who was now an orphan.

Unsurprisingly, the *Islington Gazette* gave wide coverage to the fate of the Bible class from the Cowcross Mission although, like others, got a bit confused about the numbers which ranged from thirty, plus the two benevolent ladies and a few children, to a total of forty-eight. They quoted the *City Press*[2] who made the telling point that in no part of the metropolis had so much bereavement been concentrated within as small an area as in the crowded courts and alleys adjoining the Mission Station. 'In places like Faulkner's-alley and Whitehorse-alley, every other house is literally a house of mourning, for one or more members of the family have perished.'

The *Islington Gazette*, however, got a little confused in its coverage, doubtless overwhelmed by the size of the event. When reporting on 13 September of a 'sorrowful meeting' of friends and neighbours of two of the latest members' bodies to be found (Mrs Matilda Gullifer, aged fifty-six, of 12 White Horse Alley and Mrs Caroline Smith, of 12 Benjamin Street) they stated that the only surviving member of the thirty-two strong party was Mrs Brent, of 7 Faulkner's Alley, 'who could not go on the trip, having to take a sick child to the hospital'. In fact, Mrs Mary Brent *had* gone on the trip and, what's more, had claimed in the *Islington Gazette* four days earlier that her survival was largely due to the fact that she was wearing her alpaca dress and petticoat which had kept her afloat.

Three more Bible class party members had survived: Jane Green, who had been a servant to 60-year-old Miss Barden, who was lost, and two children of Mrs Eliza Haist, who had gone around announcing 'Today's the day!' Eliza herself and her three other children died.

Later, that day an exceedingly well attended service was held at the Cowcross Mission Hall where a list of those lost was read out and an outline of their conversion to Christ delivered by Mr Catlin, the superintendent.

For his address to the Tufnell Park Congregational Church the

Reverend E.H. Palmer chose Ecclesiastes 9, 12 as his text. He, too, drew the lesson that we should listen to the warning voice of this lamentable occurrence which demonstrated that you never knew when your time would come.

> 'Up to the time of the catastrophe everything went well with us,' say the survivors. Such is generally the case, everything may seem to be going well with us, but by a flaming house, a railway collision, a runaway horse, a flash of lightning, or a thousand other causes we may be swiftly swept into the spirit world.

We should be prepared, he went on, by striving for a spiritual life. Then he overdid it somewhat by going on about the drowning, 'struggling in the cold river, crying piteously, with wild despairing eyes for help which came not!' He concluded his extremely long sermon with a verse:

> They are out of a life of commotion,
> Tempest-swept, oft as the ocean,
> Dark with wrecks drifting o'er,
> Into a land calm and quiet;
> Never a storm cometh nigh it,
> Never a wreck on its shore.[3]

The Reverend Styleman Herring, Vicar of St Paul's, Clerkenwell, had already sent back a dispatch from the front to the *Islington Gazette*, having gone down to the scene early on to seek 'a valued missionary' whom he had heard was lost. 'The corpses,' he reported back were, 'mostly women of a respectable class'. He described how he had looked after, then sent home, a widowed parishioner who was mourning over the loss of an aged sister who, with two ladies and thirty mothers from a Quakers' meeting, had gone for an excursion, and alas, not returned. 'No one', he said 'but the stoutest hearts ought to see these rows of mangled, swollen and distorted corpses – each seemed convulsively grasping something'.[4]

For his text before the congregation at St John's, Clerkenwell, the Reverend W. Dawson took chapters 19 and 20 of the Gospel of St Matthew, from which he drew the message that in the midst of life we are in death and that, even in that hour of terror, darkness and despair, God was present and saw what passed. The offertory, he concluded, would be sent to the Mansion House Relief Fund.

The Mansion House Relief Fund was the Lord Mayor of the City of London's fund for the relief of those who had suffered from the disaster. To fill its coffers, theatres and music halls held special fundraising performances. Collection boxes, placed at hotels and outside the Mansion House, were constantly filled. The National Sunday League and 'S' Division Police Band joined forces to give a concert in Regent's Park and a north/south cricket match took place for the aid of the combined *Princess Alice* and Welsh Colliery Disaster funds. The teams included many well-known cricketers, including W. G. Grace, and the Australian cricket team, before leaving for home after a 'sensational' four-month season countrywide, donated £100.

Members of the Stock Exchange gave over £1,000, the traders at Smithfield Meat Market £172.2s and 400 francs came from workmen in a Parisian pottery who had not forgotten that London sent bread to a famished Paris in 1871. For the same reason, the *Comédie Français* in Paris, 'preserving an appreciative recollection of the good help which was rendered to them in 1871', sent a cheque for £50.[5]

Most pertinently, members of the Alliance Club of the Swimming Associations of Great Britain unanimously resolved to invite all their members to collect subscriptions on behalf of the sufferers. Swimming, or the inability of most of the population to be able to do so and the patent lack of facilities to learn, had become a very hot topic on the letter, leader and feature pages in the newspapers.

As for the paying out of all these monies collected, the aforementioned Reverend W. Dawson of St Paul's Church Clerkenwell, had done a two-day stint at the Woolwich dockyard gates on behalf of the Lord Mayor, for the purpose of handing out 'immediate relief in the shape of money in all necessitous cases', and the Mansion House organizers announced themselves anxious to receive applications from bereaved relatives

Possibly the first attempt to fraudulently collect donations on behalf of the victims was made by Mary Barclay, 'a respectable-looking upholsteress'. She called on three homes in Edmonton, north London, claiming that she was collecting for a relief fund 'got up by the ladies of Edmonton' and her uncle, the local vicar. She had garnered 2/6d from each of three persons thus approached before she was halted and given a month's hard labour for her trouble. Mary claimed she had done it on the impulse of the moment and, *The Times* reported, 'expressed her very great sorrow for what she had done, and stated her intention of entering a home as soon as she was able'.[6]

Among the royal donors to the Mansion Fund were Queen Victoria, who gave 100 guineas, the Prince of Wales, who sent £50 with a nice letter, and Prince Leopold, who gave £25. The Grand Duke and Duchess of Hesse (the real Princess Alice) agreed to be patrons of a concert to be held at the Exeter Hall on The Strand. Since the hall's two auditoriums held audiences of 1,000 and 4,000 the takings for this were likely to be considerable.

Princess Alice had also known tragedy. In 1861 she had nursed her beloved father, Prince Albert, while he was suffering from typhoid, then borne the brunt of her mother's almost demented grief following his death. Alice's much-postponed marriage to the then Prince Louis of Hesse Darmstadt finally took place in June 1862 in an atmosphere, according to Queen Victoria, 'more like a funeral than a wedding'.[7]

Alice, like her older sister Princess Victoria (by then three years married to Prince Frederick William of Prussia), had been educated and encouraged by her father to have an inquiring mind, to think for herself, have a capacity for hard work and a sense of duty. Prince Albert had hoped that these marriages of his duty-driven daughters might help achieve his dream of a unified and democratic Germany, which at the time was divided into many states. In Princess Victoria's case, pursuance of this dream had ruffled feathers in Prussia and earned the implacable hatred of Otto von Bismarck, who had his own ideas about what was best for his country and was of the opinion that women, all women, were the last people to know any better, nor should they have any opinions on the subject.

Although Princess Alice had also startled the natives of her new home city with her forward ways, her dutiful efforts leaned more towards improving the lot of Darmstadt's poor, sick and disabled. She was also keen on improving the work and social prospects of women and, after regularly consulting with Florence Nightingale, set up nursing organizations. When she set up a hospital and nurse's training school in Darmstadt, she went to great efforts to ensure that the matron was trained at the Florence Nightingale School at St Thomas's Hospital in London and at a Liverpool Hospital.

Indeed, Princess Alice was relentless in her efforts to help people. Even while she was supposedly recuperating from overwork at Eastbourne (on a holiday provided by her mother), she was busily inspecting the conditions of the poor in that coastal resort and visiting the local hospital and a rescue home for prostitutes.

Her husband, who by 1878 had become the Grand Duke of Hesse, was apparently a kind man and a fond father to their seven children, but he was clearly a simpler soul than she and more interested in the aristocratic pursuits of hunting, shooting, fishing and parading his troops.

This left Alice feeling bereft of intellectual stimulus. The two great tragedies of her life had been the early death of her beloved father and, in 1873, the death of her 3-year-old son, Fritz or 'Frittie', who had fallen out of his mother's bedroom window. Like his uncle, Prince Leopold, Frittie was a haemophiliac and the condition may well have exacerbated the bleeding on the brain from which the child died without regaining consciousness.

CHAPTER TEN

Meanwhile

The *Princess Alice* Thames pleasure steamer had (inadvertently) been part of an earlier tragedy; in 1873, when she was moored off Woolwich during a dense fog, a waterman's boat carrying workmen from Woolwich to Beckton Gasworks was pulled under her. The boat capsized and nine workmen were drowned. And in the days following the horrendous accident of 3 September she was to be the inadvertent cause of more accidents.

The morning after the *Princess Alice* accident, the barge *Mary Scott* was rammed by the screw steamer, the *Norman*, in Gallions Reach. The crew were saved by the Thames Police.

A few days later, paddle steamer *Hoboken*, coming downstream, struck a barge and was thrown broadside across the river. The *Ariel* paddle steamer, which had been following, tried to pass but miscalculated. She, also, ran into the barge and was severely damaged. Some passengers, understandably panic-stricken, jumped overboard onto the barge, two of them injuring their legs. Fortunately, they were the only casualties.

And there had also been deaths immediately following and related to the sinking of the *Princess Alice*. The inquests on them were heard by Mr Carttar, the Woolwich Coroner, and the inquest jury. On the day after Burial Monday a young man, named Alfred Barnes, had been on the *Cupid* saloon steamer (belonging to the London Steamboat Company) on his way to search for the bodies of relatives. The guardrail, on which Alfred was sitting, collapsed. He fell into the engine room and suffered a blow to his abdomen from the crankshaft which killed him. He was identified by his sister who had been coming down to Woolwich with him.

Another boy, named Smith, went out in a boat to see the retrieved wreck, fell into the river and was drowned. Yet another boy, 13-year-old John George Woodley, was on a boat from which he had been swimming when the Thames Conservancy boat on *Princess Alice* business caused a swell as it passed, causing John George to fall in. It seems John George was only just learning to swim and, though his young friend Fredrick William Wilson (who was able to swim) dived in after him, he was unable to find him. At John George's inquest Mr Carttar commended young Frederick William on being able to swim, commenting that the wreck of the *Princess Alice* should stimulate everyone to do so.

Although the day after the disaster *The Times* had mentioned one very pertinent accident, that of the *Metis* and *Wentworth*, oddly enough it came up very little after that apart from in the provincial press, possibly because they had little local interest in the survivors and victims with which to fill their pages. It was pertinent because it had been a collision between a Woolwich Steamboat Company's pleasure steamer (the *Metis*) and a Tyne collier (the *Wentworth*) one early September evening at almost the same spot eleven years earlier. And not only were the boats, the timing and the venue similar, but the *Wentworth* had been going downstream to head back home to Newcastle while the *Metis* had been heading upstream after leaving Gravesend carrying seventy excursionists, some of whom were dancing on the deck.

The *Metis* was virtually cut in two by the *Wentworth* and at first no one knew how many passengers had been lost. Fortunately, in that particular case, both vessels were near the shore and the forepart of the *Metis* was driven onto the south bank where some passengers were able to leap ashore. Others were saved by small craft and soldiers from nearby barracks.

At first it appeared that only three of the *Metis* passengers had died: two children and a man called Edward Cheesman who had been at the wheel. But, shortly afterwards, another succumbed: Police Sergeant Parry of 'K' Division, who died not long after rescue. His 9-month-old baby daughter had been one of the two drowned children.

Accusations and counter accusations had been bandied about in the wake of that accident: drunkenness, of the captain of the pleasure steamer; the *Metis* crew had not kept a proper lookout; she was hugging the shore but changed her mind at the last moment; once the accident had happened, the captain of the Tyne collier had responded wrongly. (To add to the eerie coincidences there had even been shouts of 'Where are you coming to?') Such accusations were about to be discussed, pulled apart, refuted and counter-claimed in the case of the *Princess Alice* and the *Bywell Castle*. The *Metis* and *Wentworth* incident was like nothing so much as a forewarning, a dress rehearsal for the real thing: the greatest civilian disaster England's waterways had ever seen. Unfortunately, at that time no one was taking any notice.

Death by drowning continued to occupy the pages of the mainstream British press, particularly their letters pages. Here, the flow of ingenious ideas to prevent that fate continued despite a *Times* leader pointing out that the offer of advice to excursionists would be very opportune if there were the remotest chance that any attention would be paid to it.

> They are enjoined to learn to swim before embarking for Gravesend. They are told that no man or woman should go onboard a river steamer without a life-belt. Precautions which implied anticipations of death as a result of a trip down the river would kill the pleasure of most holiday makers.[1]

All this advice, they went on, should be aimed at those who order the excursions, not those who make them. Was it too much to ask that steamers be compelled to use fog signals after dusk, as the Venetian gondolier notifies his approach when he drives into a side canal? (A rather strange comparison under the circumstances.)

Still the life-saving ideas came and still *The Times* and other newspapers published them.

A Mr R. Barclay Jamieson who suggested 'an extremely simple contrivance whereby those who cannot swim may at least manage to keep afloat for a much longer time – an umbrella – an indispensable article – almost universally carried nowadays in this uncertain climate by the pleasure seekers of all kinds'. Several hundred umbrellas had been found floating on the river and in the cabins of the *Princess Alice*, he claimed but in every instance, he believed, they were found closed and neatly wrapped up.

Had each owner retained sufficient presence of mind to have opened his or her umbrella, and when in the water held it handle downwards by means of the ferule end ... they would have found the inflated dome would have supported at least one person comfortably, if not more in the case of children. The umbrella would simply have floated with the tide, supporting and carrying those who continued to cling to it until timely help arrived.

He had known, he added, 'this exceedingly simple contrivance' save more than one precious life.[2]

Of course umbrellas then were nothing like the compact little objects we now slip in our pockets or handbags. Many were substantial items with ample domes 2 or 3 ft wide but, even supposing such a 'contrivance' *would* support a person in the water, to suggest it might have saved *Princess Alice*'s passengers' lives overlooks the manner in which they were suddenly thrown into the water, on top of each other, pushing each other down and struggling not just to stay afloat but to find space. Even supposing they had their umbrellas to hand, which is unlikely, they would scarcely have been able to undo the wrapping, raise them up and float to safety. But, wouldn't you know, shortly afterwards, one of the survivors, a Mr J. J. Wharton, claimed that his opened umbrella had supported him until he quitted it for a plank.

N. A. recommended the use of inexpensive life-saving fittings that were then in partial use onboard several of the Clyde steamers – these were seat cushions made of cork and covered with painted canvas.

A Flag Officer came up with more advice, much of it regarding the vessels themselves and their handling, but also including the theory 'to ride my own hobby horse', which was that all who went afloat in close waters should carry something about them which would support and enable them to reach the shore, such as an air-tight lining in some convenient part of the dress or a cork belt or jacket. Of course, the cork belt or jacket would not require the time and presence of mind required for dress inflating and they could be covered with silk or made ornamental. To be able to swim was good, of course, agreed the Flag Officer, but even good swimmers were frequently drowned from various causes. In any case, women could rarely swim 'even without their dresses. With the inflated dress or belt they cannot sink if they try'. When they were in fashion he had heard of women being kept afloat by a crinoline 'though the centre of gravity of the human being is not generally favourable to these obsolete articles of dress as life preservers'. But what about a very small crinoline above the waist which, like his inflatable overcoat, had a small tube attached through which to inflate them?[3]

Naturally, the subject of swimming did come very much to the fore. Mr George Hayes of Pimlico referred to the young lady who had swum to the riverbank and pointed out that it was important that girls as well as boys should be taught and British mothers should overcome their prejudice against their daughters learning to swim. Curious to lay the blame on the sex which was utterly powerless when it came to decisions about such facilities.

Even before the accident, there had been a growing concern about the fact that so few people could swim. Around 2,000 annual deaths from accidental drowning were recorded and the wreck of the training ship *Eurydice*[4] off the Isle of Wight less than six months earlier, when 317 sailors, most of them cadets, had drowned, had concentrated minds on the subject.

Even if people were keen to learn to swim there were very few swimming pools where they could practice. Islington, an area which had suffered greatly from the *Princess Alice* tragedy, had the private Wenlock Baths, where a couple of clubs, the Albion and the Sandringham, held regular swimming competitions. The Wenlock Baths were no distance from the Mission Hall in Cowcross Street from which the Bible party had set out.

In a letter to the *Islington Gazette* (published on 30 August 1878, only four days *before* the disaster) a 'CONSTANT READER' suggested that the now-disused site of the Highbury Barn (an Islington pleasure garden) would be a good place to install a large swimming bath for women, making the point that there was nowhere in this large and important parish for them to learn the art.

Another letter, in the same issue, from Mr J. Garratt Elliott, Honourable Secretary of the London Swimming Club, said that every park should have a swimming pool. The opening hours of the limited accommodation at the Serpentine and Victoria Park Lake were so curtailed as to be almost useless. Whereas on the banks of the River Trent in Nottingham there was a bathing shed where a couple of thousand people could, and did, undress at one time. Mr Elliott revealed that in some parts of London men took the matter into their own hands:

> The casual Sunday stroller by the River Lea is at all points shocked by crowds of naked men, thus depriving the fair sex of a constitutional walk by its winding banks; whereas, if the Conservators of the Lea would erect bathing sheds here and there, where the bottom is safe, bathers (who I cannot blame) would resort thereto and pay a penny toll, which would amply pay for maintenance, the innumerable accidental drownings would be minimized, and genuine recreation founded for the people.

Indoor facilities could also be provided in the capital city, insisted Mr Elliott. The commissioners of bathing establishments were seeing the error of their ways. The St Pancras authorities had erected 'the best appointed bath in England' in Tottenham Court Road. (St Pancras was the adjacent borough to Islington.)

Mr Elliott ended his long letter by offering the services of his members who were willing to attend any bath to give a display of fast and ornamental swimming. They would also teach anyone to swim. If they sent him a stamped addressed envelope, he would let them have a voucher for an initial free lesson. Workhouse and school children particularly should learn.

The London Swimming Club were as good as their word and, on the Saturday afternoon three days before the disaster, at the Caledonian Asylum in Holloway, the boys were sat on stools and given a drill to perform which showed them how to use their hands and legs simultaneously. Then they were taken to the baths where, in 'the sling belt, twenty-five of them were given their first lesson'.[5] (There is no mention of a similar exercise for the girls.)

The Honourable Secretary of the Swimming Club of Great Britain also put his oar in with the statistic that of London's four million inhabitants not five per cent could swim, while Edwin Guest thought it was time the Englishman renounced their pretension of being a common sense, practical, self-helpful race and submitted to being judged by history as an indolent, self-indulgent one. Apart from its value in moments of peril, swimming was a new means of enjoyment for the whole family. 'After "spelling bees" and "rinking",[6] why should not "swimming" become the "rage" – the "craze" if you will.' A teacher from Hammersmith admitted that, 'In my school out of 170 boys, two can swim imperfectly, and the rest not at all; while of three pupil teachers, two have just learnt to swim'. 'A Father' in Brighton said that men and boys there could, at certain places and certain times, bathe for free, but what about the women?[7] Interestingly, at the same time, there was a flow of correspondence in *The Times* concerning the 'Rescue of Drowning Persons'. Among the letters was one from a surgeon to the Orphan Working School at Tavistock Hill that described in detail how swimming and the correct life-saving method were taught to all their pupils. Obviously there was already a stirring of interest in the subject life-saving and 'imitation of breathing' and an increasing awareness of the vulnerability of those unable to swim.

Once the dreadful disaster had occurred a famous name added his voice to the clamour. Captain Webb,[8] the first man to swim the English Channel, commented:

> A simple easy movement of the limbs enabled me to swim from Woolwich to Gravesend and back; and yet, because so few take the trouble to learn this movement, they perish within a couple of hundred yards from the shore.[9]

The 'Directions for Restoring the Apparently Drowned', offered in the post-accident booklet, *The Wreck of the Princess Alice*, explained, 'to imitate breathing' one first should try to 'excite the nostrils with snuff, hartshorn,[10] and smelling salts, or tickle the throat with a feather, etc., if they are at hand'.

As for the artificial respiration these were an amalgam of the principles of the late Dr Marshall Hall and those of Dr H.R. Silvestre. One was advised to begin with Dr Marshall's method, which amounted to placing 'the patient' on his face, then on his side, then turned back onto his face, back and forth about fifteen times a minute. Should that not work in about five minutes then recourse to Dr Silvestre's method was advised. For this, one placed the patient on a tilted surface with head and shoulders supported on a small firm cushion or 'a folded article of dress' and kept his tongue projecting beyond his lips with an elastic band or a piece of string or tape over it and under the chin. The rescuer then stood at the patient's head, grasped his arms just above the elbows, raised them up and kept them stretched for two seconds then put them down again pressing them against the sides of his chest for two seconds.

More than a dozen local Islington children had drowned in the *Princess Alice* disaster, most of them girls, and even more adults. As a consequence, in their issue of 11 September 1878, the *Islington Gazette* went for their vestry's jugular. While conceding that most vestries had not taken advantage of the Public Baths and Washhouses Act,[11] they accused Islington's of having shown something like a prejudice against the measure and even stooping to misrepresentation of the facts.

One of the reasons for Islington 'burking the baths and washhouses question', the *Islington Gazette* claimed, was that free libraries had also been proposed and the strong prejudices against the free libraries doubtless influenced their decision. To put through Baths and Washhouses would be the thin end of the wedge 'allowing for the adoption of further permissive acts'.

Not so St Pancras, a parish similar in character to Islington, 'but with less pretensions among the administration to refinement and intelligence'. *They* had taken to it in a most liberal spirit.

It was scarcely necessary for the *Islington Gazette* to hammer home the suffering of people in Islington due, in part, to their inability to swim. The evidence lay alongside their leader column in the endless inquest and funeral reports.

Other drowning accidents were now featured in the newspapers. There had been several during the past week, reported the *Illustrated London News* on 7 September 1878. One accident had occurred when three young ladies went rowing on a lake adjoining Brymston House in Somerset, the seat of the de Vesci family. The boat capsized, two of the young ladies were saved, but the other, 18-year-old Miss Ellen Ponsonby, third daughter of the Honourable Spencer Ponsonby Fane, had drowned.

CHAPTER ELEVEN

What Are They Hiding?

On Tuesday 10 September, after carrying out their usual task of viewing the bodies recovered the previous day, the Woolwich coroner and his jury trooped back to the town hall, where he opened the day's proceedings with one of his statements. This one included a rather curious plea to the press.

Mr Carttar was still preoccupied with the problem of ascertaining the exact number that had been onboard the *Princess Alice*. Understandably so, since he needed to know when these long days of listening only to identification evidence were going to end. Then they would be able to begin looking at what had caused the accident, who was to blame and exactly how and why all these people had died. In estimating how many had been onboard, he now complained that he was 'not receiving as much assistance as he ought to do from the survivors.' The next day, *The Times* reported his surprising plea:

> It would materially aid him in forming his estimate if all those who had been saved came forward to say so, but from some false delicacy, as he supposed, on their part, many of them seemed ashamed to avow that they had been near the vessel at all. Why it should be so, he could not tell, but he hoped that the sentiment would no longer be allowed to stand in the way of the public interest, and that all of those, without exception, who had been saved would acquaint him with the fact.

Where he had got this impression is not quite clear and, if it was true, why? Perhaps some of the male survivors (and, as we have noted, it was mostly men who survived) were ashamed that they had not been able to save anyone but themselves, not even their own family, even though this may well have been impossible? Or perhaps they ought not to have been onboard? Maybe they had been taking an illicit day off work? Or were they with someone they ought not to have been with?

When author Maureen Nichols was researching the loss of her great aunt, Mary Ball, in the *Princess Alice* disaster, she was surprised to find that young Mary, who was in service, had been with a married man.

Returning to the matter of the numbers onboard, a juryman pointed out that several of them had taken note of the statements of witnesses as to the size of their parties and by this means they could arrive at an approximate number of those onboard.

'It is not an *approximate* number, it is the *accurate* number we want', the coroner retorted testily.

So began another day in which sad people paraded before the inquest jury to swear as to why they thought one of the bodies lying in the dockyard or buried unknown was a friend or dear one.

Among those identified that day by her father was 14-year-old Ruth Elizabeth Leaver, the last of the Leaver children to be found. Rosa Hennessey, daughter of a surgeon living in India and one of the Tufnell Park school party, was identified by its surviving member, Elizabeth Mary Randall, who told the court she had been promising her pupils the trip for some months. More members of the Bible party were also recognized.

The Times reporter found one identification 'more than unusually touching'. That of Charlotte Sophia Nares, aged twenty-five, the wife of George Nares, the son of the polar explorer George Strong Nares. A surgeon by the name of Thomas gave the required evidence. The husband, 'a tall, powerful young man, one of the saved,' also endeavoured to do so, 'but his emotion completely overcame him, and he had to be carried out of court'.

Unsurprisingly, despite the admirable identification arrangements, errors were beginning to surface. Mrs Nares's rings were no longer on her fingers and the rest of her jewellery was also missing, but a packet of things which did not belong to her was attached. A juryman suggested the obvious, perhaps Mrs Nares's jewels had been accidentally transferred to another body? *The*

Times thought not and that one of the watermen had probably taken them. 'A similar suspicion', they reported, 'attaches in the case of the corpse of a wealthy man, who was found with only 6½d in his pocket on his being searched at the dockyard.'

A baby had also been mislaid. William Samuel Page, another lone man among his party to be saved, had come to collect the already identified body of his infant son only to find it had been taken away by someone else. It was thought, the coroner was informed, the boy had been mistakenly removed by an under-taker from Barking but the police were doing their best to rectify the mistake.

Mr Page also wanted his wife's body but it had been 'buried unknown'. Could he have her exhumed? The coroner was doubtful: 'Only by obtaining permission from the Secretary of State', Carttar told him 'and the consent of the Bishop of the Diocese – it's a very expensive process'. Mr Page assured him that he did not mind the expense.

The reporter was also touched by the plight of a father, publican Edmund Wool (who had not been onboard), 'now left alone' after his entire family of six plus two servants had 'been swept away'.[1]

The following day, to assist identification, Mr Hinds, the Superintendent of the Dockyard Division of the Police, displayed photographs of a number of the so far unrecognized dead. They were 'by no means pleasing pictures,' *The Times* somewhat unnec-essarily informed its readers, 'only less pleasing to look upon than the wan faces of a few sorrowful women in mourning who still flit about the dockyard in the hope of finding a lost figure'.[2]

At 1 p.m. the parish authorities had informed by telegraph all the friends of the identified who lay unburied that if they were not removed they would be deposited in common graves. By 6 p.m., thirty-four had been removed, including the bodies of Captain Grinstead and his brother. The photographs, along with the trinkets in the little glazed cigar boxes proved effective. Twenty-two out of the thirty-nine unclaimed bodies displayed were identified that day. Police boiled and disinfected the clothes of those remaining and when dry they were stitched together to avoid separation or mingling. Things were winding down.

There was progress, too, on the matter of the number saved. Mr Hughes, the solicitor for the London Steamboat Company, presented Mr Carttar with a list of 130 they had drawn up saying, 'The number can be added to, but it cannot be less'. (Except, of course by extracting the at least nine who had died since rescue.) Mr Carttar was satisfied. Along with the information from the letters from those onboard, with which he had been inundated, he said he should be able to arrive at a pretty accurate estimate of the number lost.

There had been movement, too, on the question of exhumation. The Rector of Woolwich, Adelbert Anson, went to see the Home Secretary who promised a quick decision on the subject while the Chancellor of the Diocese of Rochester (in the absence of the Bishop) said he was willing to allow one mass disinterment to take place in a week or two, to give people the time to get in their applications. At the start of the Woolwich inquest on Friday 13 September 1878, Mr Carttar passed on the news that the Home Secretary had declared he had no power over burials in consecrated ground, so there was no hindrance from that quarter, and that the Chancellor of the Diocese had given his permission for exhumations.

That day's session had begun with a small spat between the coroner and Mr Harrington, the jury foreman, after Mr Harrington suggested that all future bodies should now go in the public mortuary because having numerous relatives coming and going was a serious responsibility for the dockyard store department. There wouldn't be that many more bodies coming in now anyway, he said.

The coroner, with, one suspects, some acid in his voice, told the jury that he was happy to say that he had a much more pleasing prospect to hold out 'than your worthy foreman has done'. He knew people objected strongly to having their relatives' bodies sent to the parish dead house. Fortunately, he had assurance that they had the use of the dockyard until the following Friday, the 20 September. 'Ultimately, no doubt when one or two unknown bodies may drop in, some measure such as your foreman indicated may be necessary', but in any case bodies would not be treated with any want of respect.

'I am heartily glad, Mr Coroner, to hear the announcement you have made,' said Harrington, 'and I need hardly add that I did not intend that the bodies still to be recovered be subjected to any indignity whatever'.

There was a chorus of 'No. No,' from the jury.[3]

Revealed by that day's identification came the surprising fact that Miss Jane Law, the younger of the two wealthy sisters who had arranged the Bible party outing, had been 'buried unknown'. But now her brother, banker John Law, swore he had recognized her clothing.

Teacher, Elizabeth Randall, performed her final identification duty by swearing to the clothing of the Tufnell Park school-girl, 17-year-old Ada Florence Farnum, daughter of a merchant in Demerara, Georgetown, Jamaica, who had been buried unknown.

There was another suggestion of theft from a body when the brother-in-law of baker Mr Henry Belcher claimed that there had been £28 in notes and gold in the pocket of the deceased, which Mr Belcher had taken with him to pay his miller but had been too early. The money had not been found on him before he was buried unknown. The coroner referred him to the police.

This was the final day of the first part of the inquest, the second half would commence on Monday morning, Mr Carttar announced. Therefore, he wished to thank the military author-ities and the police whose conduct had been admirable. He did so in some detail, at the conclusion of which Mr Harrington butted in to endorse all he had said but pointed out that 'some notice should also be given to the men of the Army Hospital Corps, Gilham, the Coroner's Officer, the South Eastern Railway Company and ...'

The coroner cut him off saying these details might be better gone into at a later period. He and the jury had very many more hours to spend in the company of Mr Harrington and it was not going to get any easier.

The progress of the Mansion House Fund was regularly revealed by the newspapers who listed the latest donations, among which were:

> The sum of £172.2s handed in from the salesmen of the London Central Meat Market in Smithfield. Messrs N. M. Rothschild and Son subscribed £100, and Mr Albert de Rothschild, on the invitation of the Lord Mayor, consented to join the committee of distribution.[4]

Whilst this committee pondered what the ultimate method of distribution of these funds would be the Reverend Styleman Herring, Vicar of St Paul's, Clerkenwell, paid regular visits to the dockyard gates to dole out emergency relief.

The Reverend Herring, who was Chairman of the Clerkenwell Emigration Society, had some experience in these matters, having performed a similar duty on behalf of widows and orphans in January 1873 when the immigrant ship, the *Northfleet*, carrying 300 workers, some women and children to Tasmania to build a railway, was rammed by an unknown vessel and sunk just off Dungeness with the loss of more than 300 lives. Also, in November of the following year, when the loss of another emigrant ship, the *Cospatrick*, en route for New Zealand, caught fire mid-Atlantic. There were insufficient lifeboats and those there were were badly launched. Only three out of 475 onboard survived.

But a new note was starting to be sounded in editorial musings on relief distribution; the suggestion that the families of the miners killed in the South Wales mining disaster were needier. True, the *Princess Alice* disaster might be much larger in scale and of much greater interest to the public in general, but in the mining disaster the bread winners had been lost, while in the Thames collision it had been the wives and little ones who had perished and the strong men who had been saved.

Many adoption offers for the orphaned children came in but, *The Times* reported, 'demand far exceeds the supply. A large number of children were on the *Princess Alice* but comparatively few were saved'. Indeed, children remained prominent in the lists of bodies found:

A female child, age 6, hair light brown; dress, white Holland (trimmed red riband round bottom, scarlet cuffs and pocket) black frock (two rows kilting, black buttons), three petticoats (one white with six rows of pleats, one serge maroon, of flannel), white drawers (flounced with embroidery), black ribbed stockings, elastic garters, high button boots, supposed marked 'E. Haggard, 41 High-street, Putney'.

A male child, age three months, hair light; dress, white Marcella pelisse[5] (gray flowers, white buttons), cape to match, white frock (fancy work front), three petticoats (two white with ten tucks, one flannel with two tucks), woollen boots, blue riband, blue sash around waist.[6]

It is touching to think that someone took the trouble to count the tucks on the baby's dress.

Children also remained prominent among those bodies unidentified, probably because in many cases their parents and siblings had died with them.

There was some other news regarding the *Princess Alice* disaster: the London Steamboat Company was suing the owners of the *Bywell Castle* for the sum of £20,000.

CHAPTER TWELVE

So, Who Was to Blame?

As well as criticism for allowing his log to be published, the captain of the *Bywell Castle* had been accused by various witnesses of not stopping and reversing after his collision with the *Princess Alice*.

But the many other published statements had muddied the water, including the one in the *Standard* on Monday, 9 September, burial day. It was by Abraham Deness the owner of the barge *Bonetta* that had been moored near Beckton Gasworks at the time of the collision and who had taken part in the rescue efforts. The first part was his graphic account of this. How people were like a flock of sheep in the water, about their piteous shrieks and shouts, how from their frantic exertions to save themselves he hardly thought he should get out alive. But in the published version he also apportioned blame to the *Bywell Castle*:

> It is my firm opinion that if the *Bywell Castle* had not ported her helm she would have cleared the *Princess Alice*, and if the latter had not been there she must have gone ashore ... It was just dark, but moonlight – the moon was just showing itself. The *Princess Alice* was keeping her course in a proper direction, and had no chance of avoiding a collision than by keeping the course she was going in. If the *Bywell Castle* had not ported her helm she must have gone clear. There was nothing else in her way to the northward for three-quarters of a mile.

This question of who exactly was to blame for the accident was about to be considered at great length as, on 16 September 1878, the inquest was reopened, this time for the sole purpose of investigating the cause of the tragedy.

However, before they began, Mr Carttar, the coroner, had something to say about two matters which had upset him. Firstly, one of the certified dead had sprung back to life due, of course, to an identification error. The following day *The Times* reported the gist of his speech:

> After all the pains they had taken to get the bodies identified beyond the risk of a mistake, he regretted to say – although, of course, the fact was satisfactory in one sense – that a person had been identified there and her body taken away, but it now turned out that she was alive. The case came under their notice on Thursday last, when Mrs Anne Dalton, now the wife of Leonard Dalton, stone and marble merchant, of 769, Old Kent Road, swore to the identity of her daughter, Mary Anne Cutler Drake, 20 years of age, a single woman, daughter of Stephen Drake, a woollen draper. Subsequently the clothes of the deceased person were identified as belonging to somebody else.

Carttar had received a letter that morning from Leonard Dalton in answer to his note on the question, saying he had reason to believe Mrs Dalton had made a mistake. They had heard from her daughter and were sorry to have troubled him 'but we are pleased to find her alive'. He returned the order for her clothes.

The second thing that had annoyed Mr Carttar was the publication of affidavits purported to have been sworn on oath to the Receiver of Wrecks by Captain Harrison and crew members of both vessels, and the conclusions drawn from them. He had no objection to the stories of the *survivors* being published in the newspapers. They had doubtless purged their minds of some of the horror which they had undergone. However, nothing could be more indecent, improper and calculated to pollute the source of justice than the publication of these affidavits. Never, he told the jury, in all his long experience had he met this kind of behaviour. Therefore, they must make sure they based their findings solely on the evidence about to be put before them. Easier said than done. So much printers' ink had been utilized over such a short time and so much of the material thus aired was of such intense interest to all concerned.[1]

The Times reacted sniffily to Carttar's comments. The

The striking Illustrated London News depiction of the *Princess Alice* disaster is reproduced in colour on a W. H. Wills's (Celebrated Ships No. 50) cigarette card, 1911

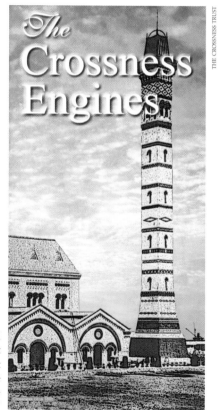

Leaflet advertising the refurbished Crossness Sewerage Treatment Works. Due to its magnificent Victorian ironwork the engine house has been dubbed 'the Crossness Cathedral'

Typical contemporary broadsheet describing and illustrating the *Princess Alice* disaster

Frantic crowds gather and overwhelm the police on duty at Woolwich Pier where many of the bodies of *Princess Alice* passengers were brought ashore

There is fierce competition among the swarms of watermen probing the river to encourage the drowned to rise so that they may claim a fee for each body

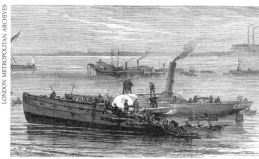

With the aid of divers and heavy lifting chains, three days after the sinking, the forward part of the *Princess Alice* is brought to the surface and towed to the south shore

Relatives identifying the bodies of the victims at Woolwich dockyard. Initially, bodies found on the northern (Essex) banks of the river could not be held at Woolwich since it was unlawful law to move them to another jurisdiction

Just prior to the collision the huge hull of the Tyne collier, *Bywell Castle*, looms over the much more fragile pleasure steamer the *Princess Alice*, while the ships' warning whistles continue to shriek and the passengers scream

Burying the unknown dead. Eventually, due to increasing decomposition, it became imperative to bury even those who remained unidentified. Their dramatic mass funeral took place on 'Burial Monday', 9 September 1878, at Woolwich Cemetery

For almost two weeks, at Woolwich Town Hall, the coroner and his nineteen-man inquest jury listened to a constant flow of relatives and friends identifying the bodies of their loved ones. Only then began the prolonged process of investigating the cause of the accident

At the start of each day the coroner took his jury to view the latest bodies retrieved and they were also taken to examine parts of the newly-raised wreck

The heavier back-end of the *Princess Alice* proved more difficult to raise. More bodies were released from the wreck as it finally surfaced on the fifth day after the collision

Relatives identifying the belongings of the dead. The number attached to each object corresponded with that placed on the victim's body: a process designed to make identification easier

The *Bywell Castle* was a powerful, iron-built, 890-ton Tyne collier. The ship's most regular coal run took it to the Eastern Mediterranean

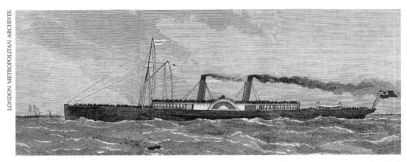

The *Princess Alice* pleasure steamer, built at Greenock in 1865, was only 219 feet long, 20 feet wide and weighed a mere 250 tons

Thames police officers searching for bodies in the drained interior of the forward part of the *Princess Alice* wreck. None were found among the debris of hats, umbrellas, souvenirs and stewards' money bags

Identifying the clothes of the dead at Woolwich dockyard. Even when a victim was 'buried unknown' their clothing was boiled and retained to aid possible identification later

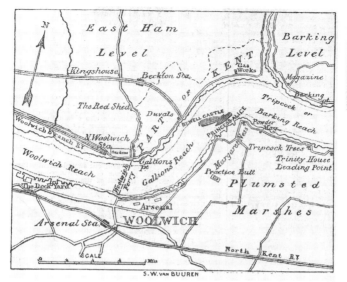

S. W. van BUUREN

An *Illustrated London News* map indicating the presumed site of the collision – close by Tripcock Point. Subsequently, there was to be much dispute amongst the witnesses and ship owners about the exact site of the accident

William Grinstead, the 47-year-old captain of the *Princess Alice*, was considered to be one of the London Steamboat Company's most experienced and careful employees and also a very nice man

Princess Alice and her family in 1876. Her ill-fated daughter, May, is seen here in her father's arms

Postcard of the Victorian panel of the Greenwich Millennium Embroideries. The *Princess Alice* disaster is shown top right

depositions were perfectly legal and their publication had been for the public benefit. Some of their correspondents had founded useful observations in them (which, of course, was the problem). The newspaper went on to quote the pertinent Section 448 of the Merchant Shipping Act at great and tedious length, then continued with their justification: the great advantage of the depositions was that they were taken while the matter referred to was still fresh and they should not be withheld from those to whom they were of use. In any case, any member of the public could purchase a copy for a small fee from the Receiver of Wreck's Office.

One sees the coroner's point of view. Leaky officialdom and unabashed trial by newspaper had become a prominent and worrying part of the British justice system and the more forceful coroners often felt the need to issue reminders of their powers and the primary importance of their inquests.

That all done, the jurors settled down to more long days at the town hall. Meanwhile, many of their businesses remained undermanned. Included among the nineteen men around that large table were two silversmiths, an upholsterer, an auctioneer, a carriage builder, two leather sellers, a milliner, a publican, a draper, a boot-maker, a grocer, a china dealer and another leather seller, most from Woolwich's main thoroughfare, Powis Street, and the surrounding area.

The jury was equipped with a survey of the river and models of the *Princess Alice* and the *Bywell Castle*. Mr Carttar began the work proper by announcing that he intended to centre the whole case on William Beechey, the first person to be identified after his wife grew worried when he didn't return from his work in the City. The verdict returned on his body would serve for all.

The first of the witnesses at the renewed inquest was Mr Herbert Oliver Thomas, surveyor to the Woolwich Local Board of Health. He produced an ordnance survey map on which he had marked the position of the wreck, but he was taken apart by the various lawyers when he admitted to not having taken any actual measurements, instead working out the position by drawing intersecting lines. Then Mr Carttar had him admit to having no previous experience of nautical surveys and (after claiming he had drawn the map of his own volition) that it had been the idea of the owners of the *Princess Alice*. Not a good start.

Clearly the coroner would have to take into account that the loyalties of the Woolwich witnesses would tend towards the *Princess Alice* and its owners. Blame had been laid at the door of the *Princess Alice* as well as the *Bywell Castle*: that she had been overloaded; that she had actually been stationary before impact and that saloon steamers made a habit of tacking recklessly to and fro across the river to 'cheat the tide'. And so on.

Next came the much-bereaved Mr William Wrench Towse, Manager of the London Steamship Company. He produced the *Princess Alice*'s passenger number certificates and her technical description: she had been built at Greenock in 1865, was 219 ft long and 20 ft wide. When loaded she drew 4–4½ ft of water, carried twelve lifebuoys in prominent places and two boats, one fitted as a lifeboat. It took her two and a half hours to get from London to Gravesend which was a distance of 23½ miles.

Then came the most eagerly awaited witnesses. Those who had actually been there on the night and thus who might reveal exactly what happened and who was to blame.

Six out of the *Princess Alice*'s fourteen crew members had survived: George Thomas Long, the first mate; John Eyres, the substitute steersman; John Richard Rand, the apprentice and lookout; Ralph Wilkinson, the second mate; Henry Young, the foremast hand; and Thomas Longhurst, the engineer.

The first of the crew to appear before the resumed inquest was one of the two men most likely (aside from the late Captain Grinstead) to be able to put them in the picture, First Mate George Thomas Long. Long had sailed the Thames for twenty-five years and had a mate's certificate of competency for a home-trade passenger ship. He had given a statement to the Receiver of Wrecks which he now went over and elaborated.

He explained that, on leaving Rosherville, Rand and Eyres had taken over the wheel, which was situated between the two funnels on the saloon deck. The captain was on the bridge which stood just over the wheel 'but rather before it'. He (Long) was on the fore-saloon acting as lookout. Wilkinson, the second mate, was on deck.

At 7.42 p.m., as they came up towards Tripcock Point, Long noticed the green light and masthead light of a steamer heading towards them midstream down Gallions Reach. It would take, he estimated, about fifteen minutes to reach them. He was sure

Captain Grinstead would have seen this oncoming vessel.

The navigation rule of the river was that vessels should pass green light to green light or red light to red light, the green light being on the left hand, or port side, and the red on the right, or starboard side. He could still see the green light of the *Bywell Castle* and expected they would pass starboard to starboard, green to green. The *Princess Alice* starboarded her helm to pass around the point and avoid the *Talbot* powder boat and line of ships moored beyond that on the left in Gallions Reach. At no time, Long insisted, were they nearer to the centre of the river than a hundred yards.

Suddenly, to his horror, he had seen all three lights of the approaching ship – which meant she was heading straight towards them. He heard Captain Grinstead shout, 'Ease her!' 'Stop her!' and then 'Stop!'

As he rushed aft to lower the starboard lifeboat he realized that the engines had stopped. Aware that they would have no time to lower the lifeboat in the normal fashion he took out his knife to cut the lashings and heard the captain shout, 'Hoy, hoy! Where are you coming to?' Then he felt the blow of the collision. Within two minutes the pleasure steamer had sunk.

The *Princess Alice* had never stopped from starboarding her helm, he insisted. Had the *Bywell Castle* been held to starboard or kept straight, Long claimed, there would have been no collision.

The jury foreman and the lawyers cross-questioned him on his knowledge of rules for navigation of the River Thames, such as 29d of the Thames Conservancy By-Laws which stated:

> If two vessels under steam are meeting end on, or nearly end on, so as to involve risk of collision, the helms of both shall be put to port, so that each may pass on the port side of the other.

It was clear he had not heard of such a rule, but also that there seemed to be general confusion about this, and neither did there appear to be any clear rule regarding whether a ship was going up or downstream.

'Was the captain sober?' the coroner asked suddenly.

'Yes, I never saw him the worse for liquor in all my life.'

'Were the two men at the wheel sober?'

'Yes.'

'Were they accustomed to steer?'

The questioning was becoming pointed.

'Yes.'

'Were the watermen licensed watermen?'

'Yes.'

The most pertinent question was about to be asked.

'Is there any truth in the statement that a perfect stranger to the vessel was steering; and had the wheel with the sanction of the captain?'

'That is right,' Long replied.

'Why did you not state that?'

'You never asked me that question.'

'Who was steering?'

'Eyres and Creed. Eyres was the stranger.'

Then you gave me a wrong answer when you said that he was one of the crew, and that his duty was to steer.

Creed had drowned, so it was 28-year-old John Eyres, the substitute steersman, on whom the spotlight now fell.

When it was established how Eyres came to be at the wheel, having taken over from a crew member at Gravesend, the coroner continued his interrogation.

'Of the two men at the wheel, whom do you consider was the head man?

'Creed.'

'Why Creed?'

'He was the man that belonged to the ship.'

'Yes, but inasmuch as the other man had the order of the captain to steer, did not the steering rest with the stranger?'

'No more than with Creed.'

At this juncture someone pointed out that Eyres was in court. 'Then he had better go out of court,' said the coroner, 'along with the rest of the witnesses.' Then he got back to his probing for the truth.

'When two men are at the wheel, there is but one who takes the run and the other who helps him?'

'Just so.'

'Do you mean to say Eyres was not the man really at the wheel making the movements?'

'He was at the wheel.'

'Why did you tell me Creed was the principal one?'

'Eyres was the steersman and Creed was assisting him.'

Poor Long was becoming confused. When the inquest resumed after lunch the foreman asked him which man was in charge of the wheel and he replied it was the man on the port side. When asked who was on the port side he replied 'Creed'.

'But,' said the coroner, 'you have just told us that Eyres was in charge of the wheel.'

'Yes, or rather they were both at the wheel.'

But the coroner had another potentially damaging question. Long had explained that his duty was to assist the captain.

'How was it,' inquired the coroner, 'that the moment the necessity for assisting the captain arose, you ran aft?'

'To save lives by lowering the lifeboat,' Long replied.

Captain Bedford Capperton Trevelyan Pim, MP, RN, whose colourful naval career had included long sled journeys searching for Sir John Franklin in the Arctic and suffering wounds while commanding a gunboat in the Baltic, was the barrister appearing on behalf of the relatives of the victim, Mr Bridgeman. Pim returned to this subject by asking what induced him to run aft to lower the lifeboat instead of running to the skipper to ask him whether he could be of any use.

'To save life.'

'Whose life?'

'The passengers'.'[2]

Apart from attempting to establish just who was steering the doomed vessel, the most persistent question and accusation was that the *Princess Alice* had ported her helm as she came round the point. Even, in fact, that she had been making for the north shore, as many saloon steamers did when criss-crossing the river to take advantage of tides and currents. Long denied this vehemently.

John Eyres was in no doubt who had been steering from Erith onwards. 'I was in charge and Creed, who is my half-brother, came to assist me.' That relationship was news.

Eyres said that he was a mercantile seaman who had sailed onboard fishing smacks and Mediterranean and Baltic steamers as boatswain, but he had not steered them. He was, he admitted, quite unacquainted with the river and had never steered a vessel as long as the pleasure steamer (220 ft). The only vessel he had steered on the Thames was a tugboat. He was steering purely by the orders of the captain. On rounding Tripcock Point the captain said, 'Mind your helm on account of the downtide'.

'By that understood that I was to hold the helm tight to prevent the vessel being swung off.'

A number of witnesses testified that Tripcock Point deflected an ebb tide so that an offset current ran north across the river towards Beckton Gasworks pier. A ship coming upstream, round the point, encountered two forces successively: first the cross current acting on her port bow and opposing a starboard helm, then the ebb tide assisting the helm by pressing on the starboard bow. In fact, a vessel might first be taken towards midstream, giving the impression she was making for the north shore, and then, suddenly like a top she might spin towards the south.

Eyres also blamed the *Bywell Castle* for porting its helm on approaching the *Princess Alice*. He had escaped by swimming to the *Bywell Castle*, grabbing a hawser and pulling himself onboard. He had begged the master to follow him but he declined saying he would stay at his post and telling Eyres to look after himself.

Mr Hughes, solicitor for the *Princess Alice* and her owners, asked what the captain of the *Bywell Castle* was doing when Eyres got onboard.

'Reversing his engines, and I told him the screw would cut people to pieces. He said, "What am I to do: I cannot let her drift ashore." I said, "Better let her drift ashore than cut people to pieces."'

'That would explain the injuries which many of the dead received,' said a juryman.

The inquest was then adjourned until the following morning. When it resumed, Captain Bedford Pim cross-examined Eyres. Whether the *Princess Alice* starboarded or not before impact, was the continuing bone of contention.

'The helm was kept a-starboard,' Eyres insisted. 'I am quite certain I did not give the wheel a port stroke – not half a one.'

'I may tell you,' replied Captain Bedford Pim, 'that when the wreck was examined the helm was to port.'

Eyres was not fazed. 'The tide would do that. Before we saw the screw we were on a starboard helm. We got close to the powder magazine 10–15 yd, or perhaps 20 yd.'

'When did you see all the three lights of the *Bywell Castle* and then the red light by itself?'

'About two minutes before the collision. Nothing then could

be done by either party to avoid it.'

Later Pim changed tack: 'There has been a report circulating that the captain was not perfectly sober. Tell the jury the true state of the case.'

'The man was quite sober as far as I know. I do not believe he had a glass of anything to drink that day.'[3]

Next up was 21-year-old apprentice, John Richard Rand, the *Princess Alice*'s foremast hand who had been at the wheel with Creed until Eyres took over. He did not diverge from the previous witness's version of events. He had climbed onboard the *Bywell Castle* just before Eyres and heard Captain Harrison order his ship to go astern and Eyres tell him not to or he would 'grind people up'.[4]

Then came 46-year-old Ralph Wilkinson, the *Princess Alice*'s second mate, who had been onboard for four summers and three winters. As a witness he turned out to be a bit of a disaster for the *Princess Alice* side. His duties included taking the wheel between Woolwich and London, to be about the deck looking out and coiling ropes to throw ropes at the piers when they docked.

'I have no fixed post, but I walk about, and sometimes go below to smoke a pipe or get something to eat.' He had no idea how near they had been to the screw steamer which had passed them before Tripcock Point (there had been an effort to show this had been a close shave), nor had he heard the whistle warnings to the *Bywell Castle*.

'Then you seem to know very little about the matter,' said the coroner.

In answer to Mr Myburgh, for the *Bywell Castle*, he replied that he did not know of anyone being stationed on the lookout.

Myburgh was astounded. 'Do you mean to say that on these steamers going up and down the river there is nobody stationed on the lookout?'

'I do not know.'

'Yet you were second mate onboard this vessel?'

'I hold no certificate.'

The coroner pointed out that he *acted* as second mate. Myburgh was not going to let go of this gift to his clients. 'I want to know again whether on these steamers, carrying 600–700 passengers up and down the river, there is no-one expressly stationed on the lookout?'

Wilkinson repeated that he did not know. Would he have looked out if he had heard the whistle blow?

'It was blown so often that I should have taken no notice of it.'

Neither did he look up to see what vessel had struck them, nor had he seen any of the *Bywell Castle's* lights or noticed whether the ship's paddles were going at the time, or whether or not they had been in midstream.

Had he not sworn to the Receiver of Wrecks that they were midstream?

'No, I said she was more on the south shore.'

'You come here pretending to know nothing,' exclaimed an irritated Myburgh, 'but here is your sworn statement. Have you not sworn to this?'

'Yes … I understood that I said she was more to the south shore.'

Myburgh persisted. Was his sworn statement true or not?

'It must be true if I said it,' Wilkinson said. There was laughter in court. He tried to retrack a little by claiming that the whistle was not meant for the crew but to warn the approaching vessel.

A juryman wanted to know whether it was not the duty of the second mate to look out?

'It is the duty of us all,' he replied. The captain had ordered him to act as lookout when he was not at the wheel, he now said, and if he had left his lookout he would ask someone to take his place.

Clearly the jury were becoming irritated with this seemingly simple-minded man and his conflicting evidence. 'You have not said so before,' a juryman complained. 'You have been misleading us altogether.'

More cross-questioning caused him to go back on this and claim again that there was no one on lookout.

So when the men were not at the wheel and are not coiling ropes have they any duties to perform, inquired Harrington, the jury foreman?

'They stand about on the decks.'

'What doing?'

'Passing away the time.'

'He has no orders at all,' said the coroner. He goes up and down and round about and does nothing. Do you call that the duty of a mate?'

'I do not exactly know.'

'Is it the duty of a sailor to lounge about the deck?'

'I am not a sailor.'

'There is no watch appointed?'

'No.'[5]

Henry Young, the foremast hand was, fortunately for the *Princess Alice*'s counsel, rather more observant as to the events preceding the collision and quite certain about there being lookouts. Indeed, the captain had said to him, 'It's a fine evening; keep a good lookout.' As well as himself, Rand and Arnold (a boy who drowned) were also on lookout that night. 'Rand was on the bow.' He added that the captain was perfectly sober, as were also Eyers and Creed at the wheel. 'I was sober too.'[6]

The final witness from the *Princess Alice*'s crew was Thomas Longhurst, the ship's engineer. Since he had been below he could not be an eyewitness to the collision and could not tell exactly when it happened.

> Shortly before, I had the order, 'Ease her; stop her.' As the vessel was going against the tide, she stopped almost immediately. About a minute afterwards, I had the order, 'Go on.' She had hardly got under way when I got the order to ease and stop again. Then came the crash. There were two heavy blows, then the water rushed into the engine room from below. Seeing that, I hurried on deck and jumped overboard. There were plenty of lifebelts onboard but I left them for those who could not swim.

There was nothing wrong with his engines, he insisted. They were in beautiful order and had new boilers.

'I can stop the engine in a second or two. I can work them as fast as you can talk,' he told Mr Myburgh, the *Bywell Castle* lawyer.

'Did not the giving of so many orders within so short a time look like a change of plan in the captain's mind?' inquired Myburgh.

'It looked as if there was something in the way.'

'Do you know where you were on the river when you got the first order to ease and stop?' asked the coroner.

'No, I was below.'

'We may take it for granted that that order was given for the rounding of the point, and that the others were given in view of the approach of the *Bywell Castle*,' said Carttar.[7]

Later, Edward Kell, the *Princess Alice*'s money collector, was called as a witness. However, he was only able to add that the vessel was in line with the *Talbot* powder ship when she was struck. *The Times* commented that this went against the *Bywell Castle*'s claim.[8]

CHAPTER THIRTEEN

Other Views

Amongst those who next gave evidence at the Woolwich inquest were various Thames watermen who had not only seen the tragedy unfolding from the outside but were less likely to be biased in their opinions. They were also familiar with the ways of the river and the craft that sailed upon her although not, it transpired, with the rules governing their movement. These witnesses were interspersed with surviving passengers whose evidence was less inclined to be useful.

Two new elements began to affect the atmosphere in court and the questions asked: fractious exchanges between those taking part and new suggestions as to the cause of death of some of the victims. Up until then, death had presumed to have been from drowning or, as with the saved who later died, from shock and immersion.

Among the watermen giving evidence was, of course, barge-owner Abraham Deness. He described seeing all three lights of the *Princess Alice* as she rounded Tripcock Point, as close as possible to the south shore, then the *Bywell Castle*, her red light showing clearly to him by the Beckton Pier, and what followed. He went on, in a rather garbled fashion, to give the court the benefit of his thirty-six years of working the Thames and Medway by telling them of the peculiarities and dangers he had encountered while rounding Tripcock Point.

> ... the tide will always bring us off the Point, the ebb tide coming round Bull's Point [on the north side of the river opposite Woolwich] will strike above Tripcock and will then set off to north ... so that coming around Tripcock Point a vessel

will not only have the ordinary set of the ebb tide but will have this tide which sets off the Point on her port bow … A vessel coming round the Point with such a tide as was running that night would have considerable difficulty in getting her starboard helm to act. The tide setting from the Point would have a tendency to carry her off to midstream. At times it will take all command of a vessel against her helm, even in my barge. Mine is a short barge and the longer the vessel the greater the effect would be as the vessel would round the Point, carrying her to midstream … that is the way in which many collisions do take place.

If that was to happen, he pointed out, she would present her port light to the vessel coming down Gallions Reach. He went on:

She must do so until they get her straight, and when they get her straight in midstream when the tide does not act upon her bow she would spin round like a top in towards the south shore … if I were in a steamer on the ebb tide, if I had nothing in my way and I had a quantity of people onboard as the *Princess Alice* had, I would hug the south shore and get her straight for the Reach as quick as I could by easing of [sic] her. If they go at full speed there, the tide catches her nose and they are across the river in no time.[1]

The vagaries of passage around Tripcock Point were becoming ever more pertinent. Just whereabouts the *Princess Alice* was when she was struck was a matter of great dispute between the chief representatives.

Peter Brown had been on a schooner at anchor on the north side, near Beckton Gasworks, when he saw the *Princess Alice* showing a green light as she passed the Point, close by the *Talbot* powder magazine, then stop abreast of his schooner with her head pointing towards the south shore. This made him wonder whether there was something wrong with their engine. Then he saw a screw steamer (the *Bywell Castle*) half a mile upstream, which seemed close to the vessels riding on the south shore. 'She must have starboarded her helm to come clear of them.' Further down she ported her helm and then he saw her strike the *Princess Alice*.[2]

However, there were doubts about Brown's statement. Mr Myburgh, for the *Bywell Castle*, questioned him closely about various statements he had made suggesting that the *Princess Alice* had stopped for five minutes before the collision and that she was unmanageable, and about papers allegedly signed by him with offers of money for his statement.

A different scenario had unfolded for Henry Erb, master of the barge *Sarah* from Rochester lying at the upper end of the Beckton Gasworks pier. He said he was thinking it strange that the *Princess Alice* had stopped when he saw the *Bywell Castle* coming round Bull's Point, keeping to the *north*. Had she held her course, he said, she would not have gone near the pleasure steamer, but she suddenly hard a-ported so that, had she not touched the *Princess Alice*, she would have gone ashore on the south side just below the *Castalia* (one of the vessels moored in line beyond the *Talbot* powder barge). He could see no reason for the collision because there was plenty of room.

Joseph Burnitt, the master of the schooner *Anne Elizabeth* from Goole, was at anchor about 300 yd above Beckton Pier when he saw the *Bywell Castle* coming down Gallions Reach, heading a little over to the north shore, and *Princess Alice* going fairly slowly as she rounded Tripcock Point, then stopping for half a minute before she was struck.

William Steer, the master of the topsail barge *Benjamin Riddell*, thought the pleasure steamer was making for the north shore, after coming close round Tripcock Point to cheat the tide, and keeping so until she passed the powder ship when she steered on a slight port helm. 'From my knowledge of navigation I should have said the *Bywell Castle* ought not to have ported after the *Princess Alice* starboarded – that is what brought about the collision.'[3]

The *Talbot* powder barge had a roof and was completely enclosed leaving only two little windows from which lookouts kept an eye open for vessels coming too near. However, that evening, one of the watchmen had been on a ladder outside, preparing to bring in a rowing boat, when he saw the accident. He declared that the *Princess Alice* had been at least a third of the way across the river.

It was during the evidence of Mr Henry Gordon Fry, surveyor for the Thames Conservancy Board, that irritations began to surface. He had produced a chart showing the position of the wreck. *The Times* reported what happened next:

> The witness was questioned minutely by the Foreman as to the accuracy of his measurements and the examination being somewhat tedious, several of the jury loudly expressed their impatience. This gave rise to a scene of recrimination, in the course of which one of the jurymen complained that from the opening of the inquiry up to the previous evening the Foreman had asked no fewer than 1,131 questions.[4]

The Times was not the only newspaper to report these exchanges and, at the opening of proceedings the next morning, the foreman complained that several of them had been 'animadverting' upon his conduct as foreman of the jury. He was clearly wounded:

> I take it as a most unhandsome thing to do. My hands are tied at the present and I have no chance of replying to those paragraphs.

He added that the criticisms disturbed his mind when his attention should be devoted to the inquiry alone and asked that they desist until the inquest was over. Then they could say what they liked about him.

The coroner supported Mr Harrington but, as ever, the foreman was not quite finished.

> Allow me sir to make one other remark. It is impossible for the gentlemen of the press to understand the object of the questions I put … they may imagine I am wasting their time; but if they knew how I am situated with my family they would be perfectly well aware that it is no pleasure to be kept away from them for so long.

'It is no pleasure for any of us', interjected a juryman.[5]

It was clear, however, that it was not just the press who had problems with the foreman. When Harrington insisted on seeing *not* a map but longitudinal sections of the hull of the *Princess Alice*, barrister Captain Pim (representing the family of victim, Mr Bridgeman) commented that he did not think the longitudinal sections would be of importance. The foreman retorted, 'I am sorry I differ from the learned counsel; but it is the *jury* who have to deal with the facts.'[6] Given Captain Pim's navy service and the fact that since retirement he had built up a law practice based on admiralty cases, one imagines he felt himself qualified to judge whether longitudinal sections might be of importance.

There was also an altercation between a barrister who wanted to chip in with questions and call witnesses when he had not been among those hitherto involved in the case. A juryman and Mr Harrington weighed in to defend the coroner.

The law men were also becoming impatient with each other. Captain Pim asked Mr Hughes to make the evidence of his witnesses as short as possible. 'A number of gentlemen have been examined on behalf of the Steamboat Company and the jury must have arrived at a pretty good judgement a far as that evidence was concerned.'[7] Mr Hughes was robustly defending his rights to call whatever witnesses he wished when a juryman butted in to point out that some of the evidence that had been given the day before was not at all calculated to strengthen his (Mr Hughes's) case.

This was going too far. Some knuckle-rapping was called for. 'It would have been better', said the coroner, 'not even to have made that observation. It was an expression of opinion that the jury were not entitled to arrive at yet.'[8]

But Mr Hughes continued to bring on the *Princess Alice* survivors, one of whom, reported *The Times*, appeared to know nothing about the accident. Another, clerk, Herbert Augustus Wiele, who had given quite detailed evidence to a newspaper with regard to the position of the *Princess Alice* in the river before the impact, now admitted that he had 'altered his views' after reading the evidence of other witnesses and having been to the scene of the wreck – exactly what the coroner had been worried about.[9]

Mr Nelson, who represented Dix, the pilot, was also becoming weary of all this and exclaimed that if Mr Hughes intended to call all seventy-eight persons who had made statements in the newspapers a great deal of time would be wasted.

Hughes protested again. What he wanted principally to prove was that their vessel was on the *south* shore. 'If that was admitted I could curtail my evidence materially.' Mr Myburgh countered that *his* whole case was that the *Bywell Castle* was justified, from what he saw, in supposing that Captain Grinstead intended to go to the *north* shore. Mr Hughes declared that he would call witnesses to prove that *that* supposition was inaccurate. 'The chart shows her pretty near the centre of the river,' murmured the coroner.[10] So the endless parade of witnesses giving their conflicting evidence continued.

Newspaper readers did not have to worry too much about deciding whether the evidence proved that the *Princess Alice* had been on the north shore, the south shore or the in the middle. They were advised on that in an introduction which appeared before the very detailed report of the actual proceedings. These introductions explained, for example, that what some of the endless exchanges were about was whether the *Princess Alice* was in the centre of the river, in which case the captain of the *Bywell Castle* was justified in thinking she was making for the north shore; whether she was on the south shore and therefore the *Bywell Castle* altered her course unnecessarily; or whether the impact of the collision had driven the wreck to the centre of the river, thereby giving the impression that that was where she had been in the first place.

One example of the confusion that arose after an accident like this, claimed *The Times*, was that several witnesses had sworn that the band was still playing at the moment of collision, whereas the musician, Robert Haines, gave evidence that all of them, except him, had gone below and he had been at the top of the steps preparing to follow them. (Hotelier, James Huddart, who had been deserted by his companion Emma Eatwell at that moment, was one who made that claim.) Haines said:

> I stood amazed for a moment with the bass viol in my hands, not knowing what to do with it. Then, dropping the viol, I ran up on the saloon deck, where I saw the captain, and got upon the awning. The captain blew the whistle until the steam failed. When the vessel sank under me I caught hold of a man with a lifebelt so was saved.

Oddly, Mr Hughes inquired after Haines's musical instrument. He replied, 'The bass viol floated away, but I have heard of it down the river. My bow was picked up at Gravesend'.[11]

The additional causes of death that had also been thrown into the mix were injuries found on victims which may had been caused by the propeller or screw of the *Bywell Castle* which, it was alleged, had not stopped turning following impact.

Joseph Hawes (a steward on another London Steamboat Company boat but a *Princess Alice* passenger on the fateful day and who had climbed up a rope to board the *Bywell Castle*) claimed that he overheard a row between the captain, mate and pilot as to whether to stop the engines. Mr Nelson, for the pilot, said that this evidence had nothing to do with the collision, but the feisty foreman exclaimed that it had *a great deal* to do with their inquiry. 'Some of the people may have been killed by the propeller of the *Bywell Castle*.' [12]

The other new cause of death being mooted was poisoning by the foul water into which the victims had fallen. Not surprising, given that the two sewage outlets for north and south London emptied into the Thames about this point. A *Times* editorial explained why this had become an issue:

> ... when the loss of life after the collision between the *Bywell Castle* and the *Princess Alice* was almost the only subject which engaged the attention of the public we printed a letter from 'A PHARMACEUTICAL CHEMIST', in which the writer expressed his belief that the mortality must have been due, in part at least, to the noxious character of the fluid into which the sufferers were plunged. Now that the first shock of the calamity is over, this opinion seems to be gaining ground; and today we publish other letters written for the purpose of enforcing it. Some of the evidence given at the inquest yesterday confirms that impression.[13]

The poisoning idea was much encouraged by Captain Bedford Pim who kept asking survivors if they had tasted the water. His questions had been prompted by the evidence of Miss Emma Eatwell. She had volunteered that the water was very foul and that she was still taking medicine on account of having swallowed some of it.

'Is the doctor treating you for nerves or for poison?' Pim had asked.

'For nerves, liver and other things,' she had replied, at which there was laughter in the court.[14]

In response, Pim told the coroner, 'There is a strong feeling that the death was due in many cases to the poisonous state of the water, and I should like the previous witness recalled in order to put a question to him on the subject.'

The previous witness was Mr Huddart who, when asked whether he had noticed anything peculiar in the water replied, 'Both taste and smell were something dreadful.' He had, he added, been down to the bottom and had risen with his mouth full.[15]

Compositor Charles Masters said he did not taste the water because he took good care to keep his mouth shut. As did letter-carrier, Benjamin Smith.

'Did it *smell* bad?' persisted Pim.

'I had not time to think of smell.'[16]

However, railway clerk Henry White came through for Pim with: 'The water was slimey and had a most disagreeable smell and taste.'[17]

Pim may have been after bigger fish – the Metropolitan Board of Works, rather than the Steamship Company – from whom to claim compensation for his clients, the family of the victim.

The Times continued making their poisonous water case, if somewhat rather inelegantly:

> Out of the 130 persons who landed alive, fourteen have since died; and it is reported by the Reverend Styleman Herring, one of the almoners of the Mansion House Fund, that:
>
>> many more are in a precarious state. We have not evidence how far the deaths may have been those of feeble, or aged, or previously unhealthy persons, or how far they may have been due to mental emotion or to accidental injury; but, if we set aside these possibilities, the rate of mortality among the saved, regarded as the mere effect of an immersion in water on a fine summer evening, is undoubtedly exceedingly large.[18]

There was no evidence whether it was injurious to health, *The Times* continued, but it was certainly a subject that called for further investigation. It was also unnecessary to foul the river like this as there were ways of purifying and filtering sewage.

One of their correspondents *did* know whether it was injurious. Mr Richard Dover of Hammersmith revealed:

> Those who have chanced to encounter or inhale an intensely putrid smell have found their powers of action paralyzed, of which there are so many records of fatal results from the sewerage in the sewers of London. And it is well known that the presence of 1-1,500th of sulphuretted hydrogen in the air is instantly fatal to a bird; that 1-800th will kill a dog; and that 1-150th of its volume has killed a horse.[19]

There was no answer to that.

However, apart from fractious jurymen and lawyers, screw injuries and poisonous waters, what was most concerning the coroner was that the Board of Trade had opened their inquiry into the tragedy whilst the inquest was still in progress causing witnesses to be torn between the two venues. The Board had now demanded that the *Bywell Castle* crew attend *their* court the following Tuesday when *he* required them to give evidence at the inquest on that day.

Though not a well man, the 69-year-old Carttar was in fighting mood. When Mr Mybergh, for the *Bywell Castle*, informed him that the Board of Trade had refused to accede to a postponement and had actually subpoenaed the *Bywell Castle* crew to attend, the coroner retorted that they had no power to take witnesses into custody. *He* had, however and, if necessary, would be prepared to exercise it. He had written to the Board of Trade and, if necessary, would appeal to the highest tribunal possible.

Fortunately a lighter note was sounded after the coroner announced that he had received information that representatives of the illustrated newspapers were anxious to be present with the intention of sketching the faces of the jury, but that he was not disposed to aid in the production of such a caricature. Therefore, he would give directions that if any person in the court occupied himself in that manner, he should direct his removal. He was shutting the door after the steed had been stolen, remarked Mr Nelson. 'The gentleman referred to took his sketches last Monday.' [20]

At the close of that day's inquest hearing, on Friday 20

September, it appeared that a compromise had been reached with the Board of Trade as Carttar announced that the inquest would be resuming, as planned, on the following Wednesday, the 25 September, the Board of Trade inquiry having been postponed until 14 October.

Then, the world would hear what the *Bywell Castle* crew had to say for themselves.

CHAPTER FOURTEEN

Aftermath

Every now and then the protracted proceedings of the Woolwich inquest were interrupted by a relative formally identifying the clothing and possessions of a victim who had been 'buried unknown'. Occasionally, this was followed by an exhumation request which, the relatives were told, would be carried out on the payment of twenty-five shillings and the production of a shell large enough to accommodate the retrieved coffin. Ten such exhumations were done.

Several of those thus identified had been with the Bible class party. These included Emma Stoneman, whose clothing was recognized by her daughter Isabel, and Elizabeth Haist, wife of a warehouseman. Her clothing was identified by her niece, as was that of her cousin Eleanor Haist, aged fifteen, and nephew William Fredric Haist, aged seventeen.

The search by the brother and sister of the Bible party's 73-year-old Elizabeth Hopkins had been particularly harrowing. She, it turned out, had been one of the first ('body number 3a') to be found and placed in the boardroom at Roff's Wharf. For some reason the pair had been unable to gain entrance to look for their sister – probably due to the chaos at the venue at the time – and she had been 'buried unknown'. Now they were able to identify her clothing.

The coroner remarked that the Bible class had numbered fifty-one, only one of which had survived. In fact, it was now becoming clear that five had survived: two of the Haist children, Jane Green, servant to Miss Barden (who had died), 60-year-old Mrs Martha Corfield and Mary Brent, who claimed that she owed her survival to her alpaca dress and petticoat.

Once recognized, a good many of the parcels of clothes were left behind. The best of these garments were given to the poor of the neighbourhood. The rest were burned. By 18 September only twenty-five bundles of clothing remained unclaimed. Several of these were such as might be worn by tourists, proclaimed *The Times*, although a few days later they declared that some of these were of 'so peculiar and distinctive a character that it is considered almost marvellous how they have so long escaped recognition'.

On the same day as the inquest on the reasons for the collision resumed, a meeting of the Mansion House Committee was held in the Venetian Parlour in the Mansion House and presided over by the Lord Mayor. Mr Soulsby, the secretary, informed the committee that, up to now the applicants were made up of twenty-eight widows, 163 orphans, twenty-six aged parents, thirty-five widowers with families and forty-four claims from survivors and others. More applications were flowing in.

The Reverend Herring said that 640 bodies had been recovered and over 130 people were rescued, though sixteen of these had since died. From the great number of inquiries for missing relatives still being made, he ventured to think 130 more had been drowned, though he feared few more bodies would be found. They could thus account for 786 dead or rescued. Therefore, if his supposition was correct, there had been 960 onboard.

Up to now he had only been able to investigate the cases of those whose initials of their surnames began with A and B and among these there were sixteen widows, twenty-two orphans and fifty-eight families. This, the Reverend Herring said, would give the committee an idea of the work before them. The Lord Mayor had given him £400 to expend in the relief of the distressing cases, of which he had spent nearly £300. He proposed to attend Mansion House daily at 11 a.m. to hear applications for immediate relief. It was arranged that a sub-committee would meet daily at midday to go personally into the various cases.

The rector of Woolwich proposed that the committee should not entertain applications for grants for the mere purpose of exhuming any of the dead buried at Woolwich and transferring them to other cemeteries. The proposal was carried.

A Mansion House sub-committee meeting discussed how one thing that *wasn't* helping those left behind was the fact that some friendly societies and burial clubs to which those involved had been regularly contributing were now dragging their heels paying out, thus increasing the distress. The committee were not suggesting that these agencies were not *bona fide*, merely commenting on their 'red tape system' of doing business.[1]

The Times of 20 September 1878, reported there were, 'as may be imagined, almost as many impudent, as deserving claims'.

> One survivor who had neither relative nor friend onboard, is anxious to be recouped for the loss of his hat and overcoat in saving himself; another seeks compensation for a lost umbrella; a woman complains that her clothing was damaged and torn in effecting her rescue, and still another has made pressing inquiries as to the recovery of a carpet bag of little or no value. Such applications are rejected.

The genuine cases included:

> A lady who had seen better days, and who had lately acted as governess and housekeeper to a gentleman drowned in the *Princess Alice*, is cast destitute upon the world, and is herself in a weak state of health, caused by the shock of the accident and the very narrow escape she had. She was in the water over three-quarters of an hour and was rescued almost in a dying state. She fortunately fell into the hands of working men who took her to a cottage, where she gradually recovered. It is thought likely that by publicity she may get another situation in some respectable family.

It transpired that many of the claims the sub-committee had to deal with were referred on to the clergyman or 'other reliable person in the district from which the claimant lived'.[2]

By 19 September the amount in the Mansion House Fund had risen to £23,000 and money continued to flow in. Among the latest donors were Prince Leopold (Queen Victoria's fourth son) with £25, Miss Alice Rothschild (£25) and Harrow School Chapel (£50), who donated 'a similar amount' to the Abercarne mining disaster fund.[3]

The Honourable and Reverend Adelbert Anson, the Rector of Woolwich, only wanted sixpences for his fund – so as not to interfere with the subscriptions needed for the living. He was collecting 'for the purpose of erecting a memorial over the place where so many who were lost in the terrible disaster on the Thames lie buried'.[4]

Other memorials in the form of poems made regular appearances in the press. As early as 11 September one pen – that of eminent lawyer, William Digby Seymour QC, LL.D – commemorated the sad affair with:

The Foundering of the *Princess Alice*

> There's a rippling wave and a sparkling spray
> As the fair ship steams along:
> It is seemly to close the festive day,
> With measures of dance and song –
> But, ah! those lips will be silent soon,
> And the music hushed in that bright saloon.

The poem went on to relate how gaiety and laughter died, then continued:

> Oh! Weep for the fate that befell the gay,
> For the young who too early died,
> For manhood and beauty swept away
> By that cold, unpitying tide!
> Weep for fond bosoms force to part,
> For the desolate home, and the broken heart!

The seven verses conclude:

> It is sweet when the Royal Lady sends
> Her message of Queenly love;
> It is sweeter when faith with a prayer ascends
> To a higher throne above.
> May He who the issues of life controls
> Have mercy on those eight hundred souls![5]

Out on the river, beyond the inquests and the Mansion House deliberations on how to help the bereaved, the weather remained fine and the last of the season's steamboat excursions continued to ply back and forth. It was noticed, however, that fewer women and children were onboard when previously they had been predominant.

As for the political news, shortly before the collision the *Princess Alice* passengers had sung: 'We don't want to fight but by jingo if we do!' in reference to a threatened war. That war now loomed even nearer in the form of the Second Afghan War.

As to the health of nations, infectious diseases remained a continuous threat. Yellow fever still had its grip on New Orleans and Memphis and deaths in London for the week ending 21 September included four from smallpox, two from measles, twenty-four from scarlet fever, ten from diphtheria, forty-three from whooping cough, thirty from various other fevers, and eighty from diarrhoea.

Islington had not forgotten its heavy *Princess Alice* losses. Mr Watts, proprietor of Collins' Music Hall on Islington Green, was one of the first to announce his intention of throwing open his establishment for performances in aid of the Mansion House Fund, reported the *Islington Gazette* of 23 September, 1878.

They went on to describe the morning and evening performances. The morning audiences were small and select but, 'as might be expected, the balance of the patronage was in favour of the latter'. The evening audience 'had to be packed in like sardines, and was largely composed of the working classes'.

Many prominent artists had offered their services so there was plenty of variety. Miss Stella De Vere, 'attired in glittering dresses', gave three songs of French origin 'in a decidedly piquant style'. Next, came Picardo's Piccaninnies, 'a troupe of youngsters, who carried off the premier honours of the day with their comic and sentimental singing and laughable Negro impersonations'. Comic songs, serio-comic songs and popular ballads followed as did sketches and a 'clever-grotesque' comedian. Miss Jenny Hill gave three of her character songs, 'including an artistic impersonation of a lady advocate of women's rights, whose denunciations of "those men" were highly diverting'.

But the charitable reason for the performances was not forgotten. 'At both, the following address, written by Mr Geoffrey Thorn, was delivered by Mr D. Crocker, and received hearty applause'.

> Kind friends, forgive me if a while
> I chase away a happy smile.

As he did with a long tale about the fate of the *Princess Alice*:

> When Death rode on her water way,
> And with one cruel, deadly stroke,
> The bond of life and pleasure broke!
> Oh! Dwell not on the anguish there.
> The piercing shriek – the hurried prayer –
> The cry for mercy – help too late –
> As twice three hundred met their fate!

He eventually concluded by urging them to play and sing again and announcing that the entire receipts would go to the Mansion House Fund.[6]

CHAPTER FIFTEEN

A Deep and Lasting Sorrow

Wednesday 25 September 1878, was surely a day dreaded by two particular witnesses: the captain and the pilot of the *Bywell Castle*.

Most of the preliminaries centred around the question of which of them had been in charge of the vessel at the time of the collision. Counsel for the *Bywell Castle* said that the pilot had been in charge but admitted that, as the ship was exempted from compulsory pilotage, the owners would not be relieved of civil liabilities even if the pilot had been in charge.

As it was, Captain Harrison agreed that the pilot had been in charge. Nonetheless, in his evidence, he made statements such as 'I ported hard' and 'I stopped my vessel when the collision was inevitable', which suggested otherwise.[1]

Both Mr Myburgh for the *Bywell Castle* and Mr Nelson for Dix the pilot agreed on the *Bywell Castle*'s liabilities, citing a similar case of the collision of the steamships *Ostrich* and *Benbow* only nine months earlier. The steamer, *Ostrich*, had been sailing downstream en route to Newcastle loaded with passengers and a light cargo. Coming upstream was a heavier ship, the *Benbow*, returning from Rotterdam carrying cattle and cargo. Both vessels were owned by the General Steamship Company. On collision, both suffered heavy damage, but the *Ostrich* was cut in two and sank immediately. Five people were drowned; three sleeping passengers and two crew.

This accident had occurred a little further upstream, in Woolwich Reach rather than Gallions Reach. In that instance, the vessel coming downstream, the *Ostrich*, had been the one which had suffered most damage and lost lives. But there were disputes as to which vessel had made a sudden wrong move: the *Ostrich* starboarding – making for the north shore – with the *Benbow* following suit shortly afterwards. And there was the question of who was in charge, the captain or the pilot?

The verdict reached then was that the fault lay with the *Ostrich*. The *Benbow*, coming upstream, had naturally, after rounding Hockness Point, headed for the north bank where the tide was less slack. Therefore the *Ostrich* should not have gone there. The evidence of the *Ostrich*'s captain and pilot was also judged unsatisfactory. The *Ostrich*'s pilot was found guilty of gross misconduct and the captain had his certificate suspended for six months. However, it was found that the *Benbow* was not without blame.

The question of civil liability, which Captain Pim had raised with regard to the *Bywell Castle*, was a different matter, said Mr Nelson. (Pim claimed that a ship's master, and therefore the owners, were liable for the actions of the pilot. But Mr Nelson held that in the case of an 'exempt ship' – that is, one not obliged to carry a pilot – the pilot was responsible.)

The coroner disagreed:

> Supposing that I, being the owner of a carriage, gave the reins into the hands of a friend, and that I sat beside him. If, in such circumstances, he commits a criminal act I am not liable; but, nevertheless, I should be held civilly liable for the damage done.

Mr Nelson agreed that that was precisely the state of the case here and added, 'I may say at once that the pilot of the *Bywell Castle* takes full responsibility of what was done, and is prepared to abide by the consequences before the court'.[2]

Captain Harrison described how he had seen the *Princess Alice* apparently heading for the north shore, then turning south, but suddenly starboarding her helm, which had led her under their bows. He was questioned by the *Bywell Castle*'s counsel, Mr Myburgh, as to why he was using 'runners' rather than the crew that had brought the ship into port.

Harrison explained that most of his crew had signed on in Cardiff for a voyage to Sulina on the mouth of the Danube then back to London where they had been discharged, so he had taken on runners to make up the numbers for the voyage up the coast to Newcastle. But, he insisted, these men were in no way inferior.

They were old sailors. 'They are often the best we get. We should take them to sea if we could get them to go.'[3]

Thus the possible accusation that the *Bywell Castle* was operating with a second-rate, inefficient crew was countered. Mr Hughes, for the *Princess Alice*, said he supposed that having runners saved money. Harrison agreed, but countered the suggestion that, being part owner, might have affected his judgement by pointing out that his share of the vessel was only a sixty-fourth. It was suggested that it had been unwise to be working with men he didn't know, particularly Haines, who was at the wheel, and was asked how he selected them. To this he gave the rather strange reply that he did it by their looks, whether they looked like sailors.

'Do you consider that a man's looks are a sufficient guarantee to justify you in placing him at your wheel?' asked Mr Moss, who was appearing on behalf of several bereaved relatives.

'Yes,' said Harrison.[4]

The captain had already known Dix, the pilot, having served on a sailing ship with him fourteen years earlier, though he could remember little about him, but was sure he understood the vessel thoroughly. Not that he had had any choice about the appointment of Dix; he had been hired beforehand by the majority shareholders.

A few survivors had accused the *Bywell Castle* crew of not doing anything to assist them while they were struggling in the water. This had already been refuted by a number of other survivors and was now denied by Harrison who described his actions directly after the collision:

> I knew immediately from the crash that there was going to be a very serious loss of life. I cut away the two lifebuoys on the upper bridge and threw them overboard. I went down along the main deck onto the forecastle. I saw some of my men there, and shouted out them to throw all the ropes overboard into the other vessel. I stopped on the forecastle until I saw the first men from the *Princess Alice* hauled up onboard. Then I shouted out, 'Lay aft and get the boats out as quickly as you can.'

He went up on the upper deck again where he told the chief engineer, the cook and the donkey-man to 'lay on as quick as you can and get the boats out'. Then he ran aft, where he found that the two stewards had cut the lashings of the starboard after-boat.

He sent one boat off with the chief engineer, the cook and the second mate and the other with the chief mate, the boatswain and the fireman. Then he threw over the between-deck ladder and went to assist getting the big boat out. By then they had the assistance of the men and the passengers from the *Princess Alice*. 'I am sure that every rope in the ship was thrown overboard.' (There were about thirty-six.)

How long had all this taken?

'Ten minutes. I should think all the people in the water were dead then.'

How many did they save?

'About twenty-eight, perhaps, in the boats and thirty-nine in the ship.'

But, of course, the most pertinent questions were about his and the pilot's actions just prior to the accident and whether the decisions they had made then were the right ones. Captain Harrison was sure they were. They had done all they could. However, asked under tough cross-examination whether a particular decision had been another of his mistakes the harassed captain answered, 'The great mistake was to come out of dock at all.'

They had seen the *Princess Alice* over land just before she rounded Tripcock Point and then she headed for the north shore.

Therefore he thought it right to try and run between her and the south shore?

'Yes.'

'Had you known that the *Princess Alice* was going to port and keep in shore, could collision have been avoided?' asked the coroner.

'No, there would not have been time. I lost sight for a moment of both the red and green lights under her bow.'

The coroner addressed Mr Nelson saying, 'You will now see that the tendency of this evidence of Captain Harrison is to throw the blame on the dead man, the captain of the *Princess Alice*, Captain Grinstead, and therefore I think that Mr Hughes, who I suppose represents him as well at the *Princess Alice*, ought to have the privilege of cross-examining last.'

Mr Nelson bowed to the coroner's decision.

'You see you cannot tell on whom the jury may ultimately consider the blame to rest,' explained Carttar.

There was much questioning as to whether they could have stopped their ship sooner and not ported just beforehand, but Harrison was of the opinion that it would not have made much difference.

Harrison had read in the paper that Eyres had shouted at them, 'Stop the ship, you will cut the people up', and that he, Harrison, had replied, 'What am I to do. My ship will go ashore if I do not.' Harrison refuted this. 'That is as baseless as the charge of inhumanity brought against me in the first instance, just as great a lie.'

Then came the most lethal accusation against them, made by Purcell, that they had all been drunk. Harrison stated that he, Dix and the whole crew had been sober. 'I was perfectly sober, as I always am. We cannot live without a little drop – most of us take a little drop. I take a little drop but I do not take too much. I do not get drunk. I have been a sober man all my life.'

It transpired that there had been some variation in the statements he had given to the Receiver of Wrecks and the Board of Trade. The first had said that they stopped and reversed, the second, which was correct, just said that they stopped. The reason for the discrepancy was that the first had been made when he was in a state of great agitation.

On seeing that the collision was inevitable, orders had been given to stop the engines. The order to go into reverse was also given but apparently, in the hubbub, never acted upon. That, Harrison thought, was probably a good thing as it would have taken them further away from the drowning people. They would not have been able to save so many and the passengers might have been injured by the fan of the screw.

After a long and intensive cross-examination, Harrison became confused while demonstrating the position of ships on the chart, then burst out:

> On looking at the vessel approaching over the Point and not knowing what her usual course was, I thought she was on a port helm all the time. But now, after looking into it, I am convinced that the tide must have swept her over and not her port helm. I

believe it now to be a mistake on my part that she was on a port helm, the tide must have swept her over.

But he did not accept that it was his mistake that had caused the accident.

Before standing down as a witness he said, 'I wish to express my extreme regret at this terrible occurrence. Whatever the result of this inquiry may be, the fact that I commanded the *Bywell Castle* at the time of the collision will be to me a deep and lasting sorrow'.[5]

Next into the fray was Christopher Dix who had been piloting exempted ships on the Thames for thirty-four years. He had been perfectly sober at the time of the collision having had nothing to drink all day except his usual glass or two of ale, he said. Haynes, the runner who had taken the wheel, was well known to him, had worked for him for years and was perfectly competent.

He had seen the *Princess Alice* coming out of Barking Reach at Tripcock Point when she seemed to make for the north shore to get into the slack tide. 'That is what river steamers do in nineteen cases out of twenty. It is very seldom they shave the point and come to the southwards.'

His evidence, unsurprisingly, mostly echoed Harrison's.

Next morning, after the jury foreman had again had his say regarding the necessity of being given longitudinal sections of the *Princess Alice*, Dix was recalled for cross-examination. Since the pilot had admitted to being a little deaf, this was carried out in loud voices, which meant that the forthcoming revelation reverberated around the room.

Had his licence ever been suspended, inquired Mr John Proctor, who was that day standing in for Captain Pim.

It had, Dix admitted, in April of the previous year, when a ship he was piloting in a snowstorm had 'unfortunately got ashore' on Goodwin Sands.[6] In this instance, the point was not the fearful reputation of the Goodwin Sands so much as the fact that Dix should never have been there in the first place. The Sands were about 70 miles beyond Gravesend and Gravesend was the limit of his pilot's license – the 'smooth water' section of the Thames.

As previously noted, the *Princess Alice* passenger numbers were also limited past Gravesend but, given the vagueness of passenger estimates following the accident, one wonders how strictly this restriction had been adhered to.

The Times was of the opinion that the 'most novel' of the evidence given at that day's inquest was that of the second mate, 36-year-old William Brankston, who described his actions following the collision.

> I immediately grasped a rope and slid down upon the forepart of the paddle box of the *Princess Alice*. I helped the people who had caught the ropes to climb up them, and cried to the others; but they only clambered to the highest part of the vessel. The *Princess Alice*, which was not much cut into by the *Bywell Castle*, broke in two while I was standing on her, and went down in the middle. I was just endeavouring to fasten a rope around woman's waist when this happened … I heard the fires being drowned out by the water. I went down with the mass of people, but saved myself by climbing up a rope. The first man to help me on deck of the *Bywell Castle* was the first mate, who, very much surprised, said, 'Wherever have you come from?'[7]

Then the captain had sent Brankston on one of the boats by which they rescued fourteen people.

He was asked whether he saved any by going down on the paddle box of the *Princess Alice*.

'I helped people to climb the ropes, but I did not succeed in saving the woman round whose waist I tried to tie a rope.'

The Times noted that several of the jury expressed their admiration of the witness's conduct.

More watermen and *Bywell Castle* crew gave evidence that more or less tallied with the opinion that the accident had been the fault of the *Princess Alice* suddenly starboarding her helm after making south. Dix had been recalled and in cross-examination refused to admit to error. This all became a little too much for Mr Hughes, of the *Princess Alice*, who remarked rather petulantly, 'When you sank the barge off Greenwich, the fault was all the barge's I suppose?'

'I have every reason to believe so,' said Dix and pointed out that he had since been employed by the steamer that had run her down.

Then Hughes suggested that Dix was being well paid for his evidence and that 'their side' had been 'most lavish' in their payments to witnesses. The coroner advised him 'not to go into that, unless you wish to throw a taint on everybody. It might provoke a retort'.[8] The topic, however, was not to rest there.

Like Harrison, when Dix stood down he said he could not leave without expressing his deep regret at the unfortunate accident and likewise his deep sympathy with the friends and relatives of the drowned.

The frustration felt by the *Princess Alice* lawyers must have been mitigated a little by the knowledge that the most serious allegation against the captain, pilot and crew of the *Bywell Castle* – that they had all been drunk at the time of the accident – was about to be brought into sharp focus.

CHAPTER SIXTEEN

Acute Memory Loss

For a person whose accusations had caused such a stir, witness George Purcell, cut an unprepossessing figure. He was weedy, pale, shaky and unkempt.

Led by the coroner, he told the jury that he had joined the *Bywell Castle* as a stoker on the day she left Millwall Docks and, unbidden, he added, 'As far as I could see all hands were sober.'

He then described his movements following the collision, including his trip down to Erith in one of the rescue craft.

'Did any one of you say to anybody at Erith that the collision was only what was to have been expected as the pilot had been knocking about drinking with the captain all the afternoon, and was drunk at the time?' asked Carttar.

'I cannot recollect,' said the stoker.

Carttar was having none of this and exclaimed, 'Oh yes, you *can* recollect. It is a statement you would *not* forget. Did you make it?'

'I cannot say I did.'

'Now don't fence with me,' cried the coroner, 'Did you make that statement to anybody?'

'I have no recollection of it.'

'Do you swear you did *not* make it?'

'No, I cannot swear it.'

Carttar did not give up but adopted a less confrontational tone. 'Now you must know, as a sensible man, what was said by your company or what you yourself said to persons at Erith?'

At this Purcell launched into a litany of excuses for his strange lack of recall. He had been in such a state of excitement, was half naked and shivering with cold at the time. If he *did* say it, it was an untruth. He would admit it if he *could* remember it, but could not swear that he had never said it. Neither would he swear that there was no such conversation between the crew and the people at Erith. But he had no recollection of any taking place.

He went further, 'There is no foundation whatever, to my knowledge, for saying that the captain and pilot were knocking about drinking on the afternoon of the day of sailing. It is my deliberate judgement that they were perfectly sober.' Everyone at Erith had wanted to treat them, Purcell went on, and, as well as two brandies and a beer, he may have had a glass of rum. He was also given a coat – which he was still wearing.

However, he did claim that some of the crew, who should have been in the engine room at the time of the collision, were not. Also that the *Bywell Castle*, contrary to their claims, did *not* stop the engines until *after* the collision. And also that, about twenty-five minutes after the collision, they had gone astern. When he returned from Erith he had seen the pilot Dix was in a 'very excited state', not saying anything to anybody but just walking about the deck trembling.

At the close of Purcell's evidence, Mr Moss, one of the many lawyers now appearing for relatives, commented, 'It will be necessary to have the Erith people here.'

'They will be sent for,' Carttar assured him.[1]

And on they came. George Thomas Harris, the confectioner, related how he had given Purcell a coat, a piece of cake and a ginger beer. The stoker appeared to have been drinking but was getting sober. In answer to Harris's question about what had caused the collision, Purcell had said, 'It is all on account of the booze'. To illustrate his point, the stoker had told Harris how, when they had picked up a female passenger who was still quite warm, he had asked the captain for some brandy to give her. But Captain Harrison had said he had none. 'And with very good reason. He and the pilot had been boozing all afternoon.' Purcell had gone on to declare that *all* the crew had been drunk, including himself. At the Yacht Tavern, when the stoker had repeated his claims, his mates had tried to shut him up. 'From the tone in which he spoke,' said Harris, 'I am quite sure he knew what he was saying.'[2]

William Lee, the Yacht Tavern keeper, agreed with Harris's

statement and added that, shortly after entering, Purcell had declared, 'The beasts were drunk' – meaning the captain and the pilot – and had added, 'in fact we all were.' Later, in the back kitchen, he had burst into tears and said, 'S'help my God, I mean to tell the truth.'[3]

One of the customers, fly proprietor James Coshall, gave evidence of hearing Purcell say, 'We shall get into trouble. It was our fault,' and that one of his companions had told him to hold his noise.[4]

William Pope, a general dealer, saw Purcell 'three parts intoxicated' make the same claims about the drunkenness of the crew. 'At this time,' Pope insisted, 'Purcell seemed to know perfectly well what he was talking about.'[5]

Dimelow, the *Bywell Castle*'s chief engineer, described Purcell's condition when he had come onboard that day:

> Purcell was like the generality of firemen. He was rather the worse for drink, but not so bad that he could not take his watch, his duties were purely mechanical. I saw him at half past four o'clock the next morning – he was lying on top of the stoke hole cover and I could not wake him up. The chief engineer came and complained he could not get him to take his watch; in fact he was dead drunk. I had not the slightest suspicion that Captain Harrison was not sober. I have made about seven voyages with Captain Harrison and have always found him a sober man and as steady a man as I was ever with in my life. I saw the other officers about and there is no ground whatever for the suggestion that they were not sober.[6]

Bywell Castle crew member, Henry Gribben, did rather let the side down at the inquest. He had given evidence earlier in the proceedings and Mr Hughes asked that he might be recalled. However, as *The Times* reported, 'it appeared that, although this witness was in the precincts of the court, he had had been drinking too much to be in a fit state to be examined'.[7]

George William Linnecar, Superintendent of the People's Mission Hall at Peckham, who had been a passenger on the *Princess Alice*, thought he had been the first to climb up onto the *Bywell Castle*. He told the court he was certain nobody there was under the influence of drink.

Yet another waterman witness, Walter Campfield, who had been rowing a dumb barge[8] down river just before the collision, gave evidence in favour of the *Bywell Castle*, saying that the *Princess Alice* must have starboarded very suddenly. This led to some tart questions from the *Princess Alice* side as to just how much he was receiving for this evidence.

'How much have I received? I consider it a very paltry sum,' Campfield replied.

'How much?' asked Mr Hughes.

'I have only received ten shillings towards my expenses. I have incurred a lot of expenses.'[9]

Mr Myburgh said he should ask how many days this witness had been hanging about and that it would be a far manlier thing for Mr Hughes to say at once that he really did mean to insinuate that his clients were tampering with the witness.

Mr Hughes replied that he thought there had been plenty of grounds.

Gavin Thurston, author of the 1965 book *The Great Thames Disaster* (Allen and Unwin), blames Carttar for allowing these attempts to turn the inquest hearing into a legal action or at least doing very little to restrain them. Thurston also criticizes the huge number of witnesses, many with little to add, which the coroner allowed to parade before the jury. Carttar had, at one point, gone into the history of coroners' courts 'very inaccurately', had even given wrong directions to the jury as well as allowed himself to get into undignified exchanges with them and the counsel. Thurston's criticisms were informed. He was a coroner for Westminster himself and as such had dealt with several high-profile inquests, such as those on Judy Garland and Jimi Hendrix.

One witness who *did* have some startling new evidence to add to the *Princess Alice* inquest appeared towards the end of proceedings on Tuesday, 8 October. He was Samuel Smith, a ship's painter, of 9 Byng Street in Millwall. Smith, an old sailor, told the court that he had seen the pilot, Dix, at about 2 p.m. on the afternoon of the collision near the Anchor and Hope public house in Millwall when, Smith was sorry to say, Dix had been the worse for drink. 'Knowing that he had once been in difficulty through drinking,' said Smith, 'I thought it a bad job that he should be drunk again.'

What made him think Dix was drunk?

'The way in which he carried himself and swung about his cigar. Besides, his face was red.'

'Now, be certain about what you are saying,' warned the coroner. 'It is a very serious matter. When did you come to the conclusion that Dix had been drinking?'

'I mentioned it to an acquaintance of mine the next day. I am very sorry I did now, for I did not want to have to come here.'

He and Dix had known each other for about twenty-three years, claimed Smith, and were friends until he (Smith) had become a total abstainer. After that, they had not seen each other as before because, 'when a man turns away from drink his friends don't like him. I thought,' Smith added lethally, 'that after a little misfortune he had had some time ago he would have abstained from drink as I did.'

The 'little misfortune' turned out to be 'losing his licence through drink'. Nonetheless, Smith thought no more skilful man could be found to take charge of a ship. 'Drinking was his only weakness.' He had been surprised to see him in drink that day because he had heard that, like him, Dix had become a total abstainer. Dix's companion at the time had been a man who looked like a captain: 'He wore a sealskin cap.'

Dix had been staggering, claimed Smith, although not necessarily so much that anybody else might see he was drunk. Then there was his face: 'Dix is generally a pale man, but his face gets red when he is in drink.'

Did he consider then that the pilot was in a fit state to take charge of a vessel, asked barrister Mr John Proctor, who was watching proceedings on behalf of the widow of Charles Curtis, a *Princess Alice* crew member.

'I have known him do so, and be very clever when he had had just a drop.'

'Am I to understand that he was better able to take a ship down the river when in a state of semi-drunkenness than when sober?'

'I don't know. He has been very fortunate; he has never had an accident while I have been with him.'[10]

Several other witnesses deposed as to Dix's sobriety that day but, after Smith's ringing endorsement of the man's capability when drunk, it was hardly surprising that Mr Nelson, Dix's counsel, chose to reserve his cross-examination of the witness until after consultation with his client. This would be somewhat delayed because the inquest was about to be adjourned for ten days. Therefore the accusations would have time to simmer and develop, while rebuttals would have time to be garnered.

Despite the forthcoming adjournment there was time for some more damaging revelations. One of the *Bywell Castle*'s crew members recalled the collision in Millwall Dock before they had set out that day and a mishap earlier that year when Dix had 'not got his anchor down quickly enough and had carried away a vessel's jibbon'.[11]

This late news about the barge collision in the dock inferred, said *The Times* the next day, that the *Bywell Castle* had been navigated with a want of skill throughout. They also suggested that the captain had given his evidence 'with an absence of candour' or, as modern parlance would have it, Harrison had been economical with the truth.

Captain Harrison was recalled to insist that he did not remember being *asked* about the barge accident but the damage, if any, had been very slight. It had been a trifling affair and probably the reason it had not been mentioned in his log was, he supposed, that he had forgotten it in the light of the greater calamity. And, no, he had not walked out with Dix that afternoon and although he had worn a hat that day, it was not a sealskin cap.

CHAPTER SEVENTEEN

In Context

The loss of women's lives when the *Princess Alice* sank was as nothing, claimed Dr Arthur W. Edis, in comparison with their sad mortality in childbirth. Indeed, the total number of lives lost due to the terrible accidents on the *Princess Alice*, the *Eurydice* and the *Grosser Kurfürst*[1] did not amount to a third of the women who died annually in childbirth. During 1876, Dr Edis continued, no fewer than 4,142 mothers had succumbed and this did not include the 1,034 who had died from various diseases after giving birth. This obstetric physician made these pronouncements in his inaugural address at the Medical Session of the Middlesex Hospital Medical School.[2] The number of maternity deaths at the time was certainly startling and it was clever of Dr Edis to use dramatic, high-profile, mass fatalities to bring home his point.

Of course the *Princess Alice* disaster and the Welsh mining disaster were by no means the only tragedies in 1878. Accidents great and small were frequent from gas explosions, steam explosions, railway accidents, fires, shipping accidents and collisions. The most dangerous place to be was at sea around Britain's shores. More lives were lost in wrecks around Britain's coastline in the year 1877 (776) than in the *Princess Alice* disaster. Shipping accidents on Britain's rivers caused another fifteen deaths in a year.

According to the Annual Wreck Register for 1877, the east coast, which the Tyne colliers so regularly traversed, was the most dangerous section of all. Its 1,100 wrecks (excluding collisions) were more than a third of the year's total. And a great many of these were colliers. Thus, claimed the *Standard* on 26 October 1878, 'The great coal trade of England not only claims its victims in the depths of the fiery mine, but among the hapless sailors who man the colliers of the Tyne and Wear'.

Looking on the brighter side, the newspaper applauded the growing number of National Lifeboat Institute stations that now dotted these dangerous coasts. They pointed out that, although nearly 800 mariners' lives had been lost in a year, not short of 5,000 had been brought safely ashore by the lifeboats.

On 23 October 1878, while the two *Princess Alice* inquiries were in full swing, *The Times'* list of wrecks and casualties included three collisions, one of them of involving a Tyne collier, the schooner *Inconstant*, which had been carrying coal to Trouville when it was rammed by *Agnes and Louise* and sustained serious damage.

Collisions on rivers also occurred quite frequently and during the lead up to the *Princess Alice* disaster Tyne colliers had been involved in several collisions, in some of which they had collided with each other.

Of course, in the autumn of 1878 the collision that remained at the forefront of the news was that of the *Princess Alice*. It had even begun to pop up in various forms among those cryptic personal notices in the columns of *The Times*. For example, the following appeared on 24 October 1878:

DAVID ECKLEY, of Boston, United States, left No. 79 York Street, Westminster, on 3 September last (the day of the *Princess Alice* disaster) and has not since been heard of. Letters and money wait for him, an important business requires his immediate presence in London. If dead, £5 reward will be paid for Evidence of the fact. If living he will greatly oblige by communicating with Messrs Doveton, Smyth and Bristow, Solicitors, No. 82 Rochester Row, Westminster.

And the expected quarrels over victims' estates soon surfaced. On 11 September a respectable-looking female told Mr Benson, the Southwark magistrate, that her daughter, her son-in-law and their child had all drowned in the *Princess Alice* disaster. She had claimed their bodies and paid out £2–3 for their funerals. Now the son-in-law's brother was trying to claim all their furniture, but the key to their house had been left with her. The next day, the son-in-law, also 'respectable looking', turned up expressing surprise that such a statement should have been made. He claimed that the woman had not expended a farthing on the funeral – it had been done at the expense of the churchwardens and others. The magistrate told him that neither had a legal claim and advised them to sort it out among themselves.

On 9 October 1878 came the case of Hankin and Turner at the Chancery Division of the High Court of Justice. The plaintiff, who claimed to be the half-brother of Mr James Ivory (a *Princess Alice* victim who had died intestate) moved to block the letters of administration obtained by a man whom he claimed was merely the illegitimate son of the intestate's mother. Eventually, the judge also decided that this was not a matter for him but the probate court and dismissed the claim with costs.

But the current most pressing *Princess Alice* side issue was what the newspapers termed 'the state of the river'. In other words, the question of just how much sewage was polluting the Thames and whether it had proved lethal to the drowning passengers.

The subject had gained prominence after Captain Pim's questioning of witnesses as to the smell and taste of the water in which they nearly drowned and *The Times*' leader urging the investigation of the matter.

The publicity bore fruit. At the next meeting of the Metropolitan Board of Works on 27 September 1878, a Mr Richardson moved that the subject be referred to the Works and General Purposes Committee to consider and report as to the correctness of the statements made that the water of the River Thames, where the unfortunate accident to the *Princess Alice* had occurred, was 'poisonous' and 'it's taste and smell something it was impossible to describe' and whether such state of the water, if correctly described, arose from the main drainage outfalls. The motion was carried unanimously.

This encouraged a Mr Richardson to be bolder with a motion that the committee should also consider and report on whether the sewage discharged into the river at the board's outfalls could, at a moderate cost, be purified before its discharge so as to render it innocuous and inoffensive as well as free from solid matter. This proved to be a move too far. One board member claimed that the sewage passed into the Thames formed only about 1/7,000th part of the stream. Another, a Mr Cook, said that

Richardson had made it look as if it were all down to pounds, shillings and pence. 'But if that were so, the board had been going wrong for a long time.' If they voted for this motion they would be condemning themselves as, by doing so, they would admit that they discharged into the river, at the outfalls, sewage that was noxious and offensive. Mr Richardson offered to dilute the proposal but, commented *The Times*, 'it was negatived by a majority of nineteen to seven'.[3]

Next into the arena was a Mr Henry Robinson who gave a paper on 'Purificating Sewage by Precipitation' at the Congress of the Sanitary Institute of Great Britain held at Stafford on 4 October 1878. He was followed by Mr H.C. Burdett with a paper on 'Thames Water: Its Impurities, Dangers and Contaminations'.

Mr Burdett said he had been invited to give his experience as a resident on the banks of the Thames. He agreed that the foulness of the water had added materially to the horrors of the *Princess Alice* calamity and pointed to a report that stated that one fifth of the river was pollution which moved up and down four times daily between Gravesend and Blackwall. He reminded the congress that Sir Joseph Bazalgette[4] had admitted the necessity of purification of sewage before it was allowed to enter the river. Also, that experience in Coventry[5] showed that the process was not impossible nor over-costly. London could do it for £120,000 and it should be done with the least possible delay.

The London Sanitary Committee got in on the act, urging swift action, as did the Woolwich Local Board of Health. Captain Behnna R.A., of the latter, moved that the Woolwich surveyor should be instructed to take samples of the water at the time of day and in the conditions corresponding to the circumstances when the *Princess Alice* sank. The motion was seconded by none other than our old friend Mr Harrington, foreman of the inquest jury, who said that the public had a right to know. A member of the Plumstead District Board of Works made the pertinent point that the Metropolitan Board of Works seemed content to have got the nuisance away from the centre of London, and had closed their eyes to the evil consequences on the districts downriver. Knives were drawn.

The Woolwich surveyor gave his sampling report and the analyst's conclusions to the Woolwich Local Board of Health on 23 October 1878. He had procured the loan of a steam launch from the Thames Conservancy Board, and 'accompanied by Mr Wigner, your analyst', had obtained two samples of Thames water at the places mentioned in the annexed schedule, one just below the surface and the other at about half the depth of the river and both as near to midstream as possible. Near where the wreck had been, he had taken one nearly, but not quite, at the bottom of the river. The timings taken and the grams of organic matter found in each were listed. The sewage had been running from the vicinity of the Northern Outfall sluice at 5.10 p.m., 'and the smell of the water in the vicinity was of a very offensive character'. Even more so at the Southern Outfall. The conclusion was:

> ... it would not be right to say that they [the *Princess Alice* passengers] were absolutely poisoned by the water they imbibed; but the intolerably nauseous smell, accompanied by an equally nauseous taste, may have produced sudden vomiting, so that by this means the little strength or power they possessed ... may have been lost, or in the mere act of vomiting the lungs of the unfortunate passengers might have been emptied of air and refilled with water, thus making the bodies specifically heavier and causing them to sink.

The sample of water taken between the Gasworks and the Northern Outfall.

> ... was simply an admixture of sewage and salt water. The microscope showed the presence of muscular tissue, cotton filaments in large quantity, many hairs, both animal and vegetable, and fragments of cooked farinaceous food.

Clearly, the report claimed, a source of contamination.[6]

Sir Joseph Bazalgette, the Metropolitan Board of Works chief engineer and the designer of the sewage system, fought back by presenting a report questioning the statement that the Thames water where the accident happened was poisonous and its taste and smell was something impossible to describe. He admitted he was not able to report on what it was like as no reliable observations were made at that time but he pointed out several alternative suspects.

Apparently a fire had broken out at Price and Co.'s oil works at 3.45 p.m. 'and for some hours afterwards large quantities of vegetable and animal oils ran into the river ... the bulk of these deleterious oils would have been passing the wreck at the time of the collision'. The condition of the surface of the river at the time and place may, therefore have been exceptionally bad.

In addition, the Woolwich Local Board 'without the knowledge of this board' had, in 1872, done a deal with the East Ham Board (which was beyond the metropolitan area) that allowed them, on payment of a fee, to bring sewage into the Woolwich Board's outlet, which more than doubled their usual quantity.

Then there was the fact that the Beckton Gasworks had an iron pipe, about three feet in diameter, which discharged gas refuse and sewage ('a dark, strong-smelling liquid') nearly opposite the position of the *Princess Alice* wreck for about three hours on the flood tide.

Bazalgette also argued that the Victoria Dock extension works, currently in progress, were causing an additional quantity of mud to flow into the river and that the smells erroneously attributed to the sewage arose from the surrounding chemical and artificial manure works. In any case, the lower reaches of the Thames were not perceptively impure, considering it as a navigable river and not a source of drinking water, and its banks were cleaner and freer from muddy deposits than they had been in previous years. Before deciding on large and expensive deodorising works or other local remedies, Sir Joseph suggested that members of the board go down the river in a steamer with their professional advisers, taking samples and the evidence of their own senses.[7]

CHAPTER EIGHTEEN

Unfit for Service?

Just before the Woolwich inquest was adjourned until 18 October, Mr Carttar sent out a select party of marine experts to examine the wreck of the *Princess Alice*. He wanted them to give the jury their opinions on the construction, stability and seaworthiness of the pleasure steamer at the time of the accident. Rather difficult, one would imagine, considering what she had been through since.

Their opinions did not turn out to be good news for those representing the *Princess Alice* and her owners, the London Steamship Company. Shipwright John Morday thought the *Princess Alice* was of very slight construction. Her plates were not thick enough and her frames were too far apart. Altogether, she was too slight for passenger traffic on the river, certainly not the number of passengers that she had carried, and that almost anything that touched her would have gone through her.

Edward Brown Barnard, a naval architect and marine engineer who had built steamers for use on the River Nile, in Egypt, and the River Minho, in Portugal, confirmed these conclusions 'on every point'. He thought the *Princess Alice* would have been 'uncomfortable' carrying 600 passengers. Indeed, he agreed, should she do so, she would be likely to 'quaver'.[1] She might just be fit for service to Gravesend, but she was certainly not fit to go on to Sheerness.

When asked by Mr Hughes, counsel for the *Princess Alice*, about her Board of Trade certificate he said, 'If a Board of Trade inspector spent four or five days surveying her he must have been hard up for a job. If I had been a surveyor appointed by the Board of Trade to survey the *Princess Alice* I should have considered myself guilty of culpable blame if I had given her a certificate to ply to Sheerness and Southend, having regard to her build and condition'.[2]

Marine surveyor, Charles Laing, declared that, knowing her construction as he did now, he certainly would not have ventured down the river on her when she had 600 people onboard and would have been 'very sorry' to be one of the 400 going on to Sheerness. Her saloon deck would make her unstable. However, he was also of the opinion that no ship could have resisted the *Bywell Castle*'s blow.

'Practical engineer' Captain Samuel Pether who was experienced with upriver boats that plied the quieter, more rural, part of the Thames, thought the *Princess Alice* 'unfit to work the Pool', where she came into contact with all kinds of vessels, and was too weak to withstand blows. He usually put a piece of timber 14 in deep and 4 in thick all round his boats for protection against bumping into piers and other boats.[3]

And so it went on. Mr Hughes, counsel for the *Princess Alice*, declared that he proposed to call witnesses to refute all of these opinions but Mr Carttar called a halt. The Board of Trade inquiry had begun the day before and, he felt, this matter would fall within their remit. Of course, he might have thought of this earlier and so saved time in this seemingly endless inquest. He then adjourned the inquest, yet again, for another ten days while the Board of Trade inquiry got under way.[4]

The most important thing to discover about the ship's construction was why she sank so quickly, since this had been the main reason for such a huge and rapid loss of life – there had been so little time for anyone to mount an effective rescue.

At the resumed inquest back in the Woolwich Town Hall on 29 October 1878, two Millwall dockmasters swore to Dix's sobriety on the pertinent afternoon while a dockmaster's assistant claimed he had known Dix for twenty years, seen him take out the largest steamers, but never seen him drunk.

Police Inspector Payne of Woolwich produced a list of fourteen bodies that had still not been identified: two men of about forty and fifty-eight; a boy aged five; two girls aged six and ten; and eight women seemingly aged twenty-two, twenty-four, twenty-five, thirty, thirty-five, thirty-six, thirty-eight and forty-five and one woman with no age stated.

Mr Carttar was surprised that so many people could have disappeared from their homes for so long without inquiries being made about them, but he understood more remained unidentified.

To add to the mystery, Police Inspector Phillips of Greenwich told him that there was a good deal of superior quality jewellery among the effects that had evidently been the property of people who had occupied a good position in life. The inference here being that their absence would be more likely to be noticed and, given that better-off people tended to have servants, this was not an odd assumption.

Then the inquest tackled the unpleasant matter of sewage in the water, its effect on the bodies and the likelihood that it may have hastened death.

Dr Harry Leach, Medical Officer of Health for the Port of London, said that the bodies had a kind of slime on them that you would not find if they had been immersed in clean water, but death had definitely been due to drowning. It was true that decomposition of the bodies had occurred earlier than usual and that the foulness of the water and the warm weather accounted for this. In answer to Captain Bedford Pim he said that sewage in the water would not poison a person but if they swallowed much of it, it would make them vomit. In reply to a question from Mr Hutchinson for the families he said, 'I think I could swim and vomit at the same time but I have not tried it'.[5]

Dr James Louttit, formerly a demonstrator of chemistry at Edinburgh, thought that some of the passengers appeared to have died of shock prior to immersion and some from asphyxia, and that even a good swimmer's chances of survival after imbibing a considerable quantity of foetid water would be diminished. He went on a good deal about the amount of sulphuretted hydrogen produced which, in high concentrations, could be lethal.

But medical knowledge was still very limited then, the science of bacteriology little known, and the fact that no post mortems had been carried out meant that this medical evidence could only be of limited use. Basically, it was all just supposition.

From then on it was back to those who had seen the disaster or were experienced in the ways of the river and ships that sailed upon her. This reverted to contradictory evidence about which moves each vessel had made; what moves they should have made; and, ultimately, which of them was therefore responsible for the tragedy.

An interesting addition to all this porting and starboarding and which lights had been shown and seen or not seen by each vessel was the point made by Ellis James Smith, captain of the *Conservator* steamer in the service of the Thames Conservancy. He said that Gallions Reach, where the collision took place, was very troublesome to navigators at night due to the lights of Beckton Gasworks and Woolwich Arsenal.

Then, at last, began the winding up of the Woolwich inquest. Carttar congratulated the jury on reaching the home stretch and pointed out that matters had to be gone into in such detail due to the enormous number of lives that had been lost.

Carttar complained that their freedom of judgement had been interfered with by two actions. Firstly, the publishing of the statements given to the Commissioners of Wrecks. These had confused the witnesses, made them contradict themselves and, indeed, some had changed their minds after reading the statements of others. Secondly, the holding of the Board of Trade inquiry before the inquest had been completed (in fact, their findings had already been published). It would, he said, have been more courteous, as well as conducive to the administration of justice, for it to have been withheld until they had finished.

Once Carttar had got that off his chest he proceeded to over-reach himself by giving judgement on various elements rather than merely presenting the jury with cogent and unbiased views of the facts for their guidance in coming to their verdict.

Instead, he launched into an all-out attack on the defective manning of the *Princess Alice*, which he found deplorable, and its provisions for safety, which were perfectly inadequate. He went on:

> The captain was undoubtedly a good man; he, poor fellow, is unable to tell his own story. The mate says, 'It was no part of my duty to place anybody on the lookout.' An extraordinary statement!

Carttar admitted you could not expect two men to be at the wheel from London to Sheerness and back again, so there were two who were off steering duty.

And who do we find them to be? A boy and an apprentice! The first mate admits he is a little defective in his eyesight! And when it comes to the matter of necessity, owing to the absence of one man of his asking for a holiday in the middle of a voyage, a man is engaged who is a perfect stranger to the captain and who, although he may have been a perfectly good sailor able to do the work, was still a stranger to the captain and the ship, and stranger to her mode of steering and everything else.

He took very strongly against the lookouts (the resting steerers) being a mere boy of eighteen and a young man of twenty-one. He thought it needed a practised eye. They were only looking out for dummies and small boats, and would be tired after a long day, and there would be music and dancing and singing, which were very likely to attract a boy of eighteen. 'When I was a young lad, I was more amused by music and dancing and singing than inclined to attend to any work that might be deputed to me.'

As for the second mate, Wilkinson, he was an extraordinary character who steered from London Bridge to North Woolwich and there knocked off. Then he only attended to the ropes for the gangway. If the whistle sounded, he did not care, if the vessel stopped it did not attach to him, because vessels so often stop for small boats.

Unsurprisingly, Carttar's outburst brought protest from Mr Hughes, counsel for the *Princess Alice*. 'I think,' he said, 'you have omitted the name of one man who was on the lookout you refer to.'

He was talking about Young, the foremast hand, who claimed to have gone forward in case of any small boats or other craft being in the way.

'He made no report,' said Carttar. 'He had only been onboard three days; he was on lookout but he made no report.' Besides, at the time, he had gone down to get his coat. And the point Carttar was making was the casualness of it all – the fact that the lookout was so intermittent and was performed in the laxest possible manner.

The *Bywell Castle* was a different story. The crew were efficient and the runners looked upon as the steadiest and most trustworthy seamen in the Port of London. There was, however, the question as to whether one lookout was sufficient.

He warned the jury not to rely too much on statements about time and distance, for there was no subject, in his experience, on which witnesses were so little able to form an accurate opinion.

As to the collision, the prime cause was the employment of the man Eyres at the wheel of the *Princess Alice*. He had probably allowed her to be swung by the tide off Tripcock Point towards midstream, and there was a mass of evidence to show that she did get near midstream, notwithstanding an apparent intention on the part of the captain to take her up the south shore.

The question arose whether the *Bywell Castle*, having seen the *Princess Alice*'s red light, and knowing that it was the practice of passenger steamers to go over to the north shore at that point, was justified in porting, and also whether the captain of the *Princess Alice*, finding himself in the position stated, ought not to have adopted a port helm, instead of continuing to fight for the south shore. It ought also to be considered whether the *Bywell Castle*, in the circumstances, ought not to have shown more caution by easing or stopping and reversing.

After a four hour summing up and a pained reference to the apparent ignorance of so many experienced men of the rules of the Thames Conservancy he gave the jury a list of questions he wanted them to answer:

1. Which vessel was to blame?
2. Whether the cause originated in criminal, culpable or gross negligence, or whether it was accidental?
3. Whether the other vessel contributed to the collision by any omission of a criminal, culpable, or accidental nature?[6]

The jury retired to consider their verdict at 5 p.m. and there was a stampede of reporters to the telegraph office.

As the room emptied, Sydney Harrington produced a parcel of sandwiches, remarking loudly that they were for his supper. 'If you feel like that, Sydney,' said a fellow juror, 'some of us have pocket pistols too.'[7] Coroner's Officer Gilham found Carttar a small office where he settled down to a sandwich and some brandy and water.

It was later disclosed to the press that almost the first thing the jury did was to vote on the question of blame. Six voted against the *Princess Alice*, eleven against the *Bywell Castle* and two against both. Of course, local loyalty may have swayed their opinions in favour of the *Princess Alice*.

At 8.30 p.m. Carttar went in to answer their queries and advised them he could accept a majority verdict of twelve.

At 2 a.m. *The Times'* Woolwich correspondent telegraphed his paper to say that the coroner was closeted with the jury but the prospect of a verdict was remote. 'A majority of twelve will be accepted, but it is understood that the nineteen jurymen are nearly equally divided in opinion. They have repeatedly asked to be discharged, but the coroner refuses to liberate them without a verdict.'[8]

At 4.30 a.m. Carttar was called in to help them draft a verdict agreed by a majority of fifteen, the foreman and three others refusing to sign the document. At 7 a.m. the doors were thrown open and the verdict issued:

That the death of the said William Beachey and others was occasioned by drowning in the waters of the River Thames from a collision that occurred after sunset between a steam vessel called the *Bywell Castle* and a steam vessel called the *Princess Alice* whereby the *Princess Alice* was cut in two and sunk, such collision not being wilful; that the *Bywell Castle* did not take the necessary precaution of easing, stopping and reversing her engines in time and that the *Princess Alice* contributed to the collision by not stopping and going astern; that all collisions in the opinion of the jury might in future be avoided if proper and stringent rules and regulations were laid down for all steam navigation on the River Thames.

Addenda

1. We consider that the *Princess Alice* was, on the third of September, seaworthy.
2. We think the *Princess Alice* was not properly and sufficiently manned.
3. We think the number of persons onboard the *Princess Alice* was more than prudent.
4. We think the means of saving life onboard the *Princess Alice* were insufficient for a vessel of her class.[9]

Newspapers were then the only means of rapidly dispensing news to the public and had been the sole arena on which this drama had been played out. Now one of the most prominent and respected, *The Times*, which had thoroughly recorded the proceedings throughout, gave its opinion on the inquest conclusions on Friday 15 November 1878:

> The verdict of the coroner's jury, which we print below, cannot be regarded with unmixed satisfaction. Where it endorses our remarks made on Tuesday as to the desirability of providing better life-saving apparatus on river steamers than was carried by the *Princess Alice*, and, as to the doubtful expediency of allowing nearly 1,000 lives to be risked in one river steamer of only ordinary strength and buoyancy, we, at least, cannot quarrel with the conclusions. The discrepancy between the report of the Board of Trade Court and the jury is nevertheless to be regretted. We are informed that at one time eleven of the jury were in favour of bringing in a verdict of manslaughter against those in charge of the *Bywell Castle*.

(The Board of Trade Inquiry had reported earlier in the week, see Chapter Nineteen.) The following day *The Times* published a letter addressed to the coroner from Mr Harrington, the inquest jury foreman, a copy of which he had sent to the newspaper.

In it, he (and, purportedly, his jury) thanked everyone concerned with the inquest and inquiry: the Local Board of Health; Assistant Commissary-General Barrington, for use of the dockyard; Assistant Commissary-General Long, for use of his ambulances; the London Steamboat Company, for use of their steamers for transporting bodies; R and R Division of the Metropolitan Police and the Dockyard Division,[10] for work of the most arduous and trying nature, and Inspectors Phillips and Dawkins, for not only arduous and trying but harrowing and loathsome work; and, last but not least, your officer, Gilham. And so it went on: General Officer Commanding, Cavalry, Artillery ... Army Service Hospital Corps, the Harbour Master ... and Uncle Tom Cobley and all. Not forgetting the coroner himself:

> We cannot, Mr Coroner, leave your court without expressing the deep sense which we entertained of the great judgement,

intelligence, courtesy, and patience with which you have conducted this lengthy investigation, and rendering you our sincere thanks for the valuable assistance you have afforded us throughout this inquiry, which we cannot but believe to have been, from the immense loss of life and the questions involved in it, the most important coroner's inquisition ever held in this country.

In leaving you we can only say, however much many of the jury may have suffered in their business affairs, and the by no means small expense we have been put to by attending this inquiry, we shall not look upon it either as a labour thrown away or money lost if from it shall arise some definite and precise rules as to the proper navigation of the River Thames.

I remain your obedient servant,

S.C. Harrington, Foreman of Jury

This was an appalling piece of impertinence (any thanking should have and was to come from the coroner himself). Following it on the page was another letter to the editor:

Sir, I took passage today from Charlton Pier[11] to Woolwich Town Pier by the London Steamboat Company's steamer *Osprey*. At 12.10 we met the North German steamer and there was not a soul on the topgallant[12] forecastle. At 12.13 we met the screw steamer *Ridge Park* without any lookout on the topgallant forecastle; and at 12.15 we were passed by one of the Trinity Corporation steamers with no one on the forecastle, but two men were close to the foremast securing buoys on decks. I drew the attention of Captain Jones and his mate to these facts, to show how little attention is paid to the law.

Your obedient servant,

S.C. HARRINGTON, Foreman of the Coroner's Jury on the *Princess Alice* Disaster

He was not yet finished. On the final day of the inquest, Wednesday 27 November 1878, as thanks were being handed out to the jury from the coroner and to the coroner from the jury and to everyone else who had lent a hand, Harrington complained that the jury had been subjected to unfair comments from the newspapers.

It had been said that they held saturnalia on the night they were considering their verdict and that quantities of wine and spirits had been brought into the jury room. He wished publicly to say that this statement was absolutely unfounded. It was true that the jury had smoked, but he was not aware that their deliberations suffered either in dignity or thoroughness on that account. During the greater part of the night there were festivities in an adjoining room, and he had several times been obliged, through the medium of the coroner's officer, to request the company there to make less noise.

One juror inquired whether they were entitled to any fees and Carttar replied that none had been given in the Staunton case, where the inquest had lasted seventeen days, and it was now the practice of all counties but Surrey not to pay fees. However, considering the unprecedented character of this inquiry, he thought an exception might be made if they drew up an application to that effect. He would certainly support it. Captain Pim said he would bring it up in Parliament as soon as possible.

Carttar said, with regard to the matter complained of by the foreman, he could testify that their conduct while considering the verdict had been perfectly proper and throughout the inquiry they had acquitted themselves most creditably.

On that final day of proceedings those jury members who had agreed with the verdict signed the 24 ft long roll of parchment that contained the names of the 518 deceased persons. It now sits among the inquest records in the London Metropolitan Archive.

Among Carttar's papers were found these anonymous verses to be sung to the tune of 'Lord Lovell':

> The foreman stood at the town hall door
> Smoking a twopenny weed,
> When up came the jury and softly said:
> 'You naughty old man, take heed.'
> You naughty old man, etc.
> 'Oh, when will you stop, old man' they said.
> 'Oh, when will you stop,' said they.
> 'When I've asked 50,000 more
> Of the silliest questions, hi, hi.'
> Of the silliest questions, etc.

He talked and he jawed in his grizzling way
Till he couldn't jaw any more,
And then the jury boiled him down
And gave him away to the poor.
And gave him away, etc.

Twelve bodies remained unidentified at Woolwich, bringing the total to 530. At the end of the year the registrar general's return of births and deaths put the total due to drowning at 574, which included forty-seven from Barking, Poplar, Mile End Old Town and Westminster. Of these 228 were males and 346 females. This did not include those who had died after rescue.

Judging by the number of inquiries addressed to him by the relatives of missing persons, *The Times* reported, 'the coroner believes that there are from sixty to eighty bodies unrecovered from the river. Thus, the total number of lives lost must have been from 630 to 650'.[13] The final number was never settled upon.

CHAPTER NINETEEN

Hisses in Court

The proceedings of the Board of Trade inquiry were to yield one or two surprises and revelations, not to mention some startling accusations, despite the fact that many of the witnesses were those who had already given evidence at the protracted inquest.

The inquiry began on 14 October 1878, and was held at the Board of Trade Court in Poplar before stipendiary magistrate Mr Balguy and three naval assessors: Captain Forster, RN, Captain Parfitt and Mr Ravenhill, a nautical engineer.

The aims were to ascertain: the cause of the accident; whether any of the certified officers were culpable; whether alterations in the Thames rules of navigation were necessary; what caused the great loss of life; and whether there should be any alteration in the conditions for granting passenger certificates.

Specific charges had been laid against Captain Thomas Harrison and the *Bywell Castle*'s engineers, Henry Dimelow and Robert Thom, and the first mate of the *Princess Alice*, George Thomas Long. Given that Captain Grinstead was not alive to answer any charges, Long was the only one representing that ship. The charges read:

Against Thomas Harrison, the master of the *Bywell Castle*:

1. That he neglected to set and keep a good and efficient lookout and to see that a good lookout was kept onboard the said steamship, *Bywell Castle*.
2. That being on the bridge and in charge of the *Bywell Castle* he failed to see the lights of the *Princess Alice* as soon as they were visible.

3. That seeing collision was inevitable he did not stop and reverse his engines in time.

Against Henry Dimelow, first engineer of the *Bywell Castle*:

That while the *Bywell Castle* was navigating the River Thames and it was his duty to have charge of the engines of the *Bywell Castle* he left and gave up charge of the engines; that he called up all hands on deck and left the engines without any competent person in charge of them, whereby the orders of the person navigating the *Bywell Castle* to the engineer were not and could not be carried out.

Against Robert Thom, second engineer of the *Bywell Castle*:

That being left in charge of the engines of the *Bywell Castle*, he neglected to observe and neglected and failed to carry out an order given by the person in charge of the ship, to go astern full speed prior to the collision between that ship and the *Princess Alice*.

Against George Thomas Long for that being first mate of the steamship *Princess Alice* on the 3rd day of September, 1878, he caused or contributed to the loss of the said steamship and great loss of life by his wrongful acts and default as follows:

1. That he neglected to station anyone on the lookout.
2. That he neglected to see that an efficient lookout was kept, and that ship's lights were properly reported.
3. That being on the lookout he sighted but neglected to report the lights of the *Bywell Castle* as soon as they were visible to him.
4. That he did not report the *Bywell Castle*'s lights to the captain of the *Princess Alice*.
5. That he neglected to pass the report of the *Bywell Castle*'s lights from the lookout station forward to the captain on the bridge.

The certificates of all the men were suspended.

The history and descriptions of both vessels were read out by the Board of Trade solicitor Mr Mansel Jones:

Princess Alice:

Length: 219 ft 4 in over all. Breadth 20 ft 2 in. Depth of hold: 8 ft 4 in. Carried four boats, two of which were lifeboats.

1863 built by Mr Caird of Greenock. First known by the name of *Bute*.

1866 became the property of what was then the Woolwich Steamship Company.

1870 an intercostal stringer placed in the boiler room and the whole of the boiler bearers taken out.

1878 surveyed by a Board of Trade surveyor who made declarations on which her two certificates were issued, one of which allowed her to carry 936 passengers in smooth water from London to Gravesend.

Bywell Castle:

Tonnage: 891 tons. Length: 254 ft 2 in. Breadth: 32 ft. Depth of hold: 19 ft.

1870 Iron screw ship built at Newcastle. Owned by Messrs Hall of Newcastle.

About a week into the proceedings came a dramatic moment during the examination of those who had witnessed the accident. Amongst them was Thomas Delves M'Dowell, the boy from the *Castalia* that was among the vessels moored on the south side of Gallions Reach, who said:

The *Princess Alice* was near the north shore, I was looking at the *Bywell Castle*, and I turned my head and saw the two vessels 50 yd from each other. She was struck half-way between the buoys below us and the powder magazine, and north of midstream. I ran forward and told the men there was a collision. Kettle and Cheeseman were the two sailors in charge, the captain being away. When the boat came along with Kettle in it, Kettle got out and Cheeseman got in. They said it was no use our going. My

brother and I got in to go to the collision. Cheeseman held the
painter[1] and stopped us from going. Cheeseman was discharged
for not rendering assistance.[2]

James Cheeseman was called to be given the opportunity to
explain why he had not gone to the assistance of the stricken
vessel. He said he had seen the two ships drifting in collision
down with the tide, but hadn't gone to help because he had to
fetch the captain from Woolwich Pier at 9 p.m. and that Kettle
had told him that the report of the collision said it was very
slight. James Kettle said he did not think the collision was as
serious as it was and so did not consider it necessary to put off in
the boat.

'The two lads wanted to go,' said Mr Balguy, 'and the two men
would not take the trouble.'

'I did not think it was necessary,' replied Kettle, at which there
were hisses in court.[3]

The next day, young M'Dowell was back 'to correct a mistake'.
It had been Kettle who had held the painter and prevented
him and his brother from going to help with the rescue, not
Cheeseman. They had threatened to summon him and were
'going on at him' outside[4]. They had both been discharged from
the *Castalia*. A clearly concerned Mr Myburgh wanted to know
whether they had threatened to do the boys any harm and
whether they needed protection. No, the boy assured him and
Mr Balguy, they had only threatened to summon him and he was
not in fear of them.

One of the other revelations occurred following the
appearance (at the request of Captain Pim) of Samuel Pether,
one of Carttar's naval experts who, at the inquest, had claimed
that the *Princess Alice* was too lightly constructed for her task.
To illustrate the weak cladding of the *Princess Alice* Pether
produced fragments of iron taken from the outside of the
paddle-steamer's hull and a piece of wood from the main deck.
Pether was questioned and rather taken apart by the *Princess
Alice* counsel, Dr W. Phillimore, who revealed that Pether's
expert qualifications were rather flimsy or, as author Gavin
Thurston put it, he was little more than 'a jobbing ship repairer
for upriver craft'. The next day, Dr Phillimore called Mr Denton,
the London Steamship Company's superintendent engineer,

who informed the court that it looked 'improbable' that the piece of wood produced had actually come from the *Princess Alice*. Not only was it of the wrong thickness, but no hole had been found from where it was supposed to have been taken. Nor did it have the necessary caulking or signs of wear and boot marks he would expect from decking. There were similar doubts about the fragments of iron plate. Consequently, the magistrate, Mr Balguy, thought it advisable that the assessors see the deck of the vessel for themselves.

Meanwhile, another construction expert, John Scott Russell, a naval architect and vice president of the Naval Architect's Society, told the inquiry that he thought the *Princess Alice was* well enough built for the work she was meant to do. She had originally sailed the landlocked sea between Wemyss Bay and Arran in Scotland, but he compared her with a similar ship, the *Cleopatra*, that had crossed the Bay of Biscay and gone on to the Mediterranean and the Black Sea. He thought the iron used on the *Princess Alice* was excellent, 'better than a good deal that is made now for such purposes'. In his opinion no ship could have withstood the blow from the *Bywell Castle*.

> I do not think any construction of the ship would have offered very sensible resistance to her being cut through the middle ... no thickness of steel or clever invention[5] could prevent her from being cut in two. Its fate was as inevitable as a vessel being pierced by a cannon ball. If I wanted to run down a ship I would aim at the spot where the vessel was struck, it was the most vulnerable part.

Indeed, not even the famous *Great Eastern* (which Russell had built), with its ¾ in plates, could have withstood the force of an 890-ton mass, like the *Bywell Castle*, moving at four knots and concentrated in a single, upright stem. As for the wooden stringer (suggested by Pether as protection) it would have been 'as matchwood'.

Furthermore, there were *not* too many passengers onboard. Their weight was as nothing to the cargo she was capable of carrying. If all the (900) passengers were very plump, large gentlemen they would weigh 80 to 90 tons. 'Ninety tons is no cargo at all for a ship that size.' If they were ordinary size men they would weigh in at about 55 tons.

Russell had not finished rebutting criticism of the *Princess Alice*. Her proportions were perfectly all right: 'I have built ships with less depth, less beam, and more length, which have not only navigated rivers but have crossed the Atlantic'.[6]

The only fault he found with the pleasure steamer was the distance between her forward bulkhead and the one behind the engine – 32 ft – which was too long for the section that carried the most weight. He was in favour of numerous, watertight bulkheads. The *Princess Alice* had five, which divided the body into six watertight compartments, which was considered adequate when she was built. More may well have prevented the ship from sinking so rapidly, although the fact that she was practically cut in two made the rapid sinking almost inevitable.

The assessors who went to the wreck to examine the site of Pether's piece of deck took him with them to indicate the site but, it transpired, he had not actually removed it himself. In fact it had not been taken from the wreck but a ship-breakers yard to which some of the decking had been removed. He had asked them to cut him a piece of the thickest and been told it was all alike. However, lying about in the open, accessible to anyone was decking from three other boat decks that had just been delivered. The fragment could have come from one of those other decks. In any case, the assessors agreed that the sample Pether had brought to court did *not* come from the *Princess Alice*. There was talk of perjury charges being brought against this unfortunate 'expert'.

A long dissertation in the *Engineer* was particularly cutting about Pim: 'Unfortunately Captain Pim called witnesses to prove that she (the *Princess Alice*) was unfit for her duties who possessed little or no weight as experts'. When discussing the ship's structure and the plank episode:

Again – perhaps from want of sufficient knowledge of the subject – Captain Pim entirely missed the true point at issue, namely the great transverse weakness of the *Princess Alice*, resulting from her extreme shallowness in proportion to her length, and the thinness of her plates; while he made a good deal of her narrowness, which had nothing to do with the matter.[7]

For some reason best known to himself, Captain Pim chose this arena to launch into an attack on both ships and the Board of Trade at whose door, he was sorry to say, the responsibility of this dire calamity rested. There had been no system of order on the *Princess Alice*, he claimed, and those handling the *Bywell Castle* were merely runners who had no interest at all in the vessel. As for the Board of Trade:

> Sir, the condition of our merchant seamen is of the deepest moment to us. There are very few British seamen left, for at least four-fifths of the crews of our merchant ships are made up of foreign and home riff-raff – the scum of the earth – who, moreover, do not know one end of a ship from another ... I have no hesitation in saying that during the last twenty-five years, since which time the mercantile marine has been under the control of the Board of Trade, our merchant service has steadily declined both as regards men and ships.

He also pointed out that there had been no instance of bravery on either vessel – with the exception of Brankston, who had abseiled down onto the stricken vessel. Considering how fast everything happened, one gets the impression that there was little time to do anything other than respond automatically to the situation and that there wasn't much opportunity for bravery.

The man appeared to be pursuing a solo cause, but one wonders what assistance this was supposed to be to his clients, the relatives of Mr and Mrs Bridgeman, whom he claimed had been 'done to death' onboard the *Princess Alice* which, he still insisted, was of the flimsiest build.

Indeed Mr Mansel Jones, who was presenting the Board of Trade's case seemed perplexed by Pim's strange attack:

> I am really at a loss to understand why Captain Pim should have chosen this court as the arena for the purpose of making such serious charges against a public department of this country, when he especially is privileged to make them in another place [the House of Commons] where they could be answered and refuted by the responsible officials at the head of that department ... It may be that he thought it was safer to do so under the shield and protection of the advocate's gown.[8]

In their final report the Board of Trade stated that it was evident that two distinct theories had been put forward. One alleging a sudden porting and great alteration in her course by the *Bywell Castle*, the other a sudden change to a hard a-starboard by the *Princess Alice* while the *Bywell Castle* ported only a little to go astern of her. 'To one or other of these irreconcilable theories the witnesses usually adhered, and in equal proportions.' Therefore, the court had been obliged to attach great weight to the evidence of witnesses not attached to either theory coupled with the position of the wreck. They had come to the following conclusion, as reported in *The Times:*

> That the *Princess Alice* rounded Tripcock Point at a short distance off the Kent shore; that she straightened up the Reach at reduced speed under a starboard helm, heading towards Bull Point, till she brought the *Bywell Castle* end on to her when the latter vessel was coming down the Reach, steering to go round Tripcock Point; that the *Princess Alice* then went on at full speed, and continued under starboard helm more or less throughout; that at one time she was brought by the porting of the *Bywell Castle* somewhat on the port side of that vessel; that she did not shut her red light in from the *Bywell Castle* till immediately before the collision, when the orders were given to put her helm hard-a-starboard and to stop her engines, both of which orders were obeyed, but too late. It is possible that the *Princess Alice* may have been set off by the tide further than usual while she was straightening up after passing Tripcock Point. This would have prevented her turning short enough to bring her green light in view by the *Bywell Castle*, and so bring green to green, before the two vessels got to be end on to each other. That the *Bywell Castle* entered Gallions Reach somewhere about mid-stream; that she then steered a course to go round Tripcock Point, at the same time seeing the *Princess Alice* coming round and showing her red light. The *Bywell Castle* continued this course till both vessels became end on; she then, by porting, brought the *Princess Alice* a little on her port bow, and that soon after the red light of the *Princess Alice* became shut in; this was immediately before the collision; that orders were then given to put the helm hard-a-port and to stop the engines, both of which orders were obeyed, but too late.[9]

It was clear, the report went on, that the *Princess Alice* had committed a breach of Rule 29, Section (d) of the Board of Trade Regulations and the Regulations of the Thames Conservancy Board, 1872, by not porting her helm when she came end on to a vessel coming in the opposite direction, whereas by suddenly putting her helm a-starboard at the last moment she ran straight across and under the bows of the *Bywell Castle*. Therefore, the *Princess Alice* was to blame and the accident was unavoidable by the *Bywell Castle*. It was the opposite verdict to the one that would soon be arrived at by the inquest.

They also pointed out that the accusations of faulty construction and unfitness for service of the *Princess Alice* were utterly unfounded and 'that the charges against the officials of the Board of Trade are likewise utterly unfounded'. They deplored the fact they had been made. They did not think the *Princess Alice* had been overloaded but recommended restriction of night travel.

As to the rules of the road, the Thames Conservancy Board should make more effort to educate people about them, particularly now that the Thames had become so crowded. Obstructions such as hulks and vessels like the *Talbot* powder barge and the *Castalia* should be removed. They added a manifesto about the future of navigation on the river:

> The traffic on the River Thames has now become so crowded, and the dimensions of vessels passing up and down now exceed so enormously those of the ships of the last generation, that the safe navigation of the river by large steamships from 250 to 500 ft in length is incompatible with the presence of small craft drifting up and down with the tide, and (not being under control) unable to follow any rules whatever. Many of the owners of barges and small sailing vessels now find it to their interest to employ steam above Gravesend, and the court is of the opinion that the time has arrived when it should be made compulsory on them to do so, and that no serious hardship would be entailed upon them by such compulsory enactment, which would conduce to the safety of river navigation more than any other change contemplated. The court is informed that the Mersey, the Clyde, and the Tyne are already in advance of the Thames, as on these rivers the bulk of the river traffic is now conducted under steam.[10]

A rather curious comment, given that both vessels involved in the accident had been steam driven, but maybe the thinking was that with fewer small craft to watch out for more attention might be given to larger, more lethal ones.

As for the culpability of those charged, Captain Harrison had *not* failed to keep a proper lookout and had given the order to stop and reverse as soon as he saw the danger of collision. Dimelow and Thom carried out the order to stop the engines promptly, but Dimelow should not have left the engine room to call on deck his second and third engineers. Long had failed to keep an efficient lookout and neglected to inform Captain Grinstead of the *Bywell Castle*'s light as soon as he saw them and to pass them on from the forward lookout. But this had not affected the outcome. All the officers' certificates were returned.

Captain Pim, (who had a reputation as the British Seaman's Friend) was not about to relinquish his campaign against the Board of Trade. His next move was to send a very long missive to its president, Viscount Sandon MP, complaining that their inquiry should not have been held while the inquest was still in progress, thus interfering with the common law process, and that the wreck commissioner, not Mr Balguy, should have presided. He demanded a further inquiry and included a number of recommendations for improving navigation on the Thames.

The reply he received from John G. Talbot MP, parliamentary secretary of the Board of Trade, pointed out that much of his complaint was based on the misapprehension that the court of inquiry and assessors were nominated by them when, in fact, they were merely the promoters. The inquiries were actually made by justices (thus, Mr Balguy) and a wreck commissioner appointed by the Lord Chancellor and the assessors were from a Home Secretary's list.

Doubtless with the best of motives, on Friday 13 December 1878, the day Parliament reconvened, Pim tabled a question for the President of the Board of Trade asking 'whether in consequence of the national importance of the *Princess Alice* calamity, the length of time necessarily occupied by the coroner and jury on the inquest (from 4 September to 27 November), and the trying character of the duties, he will recommend to the proper authorities some official recognition of their arduous services'.[11]

No action was taken on this so he also moved that an address be presented to the queen that she give directions that there be laid before the House a return of proceedings of the coroner's inquest on the loss of the *Princess Alice* plus any correspondence addressed to the coroner. This was done. However, the producing of this return added another complicated and expensive task to those already weighing Carttar down, such as who was to pay fees to the shorthand writers, the police, and for the use of the town hall, and how much would they be?

CHAPTER TWENTY

Life Goes On

The fate of the orphans had continued to exercise the Mansion House Orphan sub-committee. Adoption offers had continued to come in both to them and to the west Kent coroner, Mr Carttar. At the launch of the sub-committee the secretary had reported forty-one private offers to take girls and ten for boys.

Many people had been quite specific about their requirements: Mrs Pugh, of St Stephen's Square, wanted a girl between the ages of six and ten, bookseller Mr Wardleworth a girl between three and eight, while cab driver Mr Sear and his wife would not take a girl under two. What Mrs Taylor wanted was a middle-class girl and Messrs Hopkin and Page of Shoreditch offered to take a boy of thirteen to fifteen years into their service as an apprentice.

Many mothers had died in the accident but, even if they were still alive, there was a strong feeling that their children might be better off in an orphanage than with a mother who was likely to become poor. The sub-committee also suspected that some relatives might take on a child in the hope of receiving financial reward from the fund.

Ultimately, about half the fund money was spent on buying the children places in orphanages and subsequent apprentice-ships. At one meeting a motion was put forward by Dr Piggott, seconded by the Reverend Anson, Rector of Woolwich, that before placing any children there should be inquiries into their educational standards and class. It was carried.

The problem was solved in some cases if the father had been or was a freemason, as Captain Grinstead had. Two of his children were admitted into Masonic schools. Later, in 1882, one of his sons, William Robert, joined the Thames Police. William had been an apprentice waterman employed on the river. When he heard of the accident he had made his way to the scene and, as the Thames Police Museum web pages relate, 'spent the next three days searching the vicinity, only coming ashore when he learned that his father's body, easily recognizable by his uniform, had been recovered'.[1] When the fore part of the vessel was raised the company's flag still hung on the mast. William reclaimed it for his family and it was passed down from generation to generation before eventually being presented to the Thames Police Museum at Wapping where it remains.

Soon, John J. Powell of Temple, one of *The Times'* ever-active letter writers, was worrying whether the auditing of these charities was satisfactory given the huge amounts involved: £35,000 for the *Princess Alice* disaster, upwards of £40,000 for the Abercarne miners' families and about £1,000,000 for the Indian Famine Fund.[2] Official auditors should be appointed who would publish the results. This was questioned by S.R. Townsend Mayer who wanted to know:

> ... by what test would an auditor by able to decide whether excessive grants had been made to sufferers by the *Princess Alice* disaster? It is alleged that many frivolous and dishonest claims have been sent in to the Mansion House Committee. Possibly all, or nearly all, these attempts at imposition have been frustrated; but supposing, for the sake of argument, that one has been allowed, how could an auditor detect the cheat? The fact is you cannot lay down a Procrustean rule that shall be applicable to all charities.[3]

The Mansion House Fund on behalf of the victims of the *Princess Alice* disaster was wound up on 11 October 1878, having reached a total of £35,000. More trickled in after that including (according to *The Times*) 100 guineas from a gentleman in thanks for not being onboard the *Princess Alice* and another 100 because he was not a shareholder in the Glasgow Bank (which had collapsed)!

By the end of 1878, despite failing health, Carttar had resumed his involvement with local affairs and political life and his work as a solicitor and as coroner for west Kent. This meant that rather than sitting regularly in the Woolwich Town Hall boardroom he was now obliged to travel about the district to hold his inquests in public houses, as was then the custom. But Carttar's health was failing fast and his coroner's court duties were increasingly taken over by his deputy, Mr G. Collier. A glimpse of him is given in his letter of 14 June 1879, to S. H. Turner, Esq, Kentish Bank, Maidstone, regarding the ongoing saga of the *Princess Alice* inquest fees. He wrote that he wished and intended to be at the next finance committee meeting – if his doctor would allow it:

> I was anxious to get the unsettled matter of Police and Gurney's[4] fees arranged with the Finance Committee as I promised the Secretary of State, but in fear of my ability to travel so far I have written the letters enclosed and if I do not appear by noon, be pleased to present them with my apologies and state the cause of my absence and oblige.

One of the enclosures, in a shaky, pencil-written hand, asked for the sanction to reward his officers: 'I am constantly and anxiously applied to by my officers for your decision'.[5] There had been a public subscription for the police involved in coping with the *Princess Alice* disaster. This had been distributed to 500 policemen but had left out Carttar's officers. Eventually, Carttar received a County sanction to distribute £30 among them out of which Gilham received £11.10s and the others around 30 shillings each.

Extraordinarily, almost exactly a year after the *Princess Alice* disaster, Captain Pim was defending the pilot of a ship that had been involved in a serious collision in the Thames near Tripcock Point. The vessels involved were the *City of London*, a 977-ton screw steamer from Aberdeen, and the *Vesta*, a 1,050-ton screw steamer out of Hamburg. The *City of London* had been coming downriver from Limehouse at 8.20 p.m. on 13 August 1879, on its regular Wednesday run. Aboard were forty-two crew and ninety-four passengers, 200 tons of cargo and some horses. Coming upstream at full speed was the *Vesta* carrying twenty-five crew, fifteen passengers and 600 tons of cargo. The *City of London* had rounded Tripcock Point, being obliged go towards midstream to avoid some barges, when the crew saw the *Vesta* speeding straight towards them. Warning whistles failed to halt her but, just before the moment of impact, she stopped her engines and turned full speed astern, which did not prevent her from ramming the *City of London* on her port side, cutting into her engine room and causing her to rapidly fill with water and begin to sink.

'Such a calamity', commented the *Daily News*, 'should have been attended with loss of life', and indeed, the terrified passengers, some in their nightgowns and shouting for help, clearly imagined this was the *Princess Alice* all over again.[6] Most of them were taken onboard the *Vesta*, which then managed to edge the *City of London* on to the mud of Barking Reach, where she stayed. Their captain claimed that the *City of London* had suddenly turned south into her path. Déjà vu all over again.

Not only did this accident occur quite near where the *Princess Alice* had sunk, it was also close to the site of the *Metis* and *Wentworth* collision eleven years earlier. What becomes more and more clear is that there was, in fact, nothing unusual about the *Princess Alice* collision – apart from the huge loss of life. As we have seen, ships were forever colliding with each other, even out on the open sea, where one would imagine they had enough room to avoid each other. Also, that that particular spot on the River Thames was lethal.

The Board of Trade investigation was almost a mirror of the previous one. Were there sufficient lookouts on the *Vesta* and the *City of London*? What lights were shown and seen at each critical moment? Had they obeyed the Rules of the Road? And so on. The blame in this instance was laid at the door of the *Vesta*, and its pilot for not having ported his helm when the lights of the other ship were first seen.

On 12 March, 1880, the *Morning Post* reported that C. J. Carttar was 'seriously ill from the fatigue and anxiety' as a result of conducting the inquest upon the bodies in the *Princess Alice* disaster. He had, revealed the *Lancaster Gazette* on 17 March, been confined to his room for the last six weeks. A few days later there was a flurry of countrywide newspaper reports announcing the death of Mr Charles Carttar, coroner for west Kent. They cited a lingering illness, opined that he was 'another victim of the *Princess Alice* disaster', never having recovered from the immense strain of his duties and regretted that he was not relieved of at least a portion of them. Cause of death was given as heart disease (mitral and aortic valves), two years; dyspepsia and oedema, one year.

Carttar was, of course, famous not only for the *Princess Alice* inquest, but also for the Staunton case and (reminded the *London Standard*) for the inquest on the body of 'Robert Cocking, the aeronaut, who fell from a parachute in 1838, and lies buried in Lee churchyard'.[7]

The Carttars were clearly keen to maintain their position as coroners for the Greenwich or West Kent Division. Alongside the funeral announcement, the *Evening News*, Portsmouth, said, 'we understand that Mr Arundel Carttar, son of the deceased, will announce himself as a candidate for the vacant office at the end of the week'. Less than two months after Charles Carttar's passing his son, Edward Arundel Carttar, was nominated for the post. Interestingly, the qualifications of the other three nominees (one of whom, Mr G. Collier, had been Charles Carttar's deputy) were stated after their names, but in Arundel Carttar's case all that was deemed necessary was 'son of the late coroner'. An overwhelming show of hands favoured him and the result was greeted with loud applause but the nominator of surgeon, Dr Maxwell, demanded a poll. The result was 698 votes for Arundel, 157 more than his nearest rival, Dr Maxwell. Charles Carttar had been elected to the post in 1832 at the age of twenty-one in succession to his father who had held it for twenty-one years. Small wonder he had had begun to make up his own coroner's rules.

Arundel's task could have proved easier than that of his father as there was a proposal before the Kent magistrates that the late coroner's district should be divided into three: Greenwich, Bromley and Dartford. But Arundel himself opposed the move.

The returns required for Captain Pim's parliamentary address were still causing problems. On 7 June 1880, Arundel wrote to the Home Secretary saying there were no funds available at present to meet the extra expenses entailed in acquiring these returns, but by 30 June he had deposited the return with the librarian of the House of Commons.

A notice in *The Times* of 22 June announced that the Kent County Magistrates had decided to pay £250 to the representatives of the late coroner, Mr C. J. Carttar, 'for special services in conducting the inquests in connection with the *Princess Alice* steamboat disaster. The inquests lasted over thirty-seven days, and £40 of the amount awarded has been spent in respect of documents required by the government'. All too late to have assuaged Carttar's worries

As for Captain Pim, who had caused Carttar all that anxiety, he died aged sixty-one, in October 1886, at the end of a remarkably active and varied life[8] having been promoted to rear admiral on the retired list the year before. 'Seaman, surveyor, explorer, fighter, engineer, financier, politician, journalist, author, savant and lawyer', said the *Standard* of 5 October 1886, but noted that:

> ... in the latter parts which he essayed, the bluff sailor did not, indeed, distinguish himself. As a seafaring man he did really good work: but on shore he was the victim of sharper men than himself, it would have been better for his memory if his record had ended when he came home thirty years ago, badly wounded, from the Chinese War.

CHAPTER TWENTY-ONE

The Perils of Kissing

On the same day as the jury put their signatures to the *Princess Alice* inquest report, the hearing of the London Steamboat Company's claim for damages against the *Bywell Castle* began at the Court of Admiralty at Trinity House.

The day before, as though to ram home the dangers of poor navigation, yet another serious shipping collision had occurred between the Welsh sailing ship, *Moel Eilian*, and German passenger steamer *Pommerania*, this time just off Folkestone in the English Channel. The 3,382-ton *Pommerania*, which plied between Hamburg and New York, had landed a number of passengers at Plymouth, some more at Cherbourg, and was taking the remaining 109 passengers on to Hamburg, when she was rammed by the much smaller craft. She might have been small but the (1,100-ton) Welsh barque proved lethal. She made a large hole in the *Pommerania*'s hull through which water poured. She began to sink. Two of her lifeboats had been crushed and a third was swamped as it was launched. Forty lives were lost including, it was originally thought, that of the captain, although it later transpired he had been picked up by a Dutch steamer. Although badly damaged the Welsh ship survived.

The Times claimed this showed the value of watertight compartments and that the structure of the great ocean-going steamers was generally an element of insecurity rather than of safety: 'their hulls are for the most part fatally vulnerable and can be pierced by a blow of no astonishing force'. So it seems that the man who declared that even then *Great Eastern* could not have withstood the blow from the *Bywell Castle*, was probably right.

The baiting of Germany on the subject of their naval skills

seems to have been something of a national sport, for the news-paper pointed out that what the accident also showed was that the German transatlantic passengers ships of recent years had been particularly unfortunate, for example, the wreck of the *Schiller*[1] (which has since been dubbed the 'Victorian Titanic') and the ss *Deutschland*.[2] They suggested that perhaps what was needed was an inquiry by *their* authorities as searching and severe as that had been carried out by the Board of Trade in the case of the *Princess Alice*. A note in *The Times* at the end of December said cryptically: 'The captain and officers of the *Pommerania*, whose responsibility for the recent collision was inquired into in Berlin, have been acquitted'.

But the British had no cause to crow because, on the very same day, another fatal collision occurred on the Mersey. In a thick, early-morning fog, the passenger ferry *Gem*, whose passengers were largely businessmen en route from Seacombe to Liverpool, collided with the steamer, *Bowfell*, which was lying at anchor. *The Times* reported:

> The blow had hardly been struck when there was a general rush from the cabins below, and several passengers, probably fearing a repetition of the *Princess Alice* disaster, immediately jumped overboard.

By then, four passengers were known to have drowned and another fourteen were still missing.

Inevitably, the evidence before the Court of Admiralty in the *Princess Alice* case was more or less a replay of the inquest and Board of Trade hearings. On 11 December Sir R. Phillimore gave his judgement on the action by the London Steamboat Company against the *Bywell Castle*:

> It appears to us that when the *Princess Alice* was on a parallel course with the *Bywell Castle*, red light to red light, if their courses had been continued they would have safely passed. But when a very short distance (100 to 400 yd) intervened the *Princess Alice* went hard a-starboard bringing her athwart the *Bywell Castle*. It is impossible to ascertain her motive for doing this. It appears to us, moreover, that the *Princess Alice* was navigated in a careless and reckless manner without due observance of regulations as

to lookout and speed. In our opinion the *Princess Alice* is to blame for this collision.

It remains to decide whether the *Bywell Castle* contributed. It appears she was navigated with due care and skill till within a very short time of the collision. But it is certain that having seen the *Princess Alice*'s green light she ported into it. Not only the wrong manoeuvre but the worst she could have executed.

The only defence is that it happened so short a time before the collision. There have been several cases in this court where it has been held that a wrong manoeuvre at the last moment really had no effect on the collision. I have consulted with the Elder Brethren whether this wrong action could be placed in this category. They think if 'hard a-port' had not been given, though the *Princess Alice* might have received some injury, she would not have sunk. I am bound therefore to hold both vessels to blame for this collision.[3]

So now we have one judgement blaming the *Bywell Castle*, one blaming the *Princess Alice* and a third blaming them both. The case went to the Court of Appeal, which was to take its time in reporting.

In London, the 'state of the Thames water' remained a topic of concern. At the end of November, members of the Board of Works and several scientists made two trips down the Thames on a steamer taking specimens of water at various points, as suggested by Sir Joseph Bazalgette in his report to them on 22 November. He accompanied them.

Their conclusions were that the water was made much murkier by solids mixed from the soil that had been washed from the eroding riverbanks, particularly where the banks were not maintained by wharfs, walls or stone 'pitching', than by sewage solids which were 'highly decomposable'. While not denying that there was some 'offensive water' near the sewage outlets, it was far worse in front of the London Telegraph Works at East Greenwich and, more particularly, at Lawes Chemical Works at Barking Creek. This emitted an odour of sulphuric acid and the river there was pervaded by a tarry scum thought to come from the tar works 3 miles up the creek. 'The water was thicker here, than at the outfall, and the spot altogether had a very unsavoury character about it', reported the *Standard* on 30 November. 'Some of them were bold enough to swallow large draughts of it,' the *Graphic* told its readers, 'and though no very severe condemnation was expressed, we do not hear that anyone arranged for a supply to be sent home for his private use'.

Which was just as well, since the return of deaths in London for the previous week included eighteen from enteric or typhoid fever, which can be caused by faecal matter in the water. There were also seventeen enteric fever sufferers lying in the London Fever Hospital at that time. Deaths from diarrhoea (fifteen) were counted separately. Although declining a little, the other infectious diseases continued to take their toll; seven from smallpox, eighteen from measles, fifty-four from scarlet fever, eleven from diphtheria, thirty-one from whooping cough and twenty-four from different forms of fever. Lung diseases also saw off 428 that week. Even fractures could be the death of you, but at least, unlike Spain where the disease was suspected, leprosy was not a threat. Diphtheria was, of course, a particularly dreadful disease that caused death either by suffocation from the rogue membrane growing in the throat and nasal passages or cardiac arrest due to the bacilli. Although more prevalent in poorer districts, the infectious diseases had no respect for rank or class. A cryptic note in the *Morning Post* on 26 November 1878, announced that Lady Hatterly of the Red House in Norwich had just died from 'a sharp attack of diphtheria'.

The real Princess Alice was already very much aware of the suffering diphtheria could cause. On 5 November, Princess Alice's first born, the tomboyish but kind 16-year-old Princess Victoria, complained of a stiff neck, which her mother suspected might be mumps. She remarked on how comical it would be if the whole household caught it. Next morning, young Victoria was diagnosed with the dreaded diphtheria. Five days later, 6-year-old Princess Alice ('Alicky') went down with it. The next to catch it was the youngest (and thus a particular pet of her mother's since the death of her son Frittie), 4-year-old Princess Marie, known as May. During the next three days, 12-year-old Princess Irene, 10-year-old Ernst Ludwig and the Grand Duke himself also succumbed. Their mother helped nurse them, but the 4-year-old May became very ill with the worst form of the disease (laryngeal). Alice wrote in distress to Queen Victoria at Balmoral, agonizing as to whether her 'sweet little May' would get through it. She didn't. The telegram to Queen Victoria the next day even had the granite-like former gillie, John Brown, 'crying like a child', so she knew when he delivered it to her what news it contained.[4]

Rather oddly, *The Times* commented on the fact that, although she had twenty-eight grandchildren, Queen Victoria had lost only five of them:

> According to 'Lodge's Peerage; the list of these deaths is as follows:
>
> **1st**, Prince Francis Frederick Sigismund, son of the Imperial Prince and Princess of Germany, died June, 1866, aged two;
>
> **2nd**, Prince Frederick William Augustus Victor Leopold Louis, son of Princess Alice and of the Grand Duke of Hesse, accidentally killed by a fall in May, 1873, aged two and a half;
>
> **3rd**, Prince Frederick Christian Augustus Victor Leopold Edward Harold, son of the Princess Helena and Prince Christian, died May, 1876, aged one week;
>
> **4th**, Prince Alexander John Charles Albert, son of the Prince and Princess of Wales, died in April, 1871, aged one day;
>
> **5th**, the Princess Marie of Hesse, aged 4.[5]

Alice had to keep the news of May's death from the rest of her sick children, who kept asking for their little sister and sending her books and toys. They all began to recover, apart from the sensitive only son Ernst (Ernie). Eventually, when Ernie too was out of danger, she told him about the death of his little sister to whom he was especially attached. He was so upset that she broke the golden rule of no physical contact (the disease is passed on via physical contact or from the breath of the victim) and hugged and kissed him, possibly imagining that, not having caught it after all this exposure, she was immune.

Now they all seemed to be out of the woods, Alice began to feel a little more cheerful, and in a letter to her mother on 7 December talked about repapering the nurseries and going on a trip to Heidelberg. But she was not immune. A few days after comforting Ernie she fell ill and, despite the Queen sending over Sir William Jenner,[6] one of her own doctors, Princess Alice died on 14 December. This was the same date on which her beloved father had died all those years earlier.

The response to the sad news in Britain and the colonies was unrestrained: black-edged columns in newspapers relating the sequence of events in detail; flags flown at half mast on public buildings; and church bells tolling mournfully. The regret appeared genuine. The public seem to have appreciated that here was a royal of some social conscience, not just a drain on the public purse.[7]

The people of Eastbourne, which the Princess and her family had so recently visited, were particularly touched and a collection was launched for the erection of a memorial. Soon this held sufficient cash for a more suitable memorial, a small hospital. In 1881, Alice's niece, Princess Helena, laid the foundation stone for the Princess Alice Memorial Hospital and it was opened, in 1883, by the Prince and Princess of Wales. They had been particularly affected by her death. He had declared her his favourite sister: 'So good, so kind, so clever. We had gone through so much together'.[8] In fact, they had rather clung to each other when children in the shadow of their clever older sister, Victoria.

The *Sussex Advertiser*, however, did not lose the opportunity for a little German bashing, pointing out that they had heard rumours about the bad state of drainage in the old palace at Darmstadt, 'for we have an idea that in many cases this form of illness is brought on by defective sanitary arrangements and, like Typhoid fever, is infectious, whatever may have been the opinion of *savants* hitherto'.[9]

The Times noted that only the family had been infected; none of the sixty-strong household, including nurses and physicians, had caught the disease. 'It is, therefore, clear that all the cases have been produced by direct infection, doubtless by kisses.'[10] Whilst they felt the drainage of the New Palace (built in 1804) was not suspect, they did think the sanitation in the town of Darmstadt was not very satisfactory. So the dual suspects were kisses and bad sanitation.

Princess Alice was given a splendid funeral in Darmstadt and a recumbent statue of her with her little daughter May in her arms was placed in the mausoleum. A Princess Alice (Darmstadt) Memorial Fund was launched in support of the institute for training nurses at her hospital in Darmstadt, while the German

Ambassador, on opening the Home for German Governesses in London, suggested that English ladies who desired to honour the memory of Princess Alice could not do so better than by supporting an institution in which that beloved lady had taken a warm interest.

Some of Alice's children came to even more tragic ends. Her second daughter, Elizabeth, married Sergius Alexandrovitch, Grand Duke of Russia and, in 1918, the Bolsheviks threw her (alive) down a mine shaft in Siberia. Alexy married the last Russian Czar, Nicholas II, and was assassinated with him and her family at Yekaterinburg. However, her eldest daughter, Victoria, married Louis Prince Battenberg, from which, under its new name Mountbatten, Earl Mountbatten of Burma and Queen Elizabeth II's husband, Prince Philip came. Princess Alice is Prince Philip's great great grandmother.

In his foreword to Gerard Noel's book *Princess Alice: Queen Victoria's Forgotten Daughter,* Lord Mountbatten recalled being brought up on tales of his grandmother, 'the most remarkable of Queen Victoria's remarkable children'. He had often been told that his mother, Princess Victoria, took after her 'in progressive thought and ceaselessly taking the lead in discussions and conversations'.

In 1967 Lord Louis spoke to a large gathering at the centenary celebrations of the *Alice Frauenverein* (Alice's Women's Union) at Darmstadt. 'From the other speeches', he said, 'it was clear how strongly the impact of this high-minded, practical princess was still felt in Hesse.'[11]

It was to be seven months before the final judicial judgement was heard on who was to blame for the *Princess Alice* and *Bywell Castle* collision. It was given at the Court of Appeal where the owners of the *Bywell Castle* were seeking a reverse of the decision that they were also to blame. On 15 July 1879, Lord Justices James, Brett and Cotton gave their judgements. Lord Justice James pointed out that, on the evidence, they could not overrule the finding of blame with regard to the *Princess Alice*. But as to the question of the last minute manoeuvre of the *Bywell Castle* (going hard a-port), which their assessors agreed was a wrong manoeuvre, they held that it could not have had the slightest appreciable effect on the collision. Lord Justice James clearly felt this was an action that should not have been taken, saying he wanted to add his own view, 'that a ship has no right by its own misconduct to put another ship in a position of extreme peril and then charge that other ship with misconduct'. His opinion was that:

> ... if in a moment of extreme peril and difficulty, if such other ship happened to do something wrong, so as to be liable for a contribution to the mischief, that would not render her liable for damages, inasmuch as perfect presence of mind, accurate judgement and promptitude under all circumstances are not to be expected. You have no right to expect men to be something more than ordinary men. I am therefore of the opinion that the finding of the court below that the *Bywell Castle* was, for purposes of the suit, to blame, must be overruled and the *Princess Alice* was alone to blame.[12]

The other two justices, while adding more observations, concurred: the *Princess Alice* alone was to blame.

One can only agree with Lord Justice James that it was a rather strange claim for the *Princess Alice*'s owners to have made in the circumstances and it can only have added to the financial difficulties of the London Steamboat Company. One can only assume that they may have been ill-advised by their lawyers who, of course, would be the ones to gain. The judgment was to be the knell of doom for the company. By the middle of 1884 it was on its knees but, extraordinarily, something that helped keep it afloat, at least for a while, was yet another collision in the Thames to the scene of which they ferried 80,000 sightseers.

As for the on-going problem of untreated sewage in the river, this was somewhat abated by Bazelgette who, in 1887, came up with the idea of extracting solid waste materials from the cesspools that fed the outfalls and carting it out to sea in 'sludge boats'. This marine dumping did not cease until 1998.[13]

CHAPTER TWENTY-TWO

What Rule?

The navigation of the River Thames remained a hot topic. In response to all the criticism the Board of Trade appointed a special committee to inquire into it. A myriad of experts, from admirals to the secretary of the Steamship Owners Association, gave evidence at thirty-three meetings. Many more meetings were given over to deliberations on these. The committee's reports were gathered into a substantial tome (complete with attractive colourful maps of each stretch of the river) to present to Parliament. It was, *The Times* later claimed, 'a mine of useful information on the subject of the London river'.[1]

In their preliminary report the committee first pointed out that the Thames had peculiarities that distinguished it from any other rivers in the United Kingdom. They went on to describe all the bends, 'some of which are less than a right angle', the many variations in width and depth, the river's great length, the large number of docks and wharves and the huge coal trade carried on there. The result was 'that the traffic of the Thames is not only peculiar in its magnitude, but in its composite character'. Their list of all the vessels using the river presents a mind-boggling picture:

> Firstly – Sea-going steamers, varying in size from the small coaster to the ships of the Peninsular and Oriental, the National and other Companies, 450 in length. Of these the largest do not go above Blackwall; but some over 1,000 tons go as high as London Bridge, and colliers of 900 tons now go as high as Vauxhall Bridge.

Secondly – Large sea-going ships, now for the most part towed by steam tugs.

Thirdly – River passenger steamers, and excursion steamers.

Fourthly – Colliers, smacks, schooners, sloops, billyboys[2] and various small sea-going sailing vessels.

Fifthly – Sailing barges bringing hay, straw, cement, bricks and other produce from the Medway, from Essex, and other neighbouring parts of the coast, to London.

Sixthly – Above Blackwall, the barges or lighters which collect and distribute the cargoes of the ships.

Besides these, there are skiffs, wherries and small steam launches.

After giving the numbers arriving in the Port of London during the previous few years they pointed out that they were such as to have 'almost outgrown the capacity of the river'.

The committee, however, did appear rather sanguine about the number of accidents:

The casualties on the Thames are, as might be expected, numerous, but it must not be supposed from the terrible calamity in which the present inquiry originates, that the loss of life, or even of property, caused by these casualties is large in proportion to their number.

Those from the Wreck Register covering June 1878 to 1879 occurring above Gravesend were 419 of which 373 were collisions and which involved 836 vessels.

In all these cases, however, only six lives were lost. As regards property, the cases returned as total losses were only nine in number, and of the remaining casualties 121 are described as serious, and 289 of minor importance.

This does seem quite a lot to the modern eye.

Such collision figures were nothing new. Back in October, 1875, Mr A. H. Smee, a *Times* correspondent, had pointed out that in the last half of September there had been twenty-two collisions by steamers alone. Two of these had occurred in the Thames, one on the Mersey and one on the Tyne. The newspaper also reported, since the loss of the *Northfleet* two years earlier, a disturbing practice had grown up among steam captains that demanded severe punishment.

> ... namely, after he has run a vessel down he backs his steamer clear of the wreck and then steams away in the darkness without offering assistance to the crew of the ill-fated vessel, who are thus left, too frequently, to perish; and as dead men tell no tales the owner of the steamers escapes his liability for the collision.

Apparently, three such instances had occurred that month (see also the ss *Deutschland* in Chapter Twenty-One). So, in one respect, the passengers and crew of the *Princess Alice* had been lucky. But, of course, such hit and runs were much more likely to occur out at sea where there were few other witnesses.

Among the Board of Trade Special Navigation Committee's recommendations regarding pleasure steamers was 'restrictions might well be placed on the running of these vessels after dark, or at all events not beyond one hour after sunset'. They noted that it was evident that the lookout man and the men at the wheel of the *Princess Alice* were surrounded by passengers and suggested that if the men at the wheel 'could be placed at an elevation above and railed off from the passengers they would be able to do their duty in a more efficient manner'.[3]

But when it came to the tricky question of how vessels should pass each other, the decision was hedged about with all manner of provisos due to the various limitations and abilities of the vessels and the twists and turns of the River Thames. They agreed that steamers approaching each other *should* pass each other port to port – but not in all cases. In fact, it was what *The Times* termed 'an approximation of the rule', the actual rule being supplemented by other proposed regulations, such as that steam vessels navigating against the tide at certain sharp bends and corners (like Tripcock Point) should ease their engines and wait until any vessels rounding the points with the tide (and therefore under less control) had passed clear.[4] That barges managed by oars should not be allowed to drift athwart the tide, but should be kept head on. That dumb barges between London Bridge and Blackwall Reach, if they were employed on voyages which extended between the whole of those limits or beyond, should be towed. And if a steamer found it unsafe to get out of the way of a sailing vessel she might signify the same by four blasts of the steam whistle ... and so on.

The Times of 3 September 1879, exactly a year after their first report of the *Princess Alice* disaster, lamented that no rule of the road had yet become law. Indeed, it was remarked that two recent collisions had shown that the case of the *Princess Alice* had been exceptional only in the magnitude of the ruin that followed the original mistake.

However, one of *The Times'* correspondents, Rear Admiral J. R. Ward, Chief Inspector of Lifeboats at the National Lifeboat Institution, did come up with a wheeze to assist two ships meeting at night if they were unsure what the other was about to do. He suggested the use of a novel signal light, recently designed by an officer in the United States Navy, Lieutenant E. W. Very, which was very simple and inexpensive.

> It consists of a brass-barrelled, breech-loading pistol of simple, but special character, from which are discharged stars or fireballs of any selected colour to a height or distance in any direction from 300 ft to 400 ft, just as similar stars are thrown up in the common firework called a 'Roman Candle'. These stars are so brilliant and of such size that they can be seen on a clear night from a distance of 20 miles; and I have, at an official trial under the direction of Major Le Mesurier, the Inspector of Army Signalling at Aldershot, seen them at a distance of 17½ miles.

They could be so promptly used, he went on, that no less that ten could be discharged in one minute, if required. Thus, a vessel sighting another ahead could fire green or red stars, according to whether the master had decided to go to the starboard or port side.

These lights would be invaluable for signalling distress, 'since they can be carried onboard the smallest merchant vessels, in which rockets would be unmanageable', and, he added dramatically:

... in cases where stranded vessels have quickly every light extinguished by heavy seas breaking over them, and the men have to lash themselves to the rigging with no means of making their situation known to those on the land, the master would only have to hang his pistol around his neck and buckle his belt of cartridges around him before going aloft, and he could then make signals at intervals throughout the night or until answered from the land.[5]

Indeed, Very lights were adopted worldwide.

The following year came the completion of the Albert side of Royal Victoria and Albert Docks, a vast complex which opened onto Gallions Reach, thus becoming the furthest docks downriver of the London Docks. As such, they were touted as something that would make the Thames a safer river. As *The Times* of 7 May 1880, reported:

> The Royal Victoria and Albert Docks bring the quays of London 3 miles and a half lower down the river than they have yet extended, and will enable great ocean steamships to avoid the dangerous and expensive towage to Blackwall. It was just at this point where the new docks are entered from the Thames that the *Bywell Castle*, which had swung out into the stream some miles higher up, came into collision with the *Princess Alice*, and it was just above this point that the *Canada*, another large steamer, ran into a pier and carried it bodily away.[2] The new docks will help to separate the heavy goods traffic from the light omnibus trade of the Thames, and ought to contribute greatly to the safety and cheapness of navigation on the metropolitan river.

In 1883 the *Bywell Castle* went missing, not an unusual state of affairs before modern communications allowed ship-owners and other interested parties to keep fairly constant track of their vessels.

At that time, arrivals and departures were noted at ports and telegraphed to Lloyds who advised their members and listed the ships' movements in the newspapers. Additional information, pinpointing where the ship was last seen, came from sightings by other vessels or land-based observers. Thus, last seen in the Bay of Biscay, was a typical final word on a vessel.

The *Bywell Castle* had been last seen off the Portuguese coast. The *Northern Echo* of 25 May 1883, on reporting on the investigation of its loss, pointed the finger of responsibility squarely at the ship's owners for her absence from the scene:

LOSS OF THE *BYWELL CASTLE*: WARNING TO SHIPOWNERS

At the Wreck Commissioners' Court, Westminster, yesterday, Mr Rotherey concluded the official inquiry into the circumstances attending the loss of the steamship *Bywell Castle*, while on a voyage from Alexandria to Hull with a large grain cargo ... She was last reported off the Portuguese coast on January 20 last, since which time nothing had been heard of her. Mr Commissioner Rotherey, in giving the decision of the court, said that the *Bywell Castle* was in a good seaworthy condition when she left Alexandria, but she was grievously overladen. In regard to the cause of her loss, unfortunately not a single person out of twenty-two of the crew had been saved, therefore it was impossible for the court to say how she had been lost. He hoped this would be a warning to shipowners.

CHAPTER TWENTY-THREE

In Memoriam

Twenty-three thousand people contributed their sixpences to Reverend Adelbert Anson's memorial fund, which paid for a handsome 16 ft white marble Celtic cross, which was erected in May, 1880, in Woolwich Cemetery where many of the victims lay buried, and a stained glass remembrance window was placed in the parish church of St Mary Magdalene in Woolwich.

Lying alongside the flood barrier at the entrance to Barking Creek is a simple, modern (National Lottery funded), memorial plaque, which includes a tribute to the Creekmouth residents who helped with the rescue. A more colourful, modern memorial is embroidered in a corner of a panel of the magnificent Greenwich Millennium Embroideries at the Greenwich Heritage Centre in the Royal Arsenal.

Although the general public are surprisingly unaware of the tragedy (despite its prominence as the greatest British water-ways disaster), down the years an assortment of memorial songs, poems and books have appeared.

At the time, as well as the vast newspaper coverage, various broadsheets and pamphlets recorded the event. A copy of one of the more ambitious, *The Loss of the Princess Alice* (four pages, eight sides), can be seen at the National Maritime Museum at Greenwich.[1] The cover sports a dramatic, if inaccurate, illustration of the collision, before doing a big job of selling the contents. It promises (in a plethora of typefaces and sizes):

AN AUTHENTIC NARRATIVE by a SURVIVOR, not hitherto published!

HEARTRENDING DETAILS – FACTS NOT MADE PUBLIC –
NOBLE EFFORTS TO SAVE LIFE

SKETCHES BY AN EYE-WITNESS

BEAUTIFUL POEM, specially written on the event.

And so on. The publisher (alas, not named, although the whole-saler is) informs his readers that he felt 'the public at large (and more especially that section of it who are sufferers by the melancholy event of which it is a record) would like to possess such a permanent record'.

The narrative of the survivor (who is too upset to give his name) is introduced in the usual dramatic prose which has 'the river full of drowning people, screaming in anguish, hopelessly struggling and vainly praying for help'. In his previously unpublished narrative the anonymous survivor relates how he had agreed to go on the day out despite having a new job. He describes picking up his girlfriend, Lizzie, and him chaffing her mother 'about getting such a parcel of sandwiches for him to carry', 'chaffing his poor girl too, about her new fashionable hat'.

He tells how they took along Lizzie's little brother, Teddy, who was all wistful because he had had to stay in all the previous week due to not having any boots to wear. 'Poor little chap! God bless his little heart! How pleased he was! We shall never see his little curly head again ...' laments the survivor.

In the water, after the collision, he had his arm around Lizzie while holding little Teddy by the hand. But Lizzie clutched him so hard around the neck he had to let go of the boy 'for she was choking me'. As she saw her little brother floating away she tried to go after him. Later, he saw a woman he thought was Lizzie, clutched her, and held her head above water, 'but it was not my girl'. The girl he had held was saved, he believed, though he did not know her name.

He searched all night and next day but found neither Lizzie nor Teddy. He would rather have gone down as well, he told the publisher/writer, but one thing he meant to do was 'act like a son to their poor widowed mother'. An illustration, captioned 'How They Found My Poor Girl', depicts the body of Lizzie washed up on a shore.

The broadsheet's eight-verse poem, 'In Memorium', is in the

expected, over-wrought, style. But, for once, the passengers are not depicted as dancing about, carefree, in ignorance of their forthcoming fate.

The earliest book on the disaster, albeit small, was *The Wreck of the Princess Alice (Saloon Steamer)*, edited by Edwin Guest, which was published by Weldon's Shilling Library in 1878, the profits all going to the Mansion House Fund. It opens with the statement that there was only one event with which the loss of the *Princess Alice* could be compared; this was the wreck of the *Royal George* in 1782.[2] Nonetheless, Guest goes on to claim that the blackest year in British history was 1854, when 1,401 lives were lost in four great wrecks, which he lists. But these were hardly of the home-based variety, occurring as they did in the Indian Ocean, Newfoundland and on unknown seas.

> This heavy total had already been passed before the autumn equinox of 1878, by the losses in three wrecks: the *Eurydice*, the *Princess Alice* and the German ironclad, *Grosser Kurfest*.

After this assortment of mixed comparisons, Guest's book offers an interesting medley of information, mostly garnered from the newspapers of the time, including survivors' tales, some interesting life-saving information, and the opinion that most of the passengers had been upper working class.

Henry Drew, whom we know for certain was one of the survivors, later wrote a short essay titled 'Thirty Years Ago: A Reminiscence'. In looking back at Henry's 'narrative', as the newspapers liked to call them, I was reminded that, even given expected journalistic exaggeration, these sometimes went off into the realms of pure fancy. As Henry himself angrily pointed out in the *Daily News* of 7 September 1878:

> ... surely the bare facts of my case, without embellishment, are sufficiently appalling to satisfy the public crave for harrowing details; and I feel, as a private individual, I have a right to expect from the press some respect for my feelings in this calamity.

The letter demonstrates that not only was Henry intelligent and educated, but also a man of remarkable control considering he penned it only three days after the disaster. But, alas, it is the original 'narrative' which tends to be repeated now, the one with him afraid that someone would snatch his piece of wood from him and which I recently saw cited as an example of the 'desperate scrimmage'.

Henry's 'Reminiscence' makes it clear that they had been sitting on the saloon deck, (not abaft the paddle box as his newspaper 'narrative' had claimed). The saloon deck, he pointed out, had been the joy of Londoners who had previously only known the open-decked wooden steamers. He recalls that, at the time of the collision, most of the passengers had gone down into the saloons and so were caught 'as rats in a trap' and how, when the *Princess Alice* had heeled over and lay on her side for some moments:

> ... those of us who had stood upon the deck got out of the water
> and walked up her sides helpless, expecting to be blown up by
> the boiler any moment. The boiler had, in fact, gone to the bottom
> through the hole in her side. Gradually she settled down, and we
> went with her inch by inch until we were again struggling in the
> slimy water.

The next morning, Henry and his wife could find the body of only one of his daughters, that of 3-year-old Miriam Ruth. It took five more days to find the other two, 'just in time to be laid to rest with mother and sister'. (Henry's wife having died after rescue.)

One of the most reliable witnesses as to what happened on shore is the *Kent Messenger* reporter, W. T. Vincent, who was at Woolwich from the outset and knew all the local characters and the history of the place. In his *Records of the Woolwich District* he recalls that it had been a warm and muggy evening. He had been weary after 'a troublesome day's work' and was preparing for an early night but, on hearing there had been a collision on the river and that a big steamer had gone down, he cast off fatigue with his slippers and made all haste to reach Roff's Pier, endeavouring to find out more en route. A few had heard 'something' of a wreck on the river, others 'had heard nothing, and laughed at the "old woman's tale". Too soon, the matchless horror was revealed'.

Vincent reprints his first report, '(somewhat shortened) which at early morning light was told in more than 3,000 newspapers, to the people of every civilized land throughout the earth'. He was proud that there was very little from that report representing 'the first impressions derived from such hasty and excited narratives as a reporter could gather among the wailing and turmoil', that he had since wished to amend and credited this to his informants. (He did, however, give the pilot's name as Dicks.)

In his report, he even managed an interview with William Alexander Law, *Princess Alice's* second steward, who had jumped overboard with his girl on his shoulders but 'lost her' in the melee, and described a young woman at the workhouse who said her baby had been washed out of her arms. Also, a man who had reached the north shore with a life-buoy around him who stated that he had jumped overboard, after telling his wife to throw their children in and jump after him, 'but he lost them all'. Some of the editors telegraphed Vincent:

> ... all through the wretched night to 'keep on wiring' and the first train down in the morning brought an army of reporters. One 'daily' alone had nine special correspondents at work in Woolwich for the best part of a week, so eager was the public appetite to feed upon the caviare news.

But what exercised Mr Vincent the most of all in his book was, why Woolwich?

> Were we not sufficiently notorious for deeds of evil – murders, explosions, fires, floods, fogs, wrecks and riots, not to speak of a reputation founded and established on the fiendish trade of war?

His work had, of course, done much to foster that image, his newspaper reports and the *Records of the Woolwich District* and *Warlike Woolwich,* were awash with the aforementioned dreadful deeds and calamities which occurred in that volatile place.

It wasn't until Gavin Thurston's, *The Great Thames Disaster,* that a full-length, well-researched book on the subject appeared. The collision has since been included in several modern-disaster collections and more poems and songs have emerged.

There are also three-dimensional memorials. The National Maritime Museum in Greenwich has a contemporary model of the collision (dated 1878), London Transport Museum in Covent Garden exhibits a modern model of the *Princess Alice* and the disaster features among the displays at the Museum of London Docklands.

As for the real Princess Alice herself, there is a monument to her and her daughter May at the Royal Mausoleum at Frogmore House in Windsor. Countrywide there are several Princess Alice pubs, residential Drives and Ways, a retail park, hospices, a rose, and even a football club. But only some of these are in memory of either the *Princess Alice* disaster or of that particular Princess Alice. A Princess Alice Way and a Princess Alice pub exist in Thamesmead, which overlooks the site of the *Princess Alice* collision, but some others carrying the name are far from the site. Given that three other ladies by the name of Princess Alice occupy quite prominent positions in British royal history it is not surprising that some confusion arises. More so, considering the similarities in their histories, characters and interests. To aid understanding I offer:

Princess Alice, Countess of Athlone (Alice Mary Victoria, Augusta, Pauline) 1883–1981: The daughter of Queen Victoria's youngest son, Prince Leopold, and Princess Helen of Waldech and Pymont. In 1904 she married Prince Alexander of Teck, who later became the Earl of Athlone. From 1924 her husband became successively Governor General of South Africa and then (from 1940–1946) Governor General of Canada. Alice took an interest in the women's sections of the Canadian armed forces and became president of the nursing division of the St John's Ambulance Brigade. She was widowed in 1957 and lived at Kensington Palace until 1981, almost reaching the age of ninety-eight, which made her the longest lived Princess of the Blood Royal and the last surviving grandchild of Queen Victoria.

Princess Alice of Battenberg (Victoria Alice Elizabeth Julia Marie) 1885–1969: The daughter of Princess Victoria (the eldest daughter of our original Princess Alice) and Prince Louis of Battenberg, she was born in Windsor Castle and spent her childhood between Darmstadt, London and Malta, where her naval officer father was occasionally stationed. Although congenitally deaf, with encouragement from her mother, Alice learned to lip-read and to speak English and German. In 1903 she married Prince Andrew of Greece and became Princess Andrew of

Greece. The couple had five children: four girls and one boy. The boy was Prince Philip of Greece and Denmark who later married Britain's Princess Elizabeth.

During the Balkan Wars[3] the Princess acted as a nurse and set up field hospitals for which, in 1913, she was awarded the Royal Red Cross. During the next few years, as various European thrones toppled, the Greek Royal family were forced into exile twice, on the second occasion rescued by a British cruiser, HMS *Calypso*. Her daughters married German princes and her son, Prince Philip, went to stay with his uncles Lord Louis and George Mountbatten (the name Battenberg having been dropped during the Great War). In 1938 she returned to Athens where she worked among the poor. She stayed on during the war, working for the Red Cross, helping organize soup kitchens and shelters for orphaned children and hiding Jewish widow Rachel Cohen and her five children from the Gestapo. For this act she was later honoured by Israel as being Righteous among the Nations.

Alice attended the wedding of her son, Prince Philip, to Britain's future queen and, in 1953, Queen Elizabeth's coronation, to which she wore the two-tone grey, nun-like habit of the order of Greek Orthodox nuns which she had founded. She finally left Greece in 1967 following the Colonel's coup and went to live at Buckingham Palace where she died on 5 December 1969.

Like her grandmother, Princess Alice of Great Britain and Ireland, she clearly had a keen social conscience and sufficient practical sense to put it to good use.

Princess Alice, Duchess of Gloucester (Alice Christabel Montague Douglas Scott) 1901–2044: The third daughter of John Montague Douglas Scott, Scotland's biggest landowner, and former Lady Margaret Bridgeman. She married Prince Henry, Duke of Gloucester, the third son of King George V. During the war the Duchess acquired several senior armed forces, Red Cross and nursing posts and became Colonel in Chief of a dozen regiments and Chancellor of Derby University. From 1945–1947 the couple lived in Canberra, her husband having become Governor General of Australia. In 1994 she moved to Kensington Palace where, on her one hundredth birthday in 2002, she became the oldest person in the history of the royal family. She died, aged 102, in 2004.

As you will notice: more than one of these four princesses was involved with nursing or medical charities; two had husbands who became colonial Governor Generals; two were particularly long-lived; and, of course, all had German connections via marriages of Queen Victoria's offspring.

Obviously, the finest memorials to the *Princess Alice* disaster and those with the most impact and lasting benefit were the swimming pools that sprang up around London. Places like Islington, which had lost so many of its residents in the disaster and whose vestry had been heavily criticized for dragging their heels, now got moving. Indeed, as early as 16 September 1878, a letter from a Mr E. Plummer appeared in the *Islington Gazette* declaring that he had secured a most eligible site in the Blackstock Road for the erection of two very large swimming baths for the inhabitants of Finsbury Park, Highbury and Islington.

> The plans, &c, are now in hand; as soon as they are completed
> I intend calling together a meeting of such gentlemen as take
> an interest in this great subject – swimming, for the purpose
> of forming a committee to carry out the same in a first-class
> manner.

This time the vestry acted quickly. In 1892, fourteen years after the *Princess Alice* disaster, two public baths and washhouses were opened and they were impressive. The first, on Caledonian Road, in the south of the borough, had two swimming baths. One was 90 x 30 ft (first class, 6d) the other 75 x 25 ft (second class, 2d). There were also forty-two private hot and cold baths for men and sixteen for women (first class hot, 6d, cold, 3d; second class hot, 2d, cold, 1d).

The second of the new Islington baths and washhouses were on Hornsey Road (near the Blackstock Road mentioned by Mr Plummer). This one had two swimming baths for men (132 x 40 ft and 100 x 35 ft) and one for women (75 x 25 ft) plus private baths (seventy-four for men, thirty-four for women), laundry facilities and a bonnet room. The Hornsey Road Baths, although under-providing for women who had, after all, been the majority of those drowned that early September evening, was at the time the largest complex of its kind in the United Kingdom.

A third set of public baths and washhouses was opened just off the Essex Road, halfway down the borough, in 1895. Islington had clearly learned its lesson.

CHAPTER TWENTY-FOUR

Déjà Vu

When the railways began to take London pleasure seekers down to coastal resorts, the pleasure gardens, such as Rosherville, suffered. By 1880 the well-known Cremorne and Vauxhall Gardens and the lesser known Highbury Barn in Islington and Surrey Zoological Gardens had all closed. Times changed for Rosherville as well. The fine statues in the Grecian Garden had begun to show their age and where once there had been wild animals there were now performing dogs and goats. The bear had grown weary of his pit and the taunts of onlookers and seized the arm of a gentleman who had incautiously put it through the bars of the cage. Damages granted amounted to a serious £500.

' In 1877 a considerable sum of money had been spent on a new pavilion, dancing platform and steam roundabout, but to no avail. In September, 1881, the owner was declared bankrupt. Rosherville limped on under various other ownerships and in 1901 there was a suggestion that, since the gardens had brought so much local pleasure and income, they might be purchased by Gravesend local authority. But it came to nothing and the gardens fell into decay. In 1930 they were auctioned off as a factory site.

The Crossness sewage pumping station, which had been one of the more attractive sights for the *Princess Alice*'s passengers but added to their misery shortly after, was decommissioned in the 1950s and fell into disrepair. It was rescued in 1987 by the Crossness Engines Trust, set up to oversee the restoration project which is still in progress and is supported by Heritage Lottery and other funds.

The pumping station's interior is made much of not only due to its huge rotative beam engines (named Prince Consort,

Victoria, Albert Edward and Alexandra) but also its spectacular ornamental ironwork. Nikolaus Pevsner, a noted authority on British architecture, referred to Crossness as 'a Victorian cathedral of ironwork'. The building was used extensively for the BBC production of *The Crimson Petal and the White* doubling as both a cosmetic factory and the interior of a London train station.

The Moorish chimneys of Abbey Mills Pumping Station, Crossness's Byzantine twin across the water, were demolished in 1941 for fear that a bomb strike might topple them onto the pumping station. The remains of the buildings are Grade II listed and a modern pumping station now operates nearby. The old Abbey Mills Pumping Station has also been used as a film location, representing Arkham Asylum in the 2005 film *Batman Begins*.

The Beckton Gasworks, described as 'the largest such plant in the world'[1] and which manufactured gas for most of London north of the Thames, closed in 1969 after the discovery of North Sea gas rendered manufactured gas uncompetitive. Spoil heaps from the works, that were reduced and landscaped, became known locally as Beckton Alps. The Beckton Gasworks' site has been used in a number of films. The opening scene of the 1981 James Bond movie *For Your Eyes Only* (in which Bond attempts to gain control of a helicopter operated with remote control by his nemesis Ernst Stavro Blofield) was shot there. The site also doubled for the Vietnamese city of Hue in Stanley Kubrick's *Full Metal Jacket* during which much of the gasworks were selectively demolished before the platoon went in to clear it of the Viet Cong. Virtually no trace of the old gasworks now remains.

The town of Woolwich was in Kent but became part of Greater London in 1889 and is now in the newly created Royal Borough of Greenwich. The Royal Arsenal saw a massive expansion during the Great War but during the Second World War the site was considered too vulnerable to bombing and much of its ordnance production was moved away. Nonetheless, 30,000 people continued to work there during the war and quite a number were killed by bombs, flying bombs and rockets.

But the town was already in decline at the time of the *Princess Alice* disaster due to the closure of the docks and this continued into the twentieth century.[2] The closure of the Sieman's factory in 1968 and the scaling back of the Royal Arsenal, which finally closed in 1994, brought further decay.[3] As the town centre of Woolwich declined, cinemas closed and the main street became home to discount stores and charity shops. The redevelopment of the sprawling Royal Arsenal site, on which were built the new town of Thamesmead, Belmarsh high-security prison and new-build apartments, brought some improvement, as have conversions of listed Royal Arsenal buildings for residential use, a Royal Artillery Museum and the Greenwich Heritage Centre. An Arts Centre has been opened, further improvements are planned and the town was a venue for the shooting events at the recent Olympics.

The Thames Division of the Metropolitan Police is now the Marine Support Unit; it has responsibility for policing the 36 miles of river between Dartford Creek and Hampton Court. They began life in 1798 as the Marine Police Force, founded largely to prevent theft and corruption in the Port of London. When amalgamated with the new Metropolitan Police in 1839 they became the Thames Division and operated out of three riverside police stations: Wapping, Waterloo and Blackwall. Today, the Marine Support Unit fights crime and prevents disorder and drug importation. It also has four specialist teams: terrorism and crime; intelligence; tactical response (which targets crime hotspots, often focussing on other London waterways) and the underwater and confined space search team (which also carries out searches of canals, ponds, lakes and reservoirs). The unit is not a statutory search and rescue organization, but with the growth of leisure activities on the Thames, they do spend a lot of time assisting and advising private boat owners and recovering bodies. Over fifty people a year lose their lives in the Thames, about eighty per cent of these are deaths by suicide and these bodies are retrieved and identified by the Marine Support Unit.

Now and then down the years the terrible story of the *Princess Alice* has been remembered but, considering the scale of the accident, one might have expected it to attract more attention. Perhaps the horrors of two world wars have put it in the shade. However, the internet and the current popularity of family research have sparked off interest in the subject as a number of people discover that their ancestors were either victims or survivors of the disaster. There is even a Facebook meeting place for relatives or those otherwise interested.

David Ellen, who had been researching the subject for some time, discovered that his ancestor was Henry Drew, the unfortunate man who had lost three daughters in the accident after which his survivor wife died. It is heartening to know that Henry did manage to find happiness again by marrying and becoming father to seven more children. One of these, Clara, was to become David's mother.

Quite a number of pub landlords were onboard the fated ship that day and another victim's descendant, Lisa Grace Smith, told me that it was mentioned in her family that the outing 'had been regarded as the publican's equivalent of a beano'. Her ancestor was the brother of Disney Perou, beer seller of the Rising Sun Tavern in Sidney Street, Stepney, and the Brittania Beer House in Mile End. Disney's body was found washed up at Barking Creek three days after the accident. Lisa had traced the family back to a Huguenot couple, Pierre Priou and his wife, who came over to England in 1645. Indeed, Disney's father was a weaver, as was Disney on his marriage to Martha Pratt in 1843. Disney left a long and explicit will, drawn up in 1874. One of its chief beneficiaries was his daughter, Mary Ann, who was left the beer house lock, stock and barrel. She had been and was, the will explained, very useful to him in his business.

Other publicans who perished were Peter H. Moore of the Alfred Tavern in Islington, Alexander Mouflet, licensee at the Metropolitan Meat Market, plus his wife and two children; Thomas Fuller, of the Adam and Eve Tavern at Aldersgate in Kent, and his son, George Hughes of the Control Arms, Porters Green; Caroline Adelaide Dyble of the Rose and Crown off Fleet Street; and licensed victualler Sophia Finnett, of the Queen Victoria, Bromley, who had intended to board another boat but was persuaded onto the *Princess Alice* by four friends 'who were also lost'.[4] It was not reported whether her friends were also licensees or barmen and barwomen, of whom there were several. Edmund Wool, landlord of the Granby Arms in Hampstead, did not go on the outing, but six of his family did and all perished, from his wife, Annie, to their 16-month-old baby, Kate. Publican Edmund Relfe suffered a similar bereavement. He had not been on the day out either, but his three daughters, aged twenty, sixteen and thirteen, had and he was obliged to identify their bodies.

Another publican surfaced during the family research of

Maureen Nicholls. Her mother had told her that her aunt, Mary Ball, had died in a Thames accident between the *Princess Alice* and the *Bible Castle*. 'My first lesson', says Maureen, 'in names being slightly altered over the years.' Mary Ball was in service and, it seems that her mother, Bridget, had not realized that she was missing until her friends came to see her to tell her that Mary had gone out on her day off 'with a licensed victualler who was married'. The pair had chosen to go on the boat trip because they would be less likely to meet people they knew. Being off duty, Mary had worn her hair long and free and, Maureen relates, 'apparently when the boat went down and they were flung into the water Mary's man-friend grabbed her hair and swam for the shore; unfortunately when he reached the shore he found he had rescued the wrong woman'.[5] The man's name had not been passed down with the family story.

Constables Lewis and Briscoe were not the only police victims. Superintendent Aslat from the East India Dock Police and PC Robert Ginn from Cambridge Police also died, as did the two nieces Ginn had brought with him.

The three largest groups of working people onboard were shopkeepers and their assistants, artisans and servants. The servants ranged from butlers to grooms, cooks, ladies' maids and nursemaids, the latter mostly accompanying their employers for the purpose of looking after the children. Carpenters, plumbers, potters, stonemasons, gas fitters and compositors made up most of the artisans although there was occasional confusion over some of their job descriptions. One, noted as a 'tin plate worker', appeared elsewhere as a 'zinc worker'. Also quite numerous were the clerks (clerks to solicitors, publishers, stockbrokers, merchants, the civil service, builders and printers) and transport workers (cabbies, carriers, drovers, coachmen and railwaymen). Among the rest were half a dozen teachers (including a professor of music), a couple of dentists, an accountant, an organist, a shipwright, three hairdressers, three commercial travellers, two coffee-house keepers, a theology student, a brace and belt manufacturer, and one or two more 'gentlemen'.

There has long been a suggestion that Elizabeth Stride, one of Jack the Ripper's victims, had been a passenger on the *Princess Alice* and/or had lost her husband and two children in the accident. But Ripper-ologists have assured me that the claim does not hold water, for various reasons. Swedish-born Elisabeth Gustafsdottor was already a prostitute when she arrived in London where, in 1869, she married John Thomas Stride. The marriage broke down and, later, Elizabeth began telling the *Princess Alice* story, seemingly as a way of reinventing her past. Elizabeth's estranged husband, John Stride, died in a workhouse in 1884.

On 20 May, 1966, the *Wandsworth Borough News*, interviewed the last survivor of the *Princess Alice* disaster, 91-year-old Mrs Mabel Elizabeth Foster. When she was four years old, Mabel (whose maiden-name was Ogbourne) had spent a holiday with her aunt in Sheerness and was returning home on the *Princess Alice*. The aunt perished but, Mabel told the reporter, she still had the telegram which her grandfather had sent to her widowed mother on 4 September 1878. It said simply 'The child is saved'. The experience, said Mabel, had left her with a horror of water.

Ultimately, what actually caused the *Princess Alice* disaster on the Thames all those years ago was the same thing that caused all the other collisions: an overcrowded waterway, lack of discipline by those using it, lack of obedience of the rules of the road and lack of the sophisticated navigational aids we now have. The accidents not only kept happening but they increased and many of them involved Tyne colliers. They collided with each other in the Thames, the English Channel, the North Sea and the River Tyne.[6] Of course, the sheer number of them may account for this prominence.

In recent years large and handsome boats taking in the sights of London from Westminster Pier to Tower Bridge or Greenwich and the Thames Barrier have become very popular, as have smaller craft, often hired by groups of friends or office workers for cruise parties. One such was the *Marchioness*, a 46-ton pleasure craft that, one warm August evening in 1989, carried a group of 130 friends celebrating the twenty-sixth birthday of one of their party, Antonio de Vasconcellos. Some knew each other from their time at Cambridge University, others through their work in the fashion industry. Without warning, as the craft neared Cannon Street Railway Bridge, the *Marchioness* was rammed by a 1,880-ton dredger, the *Bowbelle*. It cut through the side of the small pleasure craft, which rolled over and quickly filled with water as it was pushed under. Complete immersion was estimated to have taken about thirty seconds. The majority of the seventy-four survivors had been on the upper decks. Twenty-four were recovered from the sunken hull.

Although the Thames was, by then, a much less-frequented highway than it had been at the time of the *Princess Alice* sinking, and this particular accident occurred much further up river and later at night, there were some echoes down the years: the rapid sinking of the smaller vessel; accusations on both sides of a failure to keep proper lookout; inebriation of one of the captains (it was found that the *Bowbelle*'s captain had sunk five to six pints of lager that afternoon); the loss of the captains of both sunken boats; and some victims being trapped in the lower saloons. And there was a similar aftermath, the larger vessel itself being later lost when the *Bowbelle* split in two and sunk off Madeira in March 1996. Another similarity was the lack of river-safety warning bells, as was noted by *The Times* of 24 March 2001. They reported that, back in 1983, after a series of collisions on the Thames, a Department of Transport official had warned that it was 'not a case of "IF" a serious accident occurs but "WHEN"'.

One marked difference between the *Princess Alice* and the *Marchioness* was the type of passenger. Those on the *Princess Alice* had been mostly mixed-age family groups and were largely upper working class, whilst those on the *Marchioness* were in their twenties, educated, artistic and professional, or aspiring to be. Some of the survivors felt that this fact lessened the sympathy felt for them, that it made them appear wealthy, privileged and self-indulgent, which they were not. However, the confidence their education had afforded them may well have helped them and their parents fight their long battle to win a public inquiry into the accident which was eventually held in 2000.

The subsequent report made several recommendations for the improvement of river safety and led to a multi-agency examination of the question. A major result of the inquiry was the setting up of four permanently manned lifeboat stations on the Thames at Gravesend, Tower Pier, Chiswick Pier and Teddington. These are capable of launching a boat within one minute of being alerted and reaching any point on the river between Canvey Island in the Thames Estuary and Teddington up river within fifteen minutes. During their first year of service (2002) they were called out 850 times.

There is a memorial plaque to the victims of the *Marchioness* disaster in the nave of Southwark Cathedral, not far from the scene of the accident. Let's hope there is no longer any need for memorials to pleasure boat disasters on the Thames.

South London

Identified

Aldridge,	Ann, 16
	Eliza, 32
Anckhorn,	Ellen, 47
	John, 49
Andrews,	Frances, 31
	William, 27
Aylen,	Frank
Bailey,	George, 25
	John, 25
Baker,	Mrs
	Ben Frederick
Basten,	Frederick
	Mary Ann
Bridger,	William, 40
Botrill,	Thomas
	William
Butcher,	Henry, 27
Brady,	Lucy
Butt,	Clement
Calton,	Harriet, 20
Carter,	Frederick
	Sarah
Chabot,	Ernest
	Harold
	Josephine, 40
Childs,	William
Chittlebury,	George
Clymick,	John
Crawford,	Jane,
	her mother, brother
	and two children
Dormer,	Emma
	Henry
Drake,	Mary Jane
	Cutler, 20
Durrant,	Ethel
Eldridge,	George
Elliott,	Mary Ann
	William
Fricker,	Flora, 3
Forsdyke,	Mrs
	Edmund
	Eliza
	Sydney
Frost,	Jane Amelia, 46
	Robert, 48
Furneaux,	Emily, 21
	Mary Drew, 60

Freeman,	Mr
Gissing,	Harry
Green,	Sarah
Greenwood,	George
	Joseph
	Sarah
Greenfield,	Rebecca and
	infant daughter
Grimsay,	Ellen
Gyde,	Mrs
	Clara Louisa, 1½
Haggar,	Hannah
Hallett,	Maria
Hand,	Dinah
	Thomas
Harris,	Walter
Hawkins,	Henry
Head,	Alfred
	Alice
Hilson,	Mary Ann
Hollis,	Mary
Hollingsworth,	Elizabeth
	George
	Maud
Hoskins,	Frances
	Henry
Howard,	George
Hughes,	Henry
Hunt,	Edith
Hurwood,	Rose Marie
Hutley,	Eliza
Ivory,	James, 60
	Mary Ann, 55
Jardine,	Charles, 48
Jones,	Elizabeth
	Florence
	Martha
Kempe,	Mr
King,	Mrs
	Edward, 6 months
	Francis
Larchin,	Arnold
	Harriet
Lambert,	Kate
	Lucy
	W.J.
Larner,	Samuel
Leaver,	Albert, 15
	Ben, 18
	Ruth, 14
Lee,	Amy
Lewis,	Caroline

Lynn,	Amelia	Ward,	Louisa, 16
Mansfield,	Alice	Wark,	Mrs, 38
	Jane		John
Marks,	Ebeneezer		William
	Esther	White,	Mrs
	Frank		Aaron, 50
	John		Sarah, 45
Martin,	Frederick	Weightman,	Emily, 14
May,	Fanny	Whiten,	George
M'Geary,	Joseph, 54		Mary
Morrison,	Emily, 24	Wickens,	Harry
	Evelyn, 15		Rebecca
Muncey,	Anna		
	Blanche	*Missing*	
Nares,	Charlotte		
Orr,	Alfred	Bandy,	Maria
Page,	Emily	Greenfield,	Mr
	Frederick	Hagger,	Mrs
	Thomas		and daughter
Palmer,	David	Hallett,	Mr
Pearson,	Susan, 22	Hollingshead,	Mr, Mrs and two
Pickerell,	Anne		children
	George	Hunt,	Mr, Mrs and one
	Jane		daughter
Potter,	Emma, 42	Jones,	Mr, Mrs and two
Ralph,	Kate		children
	Mary Ann	Jones,	Mr
	Sarah		Mrs
Randall,	Mary		Alice, 6
Sabine,	Alfred	Jenkins,	James
	Mrs	Marson,	Miss, 56
	and four children	Pearson,	Mrs
Sedgwick,	Joseph, 43	Reuter,	Elizabeth
Shand,	Jane	Russell,	Herbert, 18
Sims,	Martha	Stubbings,	Anne, 39
Slocombe,	Ann		William, 41
	William, 74	Welby,	William, 18
Smith,	Kate		
	Lilian	**Greenwich, Woolwich,**	
	Maria	**Plumstead, etc.**	
Spencer,	Arthur		
Stahr,	Victor, 22	*Identified*	
Standish,	John		
	Susannah	Barker,	Mary
Steele,	Grace, 12	Best,	Mary Ann
	Hannah	Bing,	Ann
	Louisa, 27	Boncey,	Frederick
	Sophia	Burton,	James, 9
Summers,	Annie, 29		and two other
	Florence, 5		children
	Sydney, 13 months		James, 38
Swan,	Anne		Maria
	James	Catlin,	Ada, 3
	Mary Elizabeth		Ann
Taylor,	John		Thomas, 3 months
Wallis,	Alice	Collis,	Nellie
	Anne		Theresa, 27
	Jane	Constable,	Caroline, 44

Coombes, Mary Ann, 67
Crofts, Amelia
Charles
Dunkley, Valentine
Ferguson, Jane
Grinstead, John
William
Halliday, George
Harrison, John
Hawkes, Eugenie
Hawkins, Henry
Hock, Mr
Holliday, John
Hooper, Eliza, 63
Jobling, Mrs Ralph
Thomas
King, Alfred, 19
Edward
Elizabeth
Rowley, Annie, 14
Walter, W., 12
Sans, Nelly Louisa
Searle, Mary Ann, 24
Smith, Hannah
Summers, Grace
Turner, Emily, 18
Towse, Barnard, 14 months
Edgar, 13
Emily, 32
Frederick
Ward, Louisa
Warmy, Ellen
Watson, Frederick
Wearing, Helen
Westhall, James
Whomes, Frederick

Missing

Collis, Willie, 18 months
King, Fanny
and son
Saury, Mr, 40
and son
Smith, Maria, 25
and infant
Vanderbilt, Mrs

East London

Identified

Alesbury, Alfred
Edith, 5 months
Eliza, 58
Elizabeth, 21
Jaber, 2
Jessie, 9

Louisa, 5
Allan, Catherine
George
Aslet, Mr W,
Francis
Beadle, Francis
Belcher, Harriet
Henry
Bilton, James
Bishop, William
Blackburn, Jessie
Louise
Bledger, Thomas
Bridges, Jane
Burman, Philip,
Charlotte
and three children
Butler, Alfred, 28
Elizabeth
Joseph, 48
Clifton, Henry
Cole, Charles
Conway, Mr F
Crocker, Emily Jane
Lewis
Matilda
Crouch, Flora
Florence
Frank
Frederick
Davis, Thomas
Mrs
and four children
Everest, Robert,
Mrs
and two children
Finnett, Florence
Sophy
Fisher, W.A.
Freeman, Sarah
brother
and two children
Green, Jane, 17
Hallett, George
Hammond, Alice
Frederick
Harden, Mrs
Harris, Jane, 15
Kate, 7
Sarah, 44
Sarah Alice 17
Howlett, Bessie, 25
Walter
Huddle, Eliza
Ernest
George
George Michael
Henry

Johnson,	Amelia, 29
	William, 38
Kidston,	Mrs Filmer
King,	Rosina
Lewis,	Alfred
	Mary Ann
Magiff,	William
Meeks,	Catherine
M'Geary,	Caroline
Mulhern,	Catherine
	James
	Margaret
Newman,	Elizabeth, 40
Northey,	John
Penney,	Katherine
Perou,	Disney, 51
Piddell,	Annie
	George
Piper,	Flora
Rackley,	Harriet, 24
Richardson,	Mr J
	William, 11
Richmond,	George
Riddell,	Arthur, 12
	Edward, 18
Roberts,	Mrs
	Emma
Savage,	Thomas
Scurr,	Michael
Sinclair,	Jane
	Mary Jane
Skelton,	George
Skillington,	William
Sutton,	William, 56
Velcher,	Henry
	and two children
Watson,	Ann
	Emily Mary
Wyatt,	Frederick
	Susan

Missing

Allan,	Mrs
Billing,	Mrs
	and child
Crouch,	Mr
Grinstead,	Jane
Hallett,	Mrs
Jackson,	Hannah
King,	Jane, 40
Macgiff,	Thomas
	Mitchel
Newman,	Charles
Potter,	William, 33
Sutton,	Mrs
Skelton,	Mrs
Taylor,	Eliza

North London

Identified

Armstead,	John, 21
Baker,	Emma Jane
	William
Ball,	Emma, 58
Bange,	Jane
Bardens,	Elizabeth, 63
Briscoe,	Cornelius
	Jane, 23
	Sarah, 5
Brodrib,	Eliza, 52
	John, 18
	and two children
Bull,	Emma
Burns,	Hugh
Campbell	Emma
	W.
Cattermole,	Julia
Chapman,	Elizabeth
Cobham,	Craven Proctor
	Elizabeth
	Mildred
Cochren,	H.J.
Copping,	Maria
Dillon,	Charles Rowe
	Sarah
Donald,	Hannah
Drew,	Elizabeth
	Mary Ann
	Miriam
Ellis,	Joseph
	Mary
Emmett,	James
Farnum,	Ada
Finney,	Gertrude
Flatman,	Phyllis
Fricker,	Sarah
Garrard,	George
Ginn,	R. William
Golding,	Charlotte
Gristwood,	Annie
Gurr,	Harriet, 40
Hambury,	Ella, 20
Harrison,	William, 24
Hennessy,	Ross
Hill,	William
Hollings,	Mary Ann
Hughes,	George
Hunt,	Mrs
	Edgar
	Eliza
	Ethel
	Sarah Jane
Ingram,	George

Ledamun,   James   Emmett,   Mary Jane, 36
               Leonard   Hughes,   Mrs
               Mary Ann   Turner,   Charlotte
Lowry,   Samuel
Maynan,   Eliza   ## West and north west London
Moore,   Edward
               Mrs   ## *Identified*
               and two children
Muddock,   Harry   Barnes,   Norman
               Henry   Bishop,   Mary
               Ross   Walter
Notman,   John, 50   Bishopp,   Minnette, 26
               Kate, 21   Besley,   Eliza
Nunn,   Hannah   Bridgeman,   Lucy, 25
Oakley,   Charlotte   William, 35
               George   Brown,   Mrs
Phillips,   Emily, 37   Channel,   Charles
Pitt   S.   Childs,   Alice, 6
               W.L.   George, 3
Rolt,   Kezia   Codling,   William
               Sarah   Coulman,   James
Rouse,   Alfred   Hayes,   Mrs
               Kate   Henderson,   Harry, 26
               Sarah   Louisa, 23
Scholz,   Maria   Hill,   Mrs
Stubbins,   Annie   George
               W. George   Hollingsworth, F.H.
Teesdale,   Miss   Howard,   George
               Mrs   Lambourne,   Thomas
               Charles, 24   Leverton,   Mary Ann, 40
Thompson,   Kate   Lee,   Eliza
Warburton,   Rosa, 23   Legg,   Edith
Ward,   Louisa   Little,   Egmontina 14
Watson,   Albert   William
               Alfred   Loder,   Maria
Watts,   Bess   Marsh,   Eustace
               George   Susan
               William   Marshall,   Annie
Wayman,   Alfred, 1½   May,   Ellen
               Drusilla, 16   Harry
               Elizabeth, 14   Michael
               Harriet, 26   Minnie
Wheatley,   Augusta   Mekins,   Robert
White,   Fanny, 15   Milsom,   Florence
               Mary, 13   Murphy,   Caroline
               Thomas   Harriet
Wool,   Annie, 42   Ridout,   Emily
               Annie Bird, 14   Ryall,   T. Chapman
               Emily, 5   Ryalls,   Thomas
               Kate, 16 months   Russell,   Martha
               Lydia, 13   Silvester,   Lucy
               Minnie, 11   Rosa
Worsfold,   Charles   Small,   Alice
               Charlotte   Smith,   Edwin
                                                    Frances
Missing   and child
                                                    Prudence
Briscoe,   Benjamin, 1½   Somerville,   Elizabeth, 25

Teesdale,	Elizabeth, 7
	Joseph
Tidy,	Sarah
Usherwood,	Harriet
	Mary Ann
Wakeham,	Fanny
Weaver,	Jane
White,	Ann
Whittington,	Louisa, 13
	Susan, 9
Wilkins,	Maria
	Robert
Wilson,	Betsey, 43
	John, 43
Wood,	Robert

Missing

Ackroyd,	Frank, 29
Beaver,	Mrs, 64
Clynch,	John, 45
Cocks,	Mrs, 50
Dawes,	Susan, 55
Flatman,	Philip
Ingram,	Eliza
Little,	William
Milsom,	Mr
	Mrs
	and two children
Sims,	Winifred
Smith	Mr A.J.
Wilson,	Edward
	Florence
	Samuel

Central London

Identified

Aldridge,	Ann, 65
	William, 35
Ball,	Mary, 26
Beecher,	William, 43
Bird,	Elizabeth
Boddington,	Elizabeth
Bolam,	Mary Ann
Bryant,	Susan
Denham,	Christopher
Dyble,	Caroline
Fricker,	Sarah
Frith,	Mrs
Fuller,	Thomas
George,	Mary Ann
Gulliver,	Mrs
	Matilda
Haist,	Eliza
	Eleanor
	Matilda
	William

Harris,	Elizabeth
Harrison,	Arthur, 20
	Brother, 12
Hayes,	Mrs
Holmes,	Sarah Ann
Hunt,	Frederick
Jenkins,	James
Jones,	Thomas
King,	Mary
Kitt,	John
	Rachel
Law,	Jane
Mouflet,	Alexandre
	Annie
	Louise
	Nancy
Neale,	Mary Ann
Quick,	Lucy
Rich,	Eliza
Roberts,	George
Ropkins,	Elizabeth, 72
Senior,	Alice
Sewell,	Elizabeth
Smith,	Christina
Stoneman,	Emma
Thurgood,	Mr
	Mrs Eliza
	Eliza, 2
	and sister
	Richard
Vivash,	Emma
Wakley,	Maria
Waddilove,	Zillah
Warren,	Harriet
Webb,	George,10
Willemot,	Ellen, 40

Missing

Hogwood,	Edward, 74
Smith,	Caroline, 62

Suburban and Provincial

Identified

Bell,	Harold, Barnet
	W.E., Barnet
	Walter, Barnet
Boncey,	Arthur, Chertsey
Bools,	Elizabeth, Sheerness
Creed,	William, Gravesend
Cully,	Jane, Croydon
Dewell,	Sarah, Surbiton
Harrison,	Arthur, York
Hosken,	Emma, Balham
	James, Balham
	Jessie, Balham

Huddart,	James, Hampton	*Missing*	
Ledger,	Mary, Chobham		
	Thomas, Chobham	Bowles,	Elizabeth, Sheerness
Marshall,	Lawrence,	Leech,	Mrs
	Birmingham		and three children,
Martin,	Mrs, Huntingdon		Hertfordshire
Welch,	Richard, Tonbridge	Room,	Elizabeth, 44,
			Birmingham

Note for Family Historians

The above list, which divides victims according to the areas in which they lived, is adapted from the 'Dead and Missing' list in Edwin Guest's 1878 book, *The Wreck of the Princess Alice.*

Guest's list includes the victims' addresses and, in some cases, gives their employment. Although he says 'a portion of those marked missing were identified by clothing or relics after being buried as unknown', I found only one or two of these in the 'List of bodies buried unknown but later identified' at the London Metropolitan Archives *(COR/PA/23-30)* whilst a good number of those in his identified section do appear in this. The London Metropolitan Archives also has a long list of the names, ages, relationships and occupations of the deceased (COR/PA/1) and a list of the 130 saved (COR/PA/30).

However, Colin Alsbury, a descendent of seven victims of that name, has compiled a list of 'Passengers, crew and others connected to the disaster' which is available online: www.alsbury.co.uk/princessalice/alice0.htm. It includes variant and erroneous name spellings (pointing out that these can vary greatly in contemporary sources), probable places of death registration, whether the individuals were dead/missing/saved/witness/possible victims or unknown/unclaimed, but not their addresses. Newspapers, of course, are another valuable source.

Endnotes

Chapter One

1. Henry VIII established his Royal Dockyard at Woolwich in 1512 for the purpose of building the *Great Harry*, the flagship of his new Royal Navy. In 1694, it was joined by the Royal Laboratory which developed into the Woolwich Arsenal, the source of many inventions as well as lethal accidents and explosions. In 1721, the Royal Military Academy brought the military to the town but, in 1869, the dockyard closed causing much distress and unemployment in the area.
2. The site's original owner was Jeremiah Rosher – hence the name. He sold it in 1837 to George Jones, who planted flowers, shrubs and trees, stocked the gardens with wild animals and exotic birds and opened it as the Kent Botanical and Zoological Gardens. But the public wanted more and he gradually added various amusements; the gardens became even prettier and the refreshment room expanded into a Baronial Hall. The fame of the pleasure gardens grew, resulting in the emergence of Rosherville waltzes, gallops and songs such as *Rose of Rosherville* by William Wilson.
3. Rosherville is mentioned in: *The Newcomes* by William Makepeace Thackeray; Francis Burnand and Arthur Sullivan's comic opera *Cox and Box*; Gilbert and Sullivan's comic opera *The Sorcerer* ('Hate me! I spent the day at ROSHERVILLE!'); P. G. Wodehouse's first Jeeves' story; and E. Nesbit's *The Story of the Amulet*, which describes Rosherville as a 'place to spend a happy day'.
4. *The Great Thames Disaster*, p.38 & *The Times*, 28 September 1878.
5. W. T. Vincent, *Records of Woolwich District*, p.76.

Chapter Two

1. A 'spritsail' barge had a fore and aft sail extended by a diagonal spar.
2. *The Times*, 10 September 1878.
3. Linda Rhodes and Kathryn Abnett, *Foul Deeds and Suspicious Deaths in Barking, East Dagenham and Chadwell Heath*, p.92; *Standard*, 6 September 1878.
4. Ibid., p.93.
5. *The Times*, 9 September 1878.
6. *The Times*, 6 September 1878.
7. Many East Enders traditionally spent their holidays picking beer hops in Kent.
8. *The Times*, 5 September 1878.
9. The *Metis* was a pleasure steamer, the *Wentworth* a Tyne collier, and the collision also occurred on a September evening.

Chapter Three

1. *Standard*, 5 September 1878.
2. *The Times*, 5 September 1878.
3. Ibid.
4. *Standard*, 6 September 1878.
5. *Morning Post*, 5 September 1878.
6. *Standard*, 5 September 1878.
7. Gavin Thurston, *The Great Thames Disaster*, p.55.
8. *The Times*, 5 September 1878.

Chapter Four

1. *Standard,* 6 September 1878.
2. Lewis's letter to Carttar.
3. 'Holland' was a linen fabric, unbleached or dyed brown.
4. *The Times,* 10 September 1878.
5. *The Times,* 5 September 1878.
6. Ibid.
7. *Standard,* 5 September 1878.

Chapter Five

1. *Standard,* 6 September 1878.
2. Ibid.
3. *Standard* and *The Times,* 6 September 1878.
   With regard to the naked bodies it had been remarked that, should you have committed a murder and wished to get rid of the body, this was a good time and place to do it. An idea which I confess I made use of in my historical crime novel, *Dead Born* (Hale, 2001) which I based around the *Princess Alice* disaster.
4. *Standard,* 7 September 1878.
5. *The Times,* 7 September 1878.
6. *The Times,* 7 September 1878, and the *Standard,* 6 September 1878.
7. *Standard,* 6 September 1878.
8. *The Times,* 7 September 1878.

Chapter Six

1. Coroners' Records COR/PA13,14,15, 22 and *The Times* 5 and 9 October 1878.
2. *The Times,* 5 September 1878 and Gavin Thurston, *The Great Thames Disaster,* p.49.
3. *Morning Post,* 7 September 1878.
4. *Daily News,* 7 September 1878.
5. *Standard,* 9 September 1878.
6. *The Times,* 5 September 1878.
7. Famous French tight-rope walker.
8. *The Times,* 6 September 1878.
9. *The Times,* 7 September 1878.
10. *The Times,* 6 September 1878.
11. *Daily News,* 5 September 1878.
12. *Ipswich Journal,* 10 September 1878.
13. *The Times,* 6 September 1878.
14. *Morning Post,* 7 September 1878.
15. *Daily News,* 7 September 1878.
16. Ibid.

Chapter Seven

1. *Standard,* 9 September 1878.
2. Chief Steward, Mr Boncey, had been on board, as his nephew had predicted.
3. *Standard,* 9 September 1878.
4. *Broadside Ballads,* The National Library of Scotland. digital.nls.uk/broadsides/broadside.cfm/id/14981
5. As quoted in 'Disaster', an article by Jon Josling in the *Warren* magazine, summer 1974.
6. *The Times,* 9 September 1878.

Chapter Eight
1. A German military spiked helmet.
2. *The Times*, 10 September 1878.
3. Ibid.
4. *Standard*, 10 September 1878.
5. *The Times*, 9 September 1878.
6. *The Times*, 10 September 1878.
7. *The Times*, 10 September 1878 and Coroners' Records COR/PA.
8. *Standard*, 10 September 1878.
9. Ibid.
10. Ibid.
11. *The Times*, 10 September 1878.

Chapter Nine
1. *The Times*, 12 September and 17 September 1878.
2. Cowcross Street was actually just over the Clerkenwell/City of London border.
3. *Islington Gazette*, 11 September 1878.
4. *Islington Gazette*, 6 September 1878.
5. During the Siege of Paris, 1870, and the city's capitulation (to the Prussians) in 1871.
6. *The Times*, 17 September 1878.
7. Gerard Noel, *Princess Alice: Queen Victoria's Forgotten Daughter*.

Chapter Ten
1. *The Times*, 7 September 1878.
2. *The Times*, 11 September 1878.
3. Ibid.
4. The HMS *Eurydice* was a very fast, 26-gun Royal Navy Corvette, refitted in 1877 as a seagoing training ship. The sinking is considered to be one of Britain's worst peacetime naval disasters and is commemorated in the poem by Gerald Manley Hopkins, 'The Loss of the Eurydice'.
5. *Islington Gazette*, 4 September 1878.
6. 'Rinking' is roller-skating at specially built rinks.
7. *The Wreck of the Princess Alice* (ed.) Edwin Guest, pp.110–11.
8. Captain Matthew Webb swam from Dover to Calais in twenty-one and three quarter hours on 24–5 August 1875. He was drowned in 1883 while attempting to swim the Niagara Falls.
9. Quoted in *The Wreck of the Princess Alice*, p.109.
10. 'Hartshorn' are shavings from the horn of the red deer.
11. The Public Baths & Washhouses Act, 1846, allowed local parishes to raise money to provide public baths and washhouses where the labouring classes could cleanse themselves and their clothing. The act was amended in May 1878, to allow for the construction of covered swimming pools.

Chapter Eleven
1. *The Times*, 11 September 1878 (that day's inquest proceedings).
2. *The Times*, 12 September 1878.
3. *The Times*, 14 September 1878.
4. *The Times*, 13 September 1878.
5. 'Marcella' is a type of cotton or linen fabric in a twill weave. 'Pelisse' is a young child's overcoat.
6. *The Times*, 13 September 1878.

Chapter Twelve

1. *The Times*, 17 September 1878 and Coroners' Records COR/PA 3,4 & 22.
2. (Long's evidence and his examination): Ibid.
3. (Eyers' evidence and his examination): *The Times*, 18 September 1878 and Coroners' Records COR/PA 5 & 22
4. Ibid.
5. (Wilkinson's evidence and his examination): Ibid.
6. Ibid.
7. (Longhurst's evidence and his examination) Ibid.
8. *The Times*, 20 September 1878 and Coroners' Records COR/PA 7 & 22.

Chapter Thirteen

1. *The Times*, 10 and 19 September 1878; *Standard*, 9 September 1878 and Coroners' Records COR/PA 6 & 22.
2. *The Times*, 20 September 1878.
3. *The Times*, 26 September 1878.
4. *The Times*, 19 September 1878.
5. *The Times*, 21 September 1878.
6. *Standard* and *The Times*, 21 September 1878.
7. *The Times*, 20 September 1878.
8. Ibid.
9. Ibid.
10. *The Times*, 19 September 1878.
11. Ibid.
12. *The Times*, 20 September 1878.
13. *The Times*, 19 September 1878.
14. Ibid.
15. Ibid.
16. *The Times*, 20 September 1878.
17. Ibid.
18. *The Times*, 19 September 1878.
19. Ibid.
20. *The Times*, 21 September 1878.

Chapter Fourteen

1. *The Times*, 20 September 1878.
2. Ibid.
3. Ibid.
4. Ibid.
5. A printed version with a black border can be found in the Coroners' Records COR/PA/44.
6. *Islington Gazette*, 23 September 1878.

Chapter Fifteen

1. *The Times*, 27 September 1878.
2. Ibid.
3. Ibid.
4. *Pall Mall Gazette*, 26 September 1878.
5. (Captain Harrison's evidence and examination): *The Times*, 7 and 9 October 1878; *Pall Mall Gazette*, 26 September 1878 and Coroners' Records COR/PA/10 & 22.
6. (Dix's evidence and examination): *The Times*, 27 and 28 September 1878.
   The Goodwin Sands were a ten-mile long sandbank in the English Channel,

notorious as a danger to ships and thus the site of many a wreck. Its perils were mentioned by William Shakespeare in *The Merchant of Venice* as being 'very dangerous, flat and fatal, where the carcases of many a tall ship lie buried' and it has since featured in Herman Melville's *Moby-Dick* and many other works of fiction, even the James Bond novel, *Moonraker*.

7. (Brankston's evidence and examination): *The Times*, 28 September 1878 and Coroners' Records COR/PA/11 & 22.
8. (Dix's recall and examination): Ibid.

Chapter Sixteen
1. (Purcell's evidence and examination): *The Times*, 4 October 1878 and Coroners' Records COR/PA/13 & 22.
2. (Harris's evidence): Ibid.
3. Ibid.
4. Ibid.
5. *The Times*, 4 October 1878 and Coroners' Records COR/PA/ 13 & 22.
6. *The Times*, 5 October 1878 and Coroners' Records COR/PA/14 & 22.
7. *The Times*, 4 October 1878.
8. A 'dumb barge' is a long, flat-bottomed barge for carrying cargo, in tow of a tug.
9. (Campfield's evidence and examination): *The Times*, 5 October 1878 and Coroners' Records COR/PA/14 & 22.
10. (Smith's evidence and examination): *The Times*, 9 October 1878 and Coroners' Records COR/PA/15 & 22.
11. A 'jibbon' is a boom on which the jib (a triangular sail stretched in front of the foremast of the ship) is spread.

Chapter Seventeen
1. The *Grosser Kurfürst* was a German Navy ironclad that collided with the *König Wilhelm* on 31 May 1878, whilst they were sailing in formation in the Strait of Dover, with the loss of 284 lives. *The Times* could not resist reporting that it had happened in broad daylight and on dead smooth water and adding that it could not have happened to British naval ships due to their different system of fleet sailing. (Apparently, the Germans ships were sailing too close together.)
2. *The Times*, 2 October 1878, published the inaugural addresses of each of the schools attached to the London Metropolitan Hospitals (which did not include St Bartholomew's or Guys).
3. *The Times*, 28 September 1878.
4. Sir Joseph William Bazelgette, the engineer who had designed and constructed London's drainage system.
5. He explained that Coventry's daily supply of sewage amounted to 2,000,000 gallons but was rendered especially foul by the dye works for which the city had long been famous. However, for the last three years the sewage had been purified by a chemical process costing £2,000 annually and the corporation was 'well satisfied with its sanitary success' (*The Times*, 5 October 1878).
6. *The Times*, 24 October 1878.
7. *The Times*, 23 November 1878.

Chapter Eighteen
1. *The Times*, 19 October 1878.
2. Ibid.
3. Ibid.

4. Ibid.
5. *The Times*, 30 October 1878 and Gavin Thurston, *The Great Thames Disaster*, p.122.
6. (Carttar's summing up): *The Times*, 14 November 1878.
7. Unidentified press cutting in Coroners' Records COR/PA/45 and Gavin Thurston, *The Great Thames Disaster*, p.147.
8. *The Times*, 14 November 1878.
9. *The Times*, 15 November 1878.
10. Woolwich and several other dockyards both in London and the provinces were guarded by the Metropolitan Police.
11. Charlton Pier is a couple of miles upriver from Woolwich.
12. The topgallant is above the topmast and topsail and below the Royal mast.
13. *The Times*, 28 November 1878.

Chapter Nineteen
1. A 'painter' is a rope for fastening a boat.
2. *The Times*, 24 October 1878.
3. Ibid.
4. *The Times*, 25 October 1878.
5. Possibly referring to the wooden stringer suggested by Captain Samuel Pether as extra protection.
6. Board of Trade Investigation into the Wreck of the *Princess Alice*: Coroners' Records COR/PA/34; *The Times*, 29 October 1878 and Gavin Thurston, *The Great Thames Disaster* p.121.
7. *The Engineer*, 15 November 1878.
8. Board of Trade Investigation into the Wreck of the *Princess Alice*; Coroners' Records COR/PA/34: *The Times*, 29 October 1878 and Gavin Thurston, *The Great Thames Disaster*, pp.156–7.
9. *The Times*, 11 November 1878.
10. Ibid.
11. *The Times*, 14 December 1878.

Chapter Twenty
1. Thames Police: History of the *Princess Alice* Disaster, 'Thames Divison Officer on Board' (5): www.thamespolicemuseum.org.uk/h_alice_5.html.
2. The Great Indian Famine of 1877–8 affected the south and south west of the subcontinent and spread northwards in its second year. Estimates of total famine-related deaths varied from 5.5 million to 8.2 million.
3. *The Times*, 15 October 1878.
4. The shorthand writers.
5. As quoted by Gavin Thurston, *The Great Thames Disaster*, p.171.
6. *Daily News*, 15 August 1879.
7. In fact, artist and inventor, Mr Robert Cocking, was killed in July 1837, after plummeting to the ground from a height of around 8,000 ft after jumping from a balloon with only his homemade parachute to support him. A surgeon opined that it had not been the speed that had killed Mr Cocking. Indeed, people had travelled on the railroad at 60 miles an hour without loss of life. It was the impact. The incident caused a sensation, not least because the landlord of the Tiger's Head, the scene of the inquest, had exhibited Cocker's body and parachute at sixpence a head. Young Carttar voiced his strong disapproval and warned anyone else who might contemplate anything similar.
8. One of Bedford Pim's more spectacular exploits was a twenty-eight-day trek across the ice to rescue the crew of HMS *Investigator* which had been

ice-bound for three years in a bay just off the Bering Strait. He displayed similar determination in his attempts to become an MP having stood twice, and failed, for Totnes, before finally making it in 1874, as MP for more the navy-friendly Greenwich.

Chapter Twenty-One

1. The ss *Schiller* was an ocean-going passenger liner which plied between Hamburg and New York until 7 May 1875, when, in a heavy fog, she hit the Retarrier Ledges off the Isles of Scilly and sank with the loss of 335 lives.
2. The emigrant passenger ship the ss *Deutschland* was en route from Bremerhaven to New York via Southampton when, on 5 December 1875, she ran aground on the Kentish Knock, a shoal off Harwich. Seventy-eight people died. Due to the delay in assistance from other vessels and accusations of negligence and looting, the British Board of Trade held an inquiry, unusual in the case of a foreign-registered vessel wrecked outside the 3-mile limit. The German authorities did not investigate.
3. *The Times,* 12 December 1878 and Gavin Thurston, *The Great Thames Disaster,* p.162.
4. Gerard Noel, *Princess Alice: Queen Victoria's Forgotten Daughter,* p.237.
5. *The Times,* 19 November 1878.
6. Not to be confused with Sir Edward Jenner who pioneered vaccination. Sir William Jenner established the difference between typhus and typhoid and tended to both Prince Albert and the Prince of Wales when they became ill with typhoid. His brother was the founder of Jenners, the famous Edinburgh drapers.
7. Queen Victoria's daughters were not sent penniless to their new homes overseas in marriage, they were given dowries and annuities. Parliament awarded Princess Alice a dowry of £30,000 and an annuity of £6,000, about which Prince Albert commented, 'she will not be able to do great things with that'.
8. Gerard Noel, *Princess Alice: Queen Victoria's Forgotten Daughter,* p.240.
9. *Sussex Advertiser,* 17 December 1878.
10. *The Times,* 12 December 1878.
11. Gerard Noel (as above), p.11.
12. *The Times,* 16 July 1879 and Gavin Thurston *The Great Thames Disaster,* p.163.
13. Jonathan Schneer, *The Thames: England's River,* p.159 and note 36, Chapter 7.

Chapter Twenty-Two

1. *The Times,* 3 September 1879.
2. A 'billyboy' is a two-masted vessel resembling an old Dutch cargo boat. Coming mostly from Goole, they were also known as Humber keels.
3. Board of Trade Enquiry into the Navigation of the River Thames & Minutes of Evidence: The National Archives MT9/160 M1925/79.
4. *The Times,* 3 September 1879.
5. Ibid.
6. On 17 November 1879, the *Canada,* an immense iron vessel of the National Line, towed by two powerful steam tugs, was passing down Gallions Reach on her way to New York when she swerved to avoid another vessel, cut off the brow of a coal hulk belonging to the London Steamboat Company, sank a barge laden with coal and crashed through and utterly demolished Woolwich steamboat pier. Only a very high tide prevented her from being grounded. Passengers waiting on the pier saw her coming and managed to run off it in time to save themselves.

Chapter Twenty-Three

1. National Maritime Museum, Greenwich (PAD 6772 and PAD 6773).
2. HMS *Royal George*, the largest warship in the world when launched, was sunk in August 1872 whilst undergoing routine maintenance work off Portsmouth with the loss of over 800 lives.
3. The Balkan Wars (1912–13) resulted in the expulsion of Ottoman Turkey from Europe with the exception of a small area around Istanbul.

Chapter Twenty-Four

1. *Wonders of World Engineering* (ed.) C. Winchester (The Amalgamated Press, 1937), pp.309–13.
2. Oddly, in 1974, Woolwich became the venue of the first UK branch of McDonald's chosen, apparently, because it was then considered to be a representative English town.
3. The famous Arsenal Football Club was founded by the Royal Arsenal workers in 1886 but moved to Highbury in north London in 1913 and dropped the prefix Woolwich.
4. *The Times*, 6 September 1878.
5. This is the fourth example of a man having saved the wrong woman. The first was Thames Police Inspector King who swam to the shore with his wife but found it wasn't her, (as reported in the *Kentish Independent* and the *Morning Post* and mentioned on p.13 of *The Wreck of the Princess Alice*). Secondly, in modern times the same story has been linked to another Thames Police officer, John Lewis. However, Lewis was never actually on the boat with his wife and children. When identifying his wife's body he told the inquest that he had last seen her when he saw her off at Sheerness. He had not wanted her to go home at that time but to wait until the following day. Thirdly, there is the anonymous narrator in the broadsheet (see Chapter Twenty-Three) who mentions supporting a woman he thought was his Lizzie, but later found was not. Edwin Guest also relates the story of the young son of John and Elizabeth Room of Birmingham who was 'an excellent swimmer'. He saved a woman who, at the time, he thought was his mother but she remained missing.
6. 1880   Returning from its first voyage, the *W.J. Taylor* collided with the *H.P. Stephenson* and sank in the mouth of the Tyne. Collier *Berwick* collided with a steam hopper in the Tyne.

      1884   Steamship *Dione* en route down the Thames collided with the steamship *Camden*. The *Dione* sank with the loss of thirteen lives.

      1887   Collier *Edward Eccles* collided in the Tyne with the steamer *Huntingdon*. Both were badly damaged.

      1891   Steam launch *Mayfly* and small passenger ferry *John Clayton* collided in the Tyne. Three people died. The schooner *Pedestrian* collided with Australia-bound steamship *Dorunda* off Dungeness. A steamer (name unknown) collided with Norwegian barque *Harmonie* in the mouth of the Mersey.

      1894   Collier *Ellington* collided with collier *Bromsgrove* in the Solent.

      1897   Brigantine *Rokewood* was rammed by the *Maine* steamship as she was going up the Thames. One death.

      1898   Collier *Ryhope* was rammed by the *Edwin* and sunk in the mouth of the Tyne. The collier *Wallsend* collided with the *Elizabeth* in the Thames. Collier *Frederick Snowdon* collided with collier *Walton* in the North Sea. The *Frederick Snowdon* put back to Tyne where it collided again (this time with the *Bradford*) and sank.

1899   Steamer *Edwin* collided with collier *Chipchase* in the Tyne. Collier
        Bolden collided with a brigandine in the North Sea. Three deaths.
1900   Collier *Stephanotis* collided with the Tyne swing bridge.
1901   Tyne colliers *Robert Ingham* and *Linhope* collided off Northfleet in the
        Thames.
1902   Collier *Idlewild* and collier *Mercator* collided in the Tyne. Collier
        Mercator and steamer *Cluden* collided in the Tyne. German steamer,
        Marie Paulig, collided with collier *Idlewild*.
1903   Tyne steamers *Jargoon* and *Baron Selbourne* collided at Gravesend.
        Tyne collier *Kent* collided with passenger steamer *London* off
        Flamborough Head. Tyne steamers *Rondo* and *Canto* collided at
        Gravesend.

Sources and Bibliography

Archives and other sources

London Metropolitan Archives

Coroners' Records for the *Princess Alice* Inquest (COR/PA)

The National Archives

Report on the Board of Trade Inquiry into the collision between the *Princess Alice* and *Bywell Castle* (M16769-1878 13051 and M1925/1879)

Queen Victoria's messages about the accident (M13451)

Reports of the Committee Appointed by the Board of Trade into the Navigation of the River Thames and Minutes of Evidence (MT9/160/M1925/79)

Cutting from the *Engineer* regarding Captain Pim's 'experts' (M17263)

Recommended restrictions on saloon steamers by Board of Trade Marine Department (M16719)

The National Maritime Museum: Caird Library

The Loss of the *Princess Alice* broadsheet (PAD 6772 & 3)

Islington Public Library Archives

The *Islington Year-Book and Almanac*, 1893

Thames Police Museum Website

Select bibliography

Allani, Magda, *Dark Waters: Chronicle of a Story Untold* (Slow Burn Publications, 2011)

Neal, Wendy, *With Disastrous Consequences: London Disasters 1830–1917* (Hisarlik Press, 1992)

Beckett, I.F.W., *Victoria's Wars* (Shire Publications, 1998)

Bennett, Daphne, *Vicky: Princess Royal of England and German Empress* (Book Club Associates, 1973)

Clifford, J.R.S., *Gravesend and Its Neighbourhood* (Smithers Bros, 1886)

Darbyshire, *The People's Guide to Rosherville and Gravesend*, 1878

Ford, C.J. and E.R. Green, *Rosherville Gardens* (The Endowed School, Hartlip and Whitehall Junior School Gravesend)

Foley, Michael, *Disasters on the Thames* (The History Press, 2011)

Guest, Edwin, *The Wreck of the* Princess Alice *(Saloon Steamer)* (Weldon's Shilling Library, 1878)

Lock, Joan, *Dead Born* (Hale, 2001)

Noel, Gerard, *Princess Alice: Queen Victoria's Forgotten Daughter* (Michael Russell, 1974)

Princess Alice, Duchess of Gloucester, *Memories of Ninety Years* (Collins and Brown, 1991)

Robins, Nick, *The Illustrated History of Thames Pleasure Steamers* (Silverlink Publishing, 2009)

Rhodes, Linda and Kathryn Abnett, *Foul Deeds and Suspicious Deaths in Barking, Dagenham & Chadwell Heath* (Wharncliffe Books, 2007)

Schneer, Jonathan, *The Thames: England's River* (Abacus, 2011)

Thurston, Gavin, *The Great Thames Disaster* (Allen and Unwin, 1965)

Vincent, W.T., *The Records of the Woolwich District* (J.P. Jackson, 1888–1890)

Vincent, William Thomas, *Warlike Woolwich: A History and Guide* (unknown publisher, 1875) (British Library, 2010)

Contemporary newspapers and periodicals

Burnley Express

Chambers Journal

Country Life

Elgin Courier

Gloucestershire Citizen

Isle of Wight Observer

Lancaster Gazette

Lloyd's Weekly London Newspaper

Pall Mall Gazette

Reynolds Newspaper

Sunderland Daily Echo

Aberdeen Journal

Belfast Newsletter

Cheshire Observer

Daily News

Dundee Courier

Edinburgh Evening News

Era

Evening Telegraph (Dundee)

Graphic

Illustrated London News

Illustrated Police News

Ipswich Journal

Islington Gazette

Kentish Independent

Lancaster Gazette

Leeds Mercury

Liverpool Mercury

Morning Chronicle

Morning Post

Newcastle Courant

Newcastle Daily Journal

Northern Echo

Nottingham Evening Post

Shields Daily Gazette & Shipping Telegraph

Standard

Sunderland Advertiser

Sussex Advertiser

The Times

Worcestershire Chronicle

Western Mail

Index